Time Series Forecasting using Deep Learning

Combining PyTorch, RNN, TCN, and Deep Neural Network Models to Provide Production-Ready Prediction Solutions

Ivan Gridin

www.bpbonline.com

FIRST EDITION 2022
Copyright © BPB Publications, India
ISBN: 978-93-91392-574

All Rights Reserved. No part of this publication may be reproduced, distributed or transmitted in any form or by any means or stored in a database or retrieval system, without the prior written permission of the publisher with the exception to the program listings which may be entered, stored and executed in a computer system, but they can not be reproduced by the means of publication, photocopy, recording, or by any electronic and mechanical means.

LIMITS OF LIABILITY AND DISCLAIMER OF WARRANTY

The information contained in this book is true to correct and the best of author's and publisher's knowledge. The author has made every effort to ensure the accuracy of these publications, but publisher cannot be held responsible for any loss or damage arising from any information in this book.

All trademarks referred to in the book are acknowledged as properties of their respective owners but BPB Publications cannot guarantee the accuracy of this information.

To View Complete
BPB Publications Catalogue
Scan the QR Code:

www.bpbonline.com

It is useless to teach you something! You can't do anything with your hands! Please choose a profession in which you do not need to work with your hands. Maybe just typing, and that's it...

Aleksandr Gridin
1960-2007

About the Author

Ivan Gridin is a Mathematician, Fullstack Developer, Data Scientist, and Machine Learning Expert living in Moscow, Russia. Over the years, he has worked on distributive high-load systems and implemented different machine learning approaches in practice. One of the key areas of his research is the design and analysis of predictive time series models.

Ivan has fundamental math skills in probability theory, random process theory, time series analysis, machine learning, deep learning, and optimization. He also has in-depth knowledge and understanding of various programming languages such as Java, Python, PHP, and MATLAB.

He is a loving father, husband, and collector of old math books!

About the Reviewer

Satyajeet Dhawale is a professional Data Scientist having strong experience in machine learning, deep learning, computer vision, inferential and descriptive statistical analysis. He has worked on many projects that involve complex machine learning and deep learning algorithms and used various data sets from different domains. In his career, he has successfully delivered many machine learning and deep learning solutions for complex data problems. You can find more professional details about Satyajeet on LinkedIn. (**https://www.linkedin.com/in/satyajeet-dhawale/**)

Acknowledgement

There are a few people I want to thank for the idea and the motivation for writing this book. I thank my adorable wife Tamara; her patience and beauty inspired me every day. I thank my elder daughter Ksenia; her courage and determination motivated me in exhaustion moments. And my little daughter Elena for waking me up earlier – you're my energizer!

I am endlessly grateful to my company AT Consulting. This company has done a lot to make me the expert I am. I especially thank my colleague Alexey Korotaev - one of the best managers I've ever seen. Also, I want to thank the head of my department, Dmitrii Sagalaev for giving me a chance to work on this book. I'm proud to be a part of this big team.

Thanks to my friends, who helped me in all my efforts. I want especially thank Alisher Alimov for his valuable help when I started to make the first steps in programming, Igor Zuykov and Denis Vasin for their help in learning programming and mathematics, Evgenii Sushinskii for his valuable tutoring in machine learning, and Evgenii Sokolov for the inspiration and fun that he brings into my life. A warm hug to Elena Abramovna Kozak (Vybe) for the amazing notebook she gave me, my good old friend Stas Vulf for sharing the best music playlists with me, Nina Kraviz for her beautiful music, and my German friends Anna and Alexander Gavrilov. This book would've been impossible without all of them.

My gratitude also goes to the book reviewer Satyajeet Dhawale. His participation and helpful advice have made this book much better.

Special thanks to BPB Publications especially Nrip Jain, for their support, advice, and assistance in creating and publishing this book.

Preface

People always tried to analyze time series data to understand the nature of events. Since ancient times, humanity has begun to wonder what lies in the essence of changes in moon cycles, weather, temperature, river water level, harvest, etc. And, the essential way is to collect time series data of certain events and try to analyze them. Mathematics, statistics and time series analysis gave a necessary tool for future prediction. These days, time series analysis is being used everywhere - from marketing and finance to education, healthcare, climate research and robotics. There are many practical and theoretical approaches to time series forecasting - mathematics, statistics, random process theory, etc. Artificial Intelligence model-based forecasting has also become a popular research tool for the past decade. The book explores how the latest advances in deep learning can be applied to time series forecasting.

Machine Learning and Deep Learning algorithms have obtained a lot of attention in recent years due to their applicability to many real-life problems such as fraud detection, spam email filtering, finance and medical diagnosis. Deep Learning models can automatically detect arbitrary complex mappings from inputs to output. Time series forecasting is challenging. Unlike the more straightforward classification and regression problems, time series forecasting adds the complexity of order dependence between observations.

Deep Learning techniques can extract complex hidden patterns in time series datasets that are unreachable to classical statistical methods. That makes deep learning a very promising tool in time series forecasting. This book demonstrates how modern neural networks and the last advances in deep learning can be applied to real-world prediction problems.

The book consists of nine chapters. The details are listed as follows.

Chapter 1 makes a short introduction to time series analysis. It shows some examples of time series problems and their importance. Also, we will examine the most famous classical methods for time series forecasting. And finally, we will get an explanation of the perspectives of the Deep Learning approach.

Chapter 2 introduces the basic deep learning techniques with PyTorch. It explains how to design and apply a neural network. And as the final step, we will demonstrate how to create our first neural network for a time series forecasting problem.

Chapter 3 describes the time series forecasting task as a supervised learning problem. After reading this chapter, the reader will know different types of prediction models. The chapter explains how to formulate a task correctly, prepare input and output data for neural networks training and estimate their effectiveness.

Chapter 4 focuses on recurrent neural networks (RNN). This chapter teaches how to construct efficient predictive models based on RNN, GRU and LSTM architectures and examines how they are applied to time series forecasting.

Chapter 5 illustrates the principles of building complex architectures for deep learning neural networks in time series. This chapter is a good start for diving into deep learning advances and designing your own custom deep learning architectures for particular time series problems.

Chapter 6 introduces the most advanced tuning, optimization and neural architecture search (NAS) techniques. This chapter will be helpful to all data scientists who want to master the latest advances in time series deep learning automation.

Chapter 7 applies complex deep learning models to different types of forecasting data problems. This chapter provides a bridge from theory to practice and shows various deep learning implementations to real-world tasks.

Chapter 8 introduces the PyTorch Forecasting package, which aims to ease state-of-the-art time series forecasting with neural networks. This chapter is a good start for exploring deep learning libraries related to time series analysis.

Chapter 9 shows the path for further study in the area of time series forecasting. The resources mentioned in this chapter will keep you notified about the latest advances.

Downloading the code bundle and coloured images:

Please follow the link to download the
Code Bundle and the *Coloured Images* of the book:

https://rebrand.ly/0a3411

Errata

We take immense pride in our work at BPB Publications and follow best practices to ensure the accuracy of our content to provide with an indulging reading experience to our subscribers. Our readers are our mirrors, and we use their inputs to reflect and improve upon human errors, if any, that may have occurred during the publishing processes involved. To let us maintain the quality and help us reach out to any readers who might be having difficulties due to any unforeseen errors, please write to us at :

errata@bpbonline.com

Your support, suggestions and feedbacks are highly appreciated by the BPB Publications' Family.

Did you know that BPB offers eBook versions of every book published, with PDF and ePub files available? You can upgrade to the eBook version at www.bpbonline.com and as a print book customer, you are entitled to a discount on the eBook copy. Get in touch with us at :

business@bpbonline.com for more details.

At **www.bpbonline.com**, you can also read a collection of free technical articles, sign up for a range of free newsletters, and receive exclusive discounts and offers on BPB books and eBooks.

BPB is searching for authors like you

If you're interested in becoming an author for BPB, please visit **www.bpbonline.com** and apply today. We have worked with thousands of developers and tech professionals, just like you, to help them share their insight with the global tech community. You can make a general application, apply for a specific hot topic that we are recruiting an author for, or submit your own idea.

The code bundle for the book is also hosted on GitHub at **https://github.com/bpbpublications/Time-Series-Forecasting-using-Deep-Learning**. In case there's an update to the code, it will be updated on the existing GitHub repository.

We also have other code bundles from our rich catalog of books and videos available at **https://github.com/bpbpublications**. Check them out!

PIRACY

If you come across any illegal copies of our works in any form on the internet, we would be grateful if you would provide us with the location address or website name. Please contact us at **business@bpbonline.com** with a link to the material.

If you are interested in becoming an author

If there is a topic that you have expertise in, and you are interested in either writing or contributing to a book, please visit **www.bpbonline.com**.

REVIEWS

Please leave a review. Once you have read and used this book, why not leave a review on the site that you purchased it from? Potential readers can then see and use your unbiased opinion to make purchase decisions, we at BPB can understand what you think about our products, and our authors can see your feedback on their book. Thank you!

For more information about BPB, please visit **www.bpbonline.com**.

Table of Contents

1. Time Series Problems and Challenges 1
Structure 1
Objectives 2
Introduction to time series analysis and time series forecasting 2
    Time series analysis 3
    Time series forecasting 4
Time series characteristics 4
    Random walk 5
        Import part 6
        Random walk generation 6
    Trend 7
        Import part 8
        Import part 10
        Result 10
    Seasonality 11
        Import part 12
        Result 12
    Stationarity 13
Time series common problems 14
    Forecasting 14
    Modelling 15
    Anomaly detection 15
Classical approaches 16
    Autoregressive model (AR) 17
    Autoregressive integrated moving average model 17
        Result 18
    Seasonal autoregressive integrated moving average 18
        Result 19
    Holt Winter's exponential smoothing 19
        Result 19

Classical approaches: Pros and cons	*19*
Promise of Deep Learning	20
Python for time series analysis	21
Pandas	*21*
Numpy	*21*
Matplotlib	*21*
Statmodels	*22*
Scikit-learn	*22*
PyTorch	*22*
Conclusion	22
Points to remember	22
Multiple choice questions	23
Answers	*24*
Key terms	24
2. Deep Learning with PyTorch	**25**
Structure	25
Objectives	26
Setting up PyTorch	26
PyTorch as derivative calculator	27
Function creation	*27*
Computing function value	*28*
Result	28
Import part	*29*
Create computational graph	*30*
Result	30
Result	31
Result	31
PyTorch basics	31
Tensors	*31*
Tensor creation	*31*
Random tensor	*32*
Reproducibility	*33*

- Common tensor types ... 33
- Tensor methods and attributes ... 34
- Math functions ... 35

Deep Learning layers ... 36
- Linear layer ... 36
  - Result ... 37
- Convolution ... 37
  - Result ... 41
- Kernel ... 41
- Weight ... 41
- Padding ... 42
  - Result ... 42
- Stride ... 43
  - Result ... 43
- Pooling ... 44
  - Result ... 46
- Dropout ... 46
  - Result ... 46
- Activations ... 47
- ReLU ... 47
  - Result ... 47
- Sigmoid ... 48
  - Result ... 48
- Tanh ... 49

Neural network architecture ... 49
- Result ... 52
- Result ... 52
- Improving neural network performance ... 52
- Do not put two same layers in a row ... 53
- Prefer ReLU activation at first ... 53
- Start from fully connected network ... 53
- More layers are better than more neurons ... 54
- Use dropout ... 55

　　　　Put Deep Learning blocks in the beginning 56
　　Training 56
　　　　Loss functions 57
　　　　　　Absolute loss 57
　　　　　　Mean squared error 57
　　　　　　Smooth L1 loss 57
　　　　Optimizers 58
　　　　　　Adagrad 58
　　　　　　Adadelta 58
　　　　　　Adam 58
　　　　　　Stochastic Gradient Descent (SGD) 58
　　Time series forecasting example 59
　　　　　　Result 60
　　　　Import part 61
　　　　Train, validation and test datasets 61
　　　　Import part 63
　　Conclusion 69
　　Points to remember 70
　　Multiple choice questions 70
　　　　Answers 71
　　Key terms 71

3. **Time Series as Deep Learning Problem** 73
　　Structure 73
　　Objectives 74
　　Problem statement 74
　　Regression versus classification 74
　　　　Time series regression problems 74
　　　　Time series classification problems 75
　　Univariate versus multivariate 76
　　　　Univariate input - univariate output 77
　　　　Multivariate input – univariate output 77
　　　　Multivariate input – multivariate output 77

Many-to-many	*78*
Many-to-one	*78*
Single-step versus multi-step	78
Single-step	*79*
Multi-step	*79*
Single multi-step model	*79*
Multiple single-step model	*80*
Recurrent single-step model	*80*
Datasets	80
Feature engineering	81
Time series pre-processing and post-processing	84
Normalization	*85*
Result	*86*
Trend removal	*86*
Result	*87*
Differencing	*88*
Result	*89*
Sliding window	89
Result	*90*
Effectiveness and loss function	91
Static versus dynamic	91
Architecture design	92
Training, validating and testing	92
Alternative model	93
Model optimization	94
Summary	94
Example: UK minimal temperature prediction problem	95
Dataset	*95*
Result	*96*
Result	*97*
Architecture	*97*
Alternative model	*100*
Testing	*101*

Import part	*102*
Making script reproducible	*102*
Number of features	*102*
Preparing datasets	*102*
Initializing models	*102*
Loss function and optimization algorithm	*103*
Training process	*103*
Evaluation on test set	*104*
Getting results	*104*
Conclusion	107
Points to remember	108
Multiple choice questions	108
Answers	*109*
Key terms	109
4. Recurrent Neural Networks	**111**
Structure	111
Recurrent neural network	112
Result	*118*
Import part	*118*
Making this script reproducible	*118*
Parameters	*119*
Preparing datasets for training	*119*
Initializing the model	*119*
Training	*119*
Evaluation	*120*
Performance on test dataset	*121*
Training progress	*121*
Gated recurrent unit	123
Result	*127*
Import part	*128*
Making this script reproducible	*128*
Parameters	*128*

  Preparing datasets for training 128
  Initializing the model 129
  Training 129
  Evaluation 129
  Performance on test dataset 130
  Training progress 131
 Long short-term memory 131
   Result 135
  Import part 135
  Making this script reproducible 135
  Parameters 136
  Preparing datasets for training 136
  Initializing the model 136
  Training 136
  Evaluation 137
  Performance on test dataset 138
  Training progress 138
 Conclusion 139
 Points to remember 140
 Multiple choice questions 140
  Answers 140
 Key terms 140

5. Advanced Forecasting Models 141
 Structure 141
 Objectives 141
 Encoder–decoder model 142
  Encoder–decoder training 145
   Recursive 146
   Teacher forcing 146
   Mixed teacher forcing 147
  Implementing the encoder–decoder model 147
   Import part 147

>
> Encoder layer 148
>
> Decoder layer 148
>
> Encoder–decoder model class 149
>
> Training 149
>
> Model evaluation 151
>
> Example 151
>
> Result 152
>
> Import part 153
>
> Making script reproducible 153
>
> Global parameters 153
>
> Generating datasets 154
>
> Initializing Encoder–decoder model 154
>
> Training 154
>
> Prediction 154
>
> Visualizing results 154
>
> Temporal convolutional network 156
>
> Casual convolution 156
>
> Dilation 159
>
> Temporal convolutional network design 160
>
> Implementing the temporal convolutional network 163
>
> Import part 163
>
> Crop layer 163
>
> Temporal casual layer 164
>
> Implementing temporal convolutional network 165
>
> TCN prediction model 165
>
> Example 166
>
> Import part 166
>
> Making script reproducible 167
>
> Global parameters 167
>
> Generating time series 167
>
> Preprocessing 168
>
> Preparing datasets 168
>
> Initializing the model 168

Defining optimizer and loss function	*168*
Training	*168*
Training progress	*169*
Performance on the test dataset	*170*
Conclusion	171
Points to remember	172
Multiple choice questions	172
Answer	*172*
Key terms	172

6. PyTorch Model Tuning with Neural Network Intelligence 173

Structure	173
Objective	174
Neural Network Intelligence framework	174
Hyper-parameter tuning	174
Search space	*175*
Trial	*175*
Tuner	*176*
Hyper-parameter tuning in action	*177*
NNI Quick Start	*178*
Import part	*178*
Defining search space	*178*
Search configuration	*179*
NNI API	*180*
NNI search space	*180*
NNI Trial Integration	*181*
Time series model hyper-parameter tuning example	*181*
Deep Learning model trial	*181*
Import part	*181*
Global parameters	*182*
Dataset, optimizer, and model initialization	*182*
NNI search	*184*
Import part	*184*

   Search space *184*
   Maximum number of trials *184*
   Search configuration *184*
 Neural Architecture Search 186
 Hybrid models 192
   Result *194*
  Implementing hybrid model *196*
  Import part *196*
  Casual convolution layer *196*
   Hybrid model *197*
   Optional casual convolution layer *197*
   Obligatory RNN layer *198*
   Optional fully connected layer *198*
   Hybrid model *198*
   Hybrid model trial *198*
   Hybrid model search space *199*
   Hybrid model architecture search *200*
 Conclusion 202
 Points to remember 202
 Multiple choice questions 202
   Answers *203*
 Key terms 203

7. **Applying Deep Learning to Real-world Forecasting Problems** **205**
 Structure 205
 Objectives 205
 Rain prediction 206
   Result *209*
  Import part *211*
  Model preparation function *212*
  Global parameters *212*
  Model hyper-parameters *212*
  Locations and features to train on *213*

Sliding window dataset 213
Train-validation split 214
Converting all datasets to tensors: 214
Initializing the model 214
Optimizer 215
Loss function 215
Training 215
Import part 220
Global parameters 220
Preparing datasets 220
Initializing the model 221
Loading the trained model 221
Making the predictions 222
Alternative predictions 222
Computing scores 222
Printing the results 222

COVID-19 confirmed cases forecast 223
Import part 229
Model preparation function 229
Global parameters 229
Model hyper-parameters 230
Preparing sliding window datasets 230
Creating train/validation datasets 230
Converting datasets to tensors 231
Initializing the model 231
Training and getting the results 231
Import part 234
Global parameters 234
Creating the input 234
Initializing the model 235
Making the prediction 235
Plotting the prediction 235
    Result 236

Algorithmic trading	237
Result	*239*
Result	*240*
Result	*242*
Result	*243*
Import part	*248*
Model preparation function	*248*
Global parameters	*249*
Model hyper-parameters	*249*
Preparing sliding window dataset	*249*
Creating train and validation datasets	*250*
Preparing tensors	*250*
Model initializing	*250*
Training	*251*
Import part	*253*
Best hyper-parameters	*254*
Global parameters	*254*
Sliding window dataset	*254*
Creating tensors	*255*
Initializing and loading the model	*255*
Evaluating	*256*
Result	*256*
Conclusion	257
Points to remember	258
Multiple choice questions	258
Answers	*258*
8. PyTorch Forecasting Package	**259**
Structure	259
Introduction to PyTorch Forecasting package	260
Working with TimeSeriesDataset	260
Import part	*261*
Creating TimeSeriesDataSet	*261*

  Working with TimeSeriesDataSet object 262
 Initializing built-in PyTorch Forecasting model 264
  Import part 264
  Making script reproducible 264
 Initializing Deep Autoregressive model 265
 Creating custom PyTorch Forecasting model 267
  Import part 267
  Defining PyTorch Forecasting model 268
  Implementing the forward method 268
  Initializing the custom model 269
 A complete example 271
  Result 276
 Conclusion 276
 Points to remember 277
 Multiple choice questions 277
  Answers 277

9. What is Next? 279
 Structure 279
 Objective 279
 Classical time series analysis 280
 Deep learning 280
 Studying the best solutions 280
 Do not be afraid of science 280
 Expanding your toolbox 281
 Conclusion 282

Index 283-289

CHAPTER 1
Time Series Problems and Challenges

Time series data are a very important source of information. People always tried to analyze time series data to understand the nature of events. Since ancient times, mankind has begun to wonder what lies in the essence of changes in moon cycles, weather, temperature, the river water level, harvest, and so on. And the essential way is to collect time series data of certain events and try to analyze them. Time series analysis gave a necessary tool for future prediction. These days, time series analysis is being used everywhere: from marketing and finance to education, healthcare, climate research, and robotics. There are many practical and theoretical approaches to time series forecasting: mathematics, statistics, random process theory, and so on. Artificial intelligence model-based forecasting has also become a popular research tool for the past decade. We start exploring how the latest advances in deep learning can be applied to time series forecasting.

Structure

In this chapter, we will discuss the following topics:

- Introduction to time series analysis and time series forecasting
- Time series characteristics
- Common time series problems

- Classical approaches
- Promise of Deep Learning
- Python for time series analysis

Objectives

In this chapter, we will make a short introduction to time series analysis. We will show some examples of time series problems and their importance. Also, we will examine the most famous classical methods for time series forecasting. And finally, we will get an explanation of the perspectives of the Deep Learning approach.

Introduction to time series analysis and time series forecasting

Time series is a sequence of observations that depends on time. **Time** is an essential feature in natural processes such as air temperature, a pulse of the heart, or stock price changes. Chronological order is an essential part of time series data that has to be present at the time of collecting the data. Time series analysis involves working with time-based data to make forecasts about the future. The period is measured in seconds, minutes, hours, days, months, years, or any other time unit.

Each time series dataset can be presented in tabular form, where the first column contains time data. Dataset is always sorted in chronological order. In the following table we show an example of a time series dataset:

London average temperature in 2020

Month	Average Temperature (Celsius)
January	6.7
February	6.4
March	6.8
April	10.3
May	12.6
June	15.1
July	15.7
August	17.2
September	14
October	10.5

November	8.7
December	6

Table 1.1: London average temperature monthly

Of course, formal mathematical models work only with data, but it is easier for humans to work with a visual representation of time series data, take a look in *Figure 1.1*:

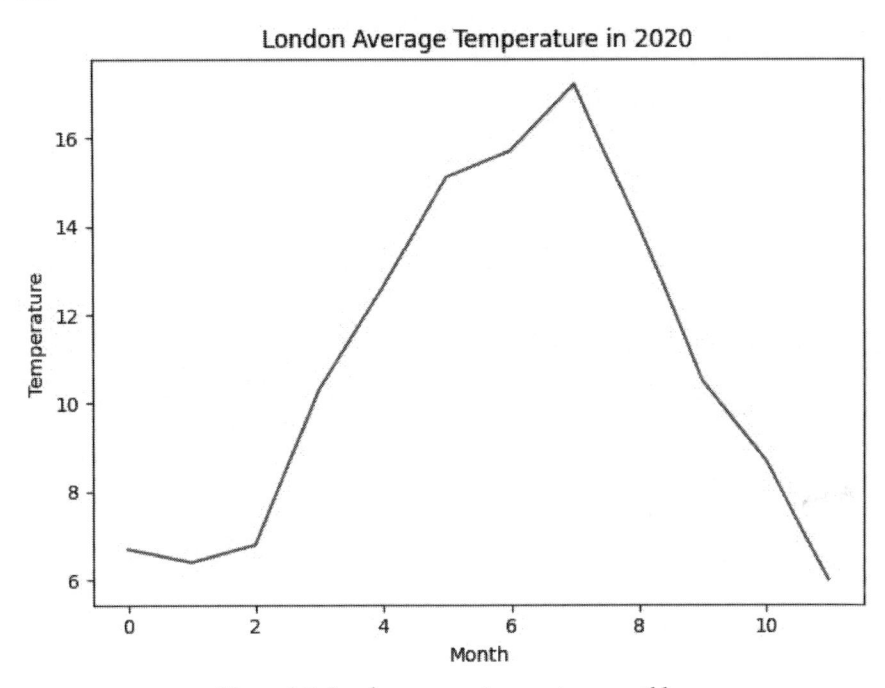

Figure 1.1: London average temperature monthly

Although we rely on complex mathematical models for solving problems, we should not underestimate the human ability to find patterns and dependencies. Therefore, the visual representation of time series data is an important part of the analysis. We'll come back to this topic later.

There is some difference between **time series analysis** and **time series forecasting**. These two fields are tightly correlated, but they serve slightly different tasks.

Time series analysis

Time series analysis recognizes the essence of time series data structure and extracts helpful information from time series: trend, cyclic and seasonal deviations, correlations, and so on.

Time series analysis solves the following tasks:
- Pre-process and perform feature extraction to get a meaningful and valid time series dataset.
- Obtain definite insights into the historical time series dataset.
- Data representation and visualization (graphical analysis, chart construction, report building)

Time series forecasting

Time series forecasting includes:
- Developing models.
- Using them to forecast future predictions.

Time series analysis is the first step to prepare and analyze time series dataset for **time series forecasting**.

> Note: In this book, we will not stick to a strict definition of the term "time series analysis". We will also mean that the term time series analysis includes the problem of time series forecasting.

Time series characteristics

We have to understand how time series differ from one another. There are different types and classes of time series. Event short glance on time series graph can explain that the two processes that generated these datasets have a completely different nature.

Let us examine the time series sample in *Figure 1.2*:

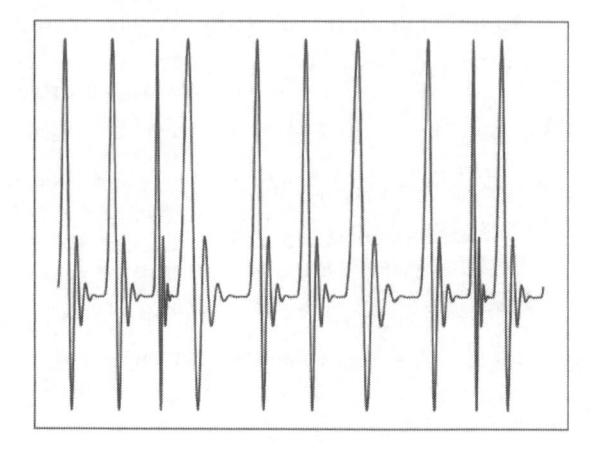

Figure 1.2: Time Series 1

What does this graph resemble? Yes, of course, this time series dataset is a cardiogram. Such time series have the following properties:

- Cycles
- Fluctuations within a certain range of values

Ok, let us take a look to another one in *Figure 1.3*:

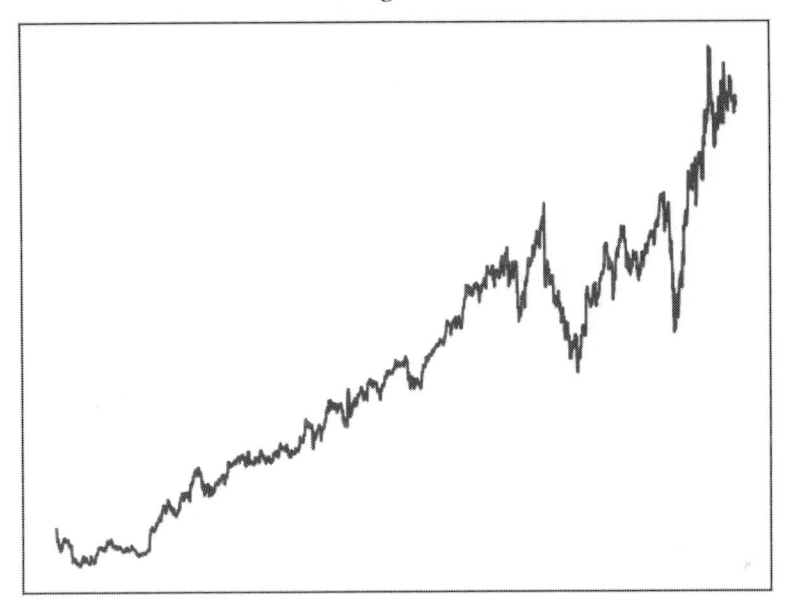

Figure 1.3: Time Series 2

Looking at *Figure 1.3*, it is already much more difficult to say what exactly this time series describes. This is the stock price of Facebook for the past 10 years, from 2011 to 2021. What can we say about this time series? This time series has the following characteristics:

- Upward trend
- Random fluctuations

Comparing *figures 1.2* and *1.3*, it is evident how different the nature of time series could be. In the next topic, we will mention the main time series types and characteristics.

Random walk

The random walk is the basic and one of the simplest time series models. A random walk is a sum of independent random variables with normal distribution: $E_1, E_2, \ldots E_N$. The following recurrence formula can describe the random walk process:

$$R_{t+1} = R_t + E_t$$

where t is the time or sequence index at which observations about the series have been taken.

It is easier to understand the nature of random walk exploring its generation **ch1/random_walk.py**:

Import part

```
import matplotlib.pyplot as plt
import random
```

Random walk generation

```
def generate_random_walk(length = 100, mu = 0, sig = 1):
    ts = []
    for i in range(length):
        e = random.gauss(mu, sig)
        if i == 0:
            ts.append(e)
        else:
            ts.append(ts[i - 1] + e)
    return ts
```

Example

```
if __name__ == '__main__':
    random.seed(10)
    random_walk = generate_random_walk(100)
    plt.plot(random_walk)
    plt.show()
```

Result

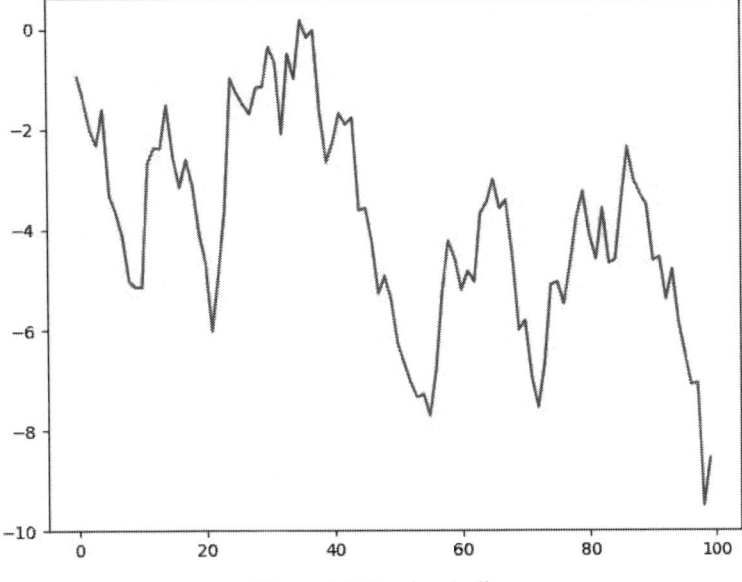

Figure 1.4: Random walk

The random walk is a fundamental stochastic process. It is an integral part of every natural time series. As we see later, each theoretical time series model assumes that it has some randomness, which is expressed as an addition of some random variable E_t to each observation.

Later throughout the book, we will denote:

- **Et – random normal variable**
- **Rt – random walk**

Trend

Trend is the main global time series direction. A quick way to check the presence of a trend is to plot the time series. Let us examine the global climate change time series for the past 100 years in *figure 1.5* (**https://data.world/data-society/global-climate-change-data**):

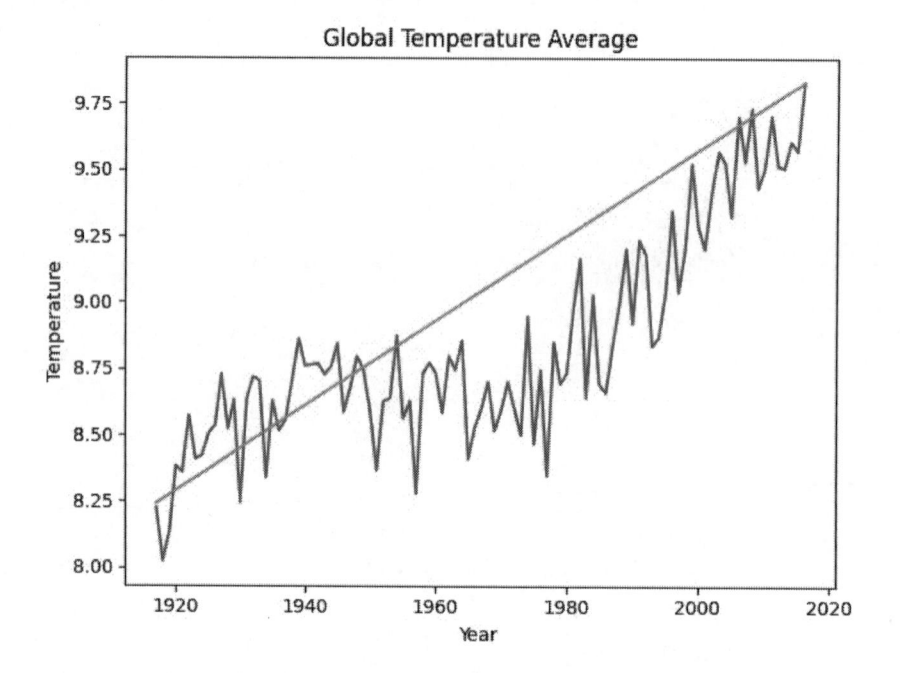

Figure 1.5: Global climate temperature

Time series shown in *figure 1.5* has an apparent upward trend, which is presented as the red line.

The following formula describes a time series with a linear trend:

$$T_t = A + B \cdot t + E_t$$

Let us check the how time series with linear trend is generated **ch1/trend_linear.py**.

Import part

```
import matplotlib.pyplot as plt
import random
```

Example

```
if __name__ == '__main__':
    random.seed(10)
    length = 50
```

```
A = 5
B = .5
C = 3
trend = [A + B * i for i in range(length)]
noise = [C * random.gauss(0, 1) for _ in range(length)]
ts = [trend[i] + noise[i] for i in range(length)]
plt.plot(ts)
plt.plot(trend)
plt.show()
```

Result

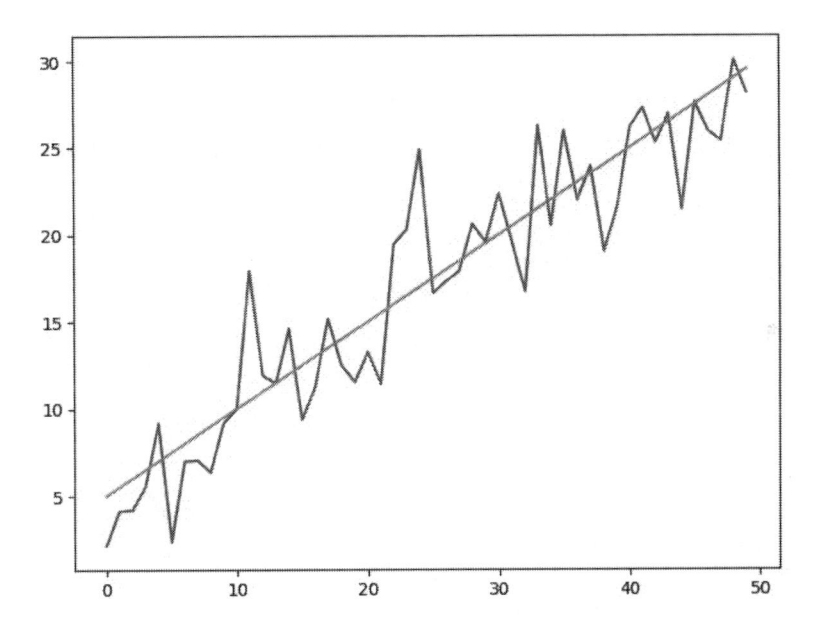

Figure 1.6: Time series with linear trend

Time series do not always have a linear trend. Often this trend can be non-linear and can be expressed using the following formula:

$$T_t = A + F_t + E_t$$

where F_t is non-linear monotonic function.

Below we provide an example of non-linear trend **ch1/trend_nonlinear.py**.

Import part

```
from math import log
import matplotlib.pyplot as plt
import random
```

Example

```
if __name__ == '__main__':
    random.seed(1)
    length = 100
    A = 2
    B = 25
    C = 5
    noise = [C * random.gauss(0, 1) for _ in range(length)]
    trend = [A + B * log(i) for i in range(1, length + 1)]
    ts = [trend[i] + noise[i] for i in range(length)]
    plt.plot(ts)
    plt.plot(trend)
    plt.show()
```

Result

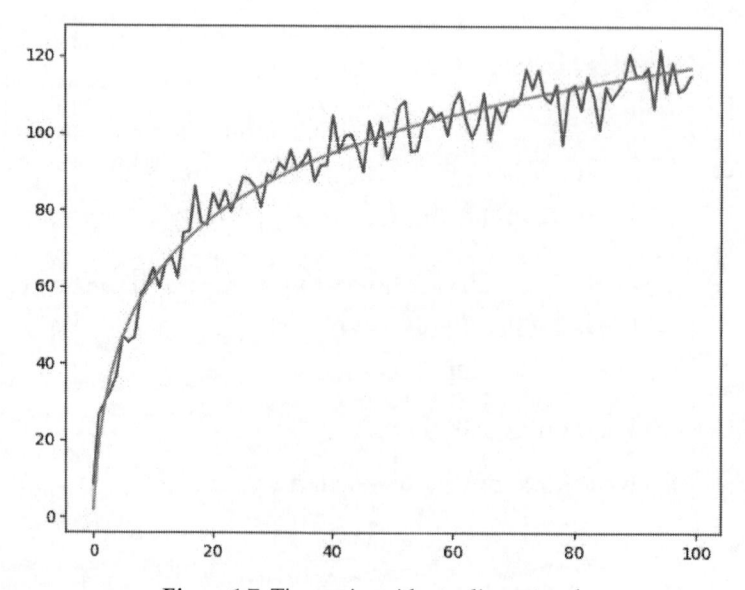

Figure 1.7: Time series with non-linear trend

Seasonality

Seasonality is repetitive variations in a time series dataset. Many processes are cyclic by their nature, and that is why these processes generate time series with the presence of seasonality. *Figure 1.8* represents monthly pneumonia and influenza deaths per 10,000 people in the United States for 11 years, 1968–1978:

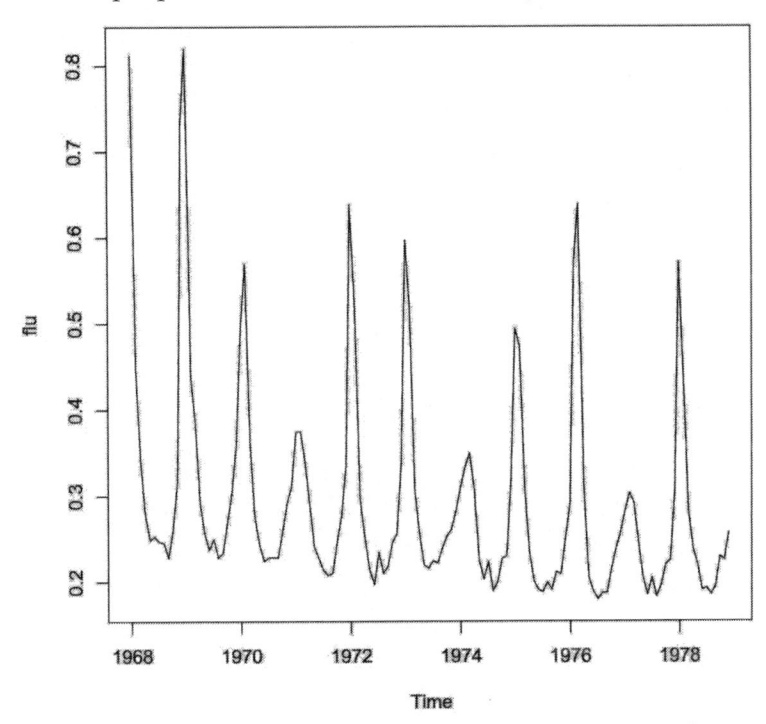

Figure 1.8: Pneumonia and influenza deaths per 10,000 people

In *Figure 1.8*, we can observe peaks each winter. And that is a rather obvious fact because during the winter, the spread of respiratory diseases increases. The same thing happens with time series, which represent temperatures, sales, water levels in rivers, and so on.

A periodic function is a function that repeats its values at regular intervals:

$$S_{t+p} = S_t$$

The most common mathematical periodic functions are trigonometric functions: $sin(x), cos(x)$.

So the formula below describes a time series with seasonality:

$$T_t = A + Bt + CS_t + E_t$$

The construction of time series with seasonality can be better understood by an example **ch1/seasonality.py**.

Import part

```python
from math import sin
import matplotlib.pyplot as plt
import random
```

Example

```python
if __name__ == '__main__':
    random.seed(10)
    length = 100
    A = 50
    B = -.05
    C = 1
    S = 3
    trend = [A + B * i for i in range(length)]
    seasons = [S * sin(i / 5) for i in range(length)]
    noise = [C * random.gauss(0, 1) for _ in range(length)]
    ts = [trend[i] + noise[i] + seasons[i] for i in range(length)]
    plt.plot(ts)
    plt.plot(trend)
    plt.show()
```

Result

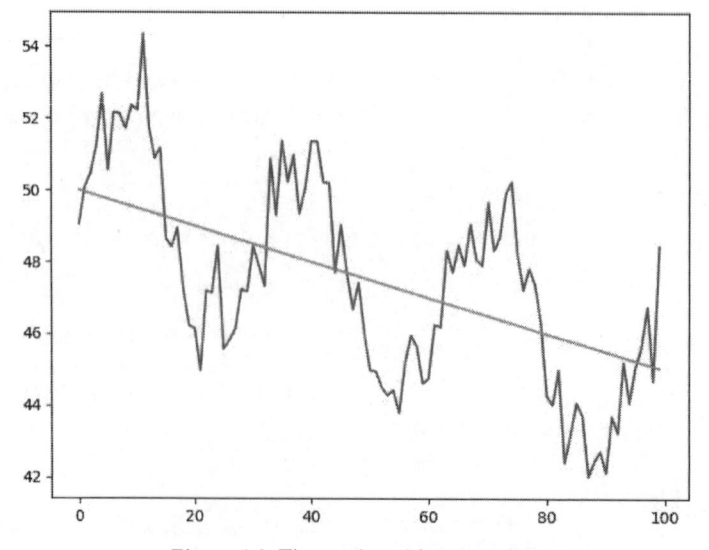

Figure 1.9: Time series with seasonality

A time series can have several seasonality factors. For example, the sales of running shoes fall in winter and raise in summer. But even in the summer period of the upward cycle, there may be sub-cycles, sales traditionally increase on weekends.

Stationarity

A **stationary time series** is characteristic does not depend on the point at which the series is observed. Thus, time series with trends, or seasonality, is not stationary. The trend and seasonality will influence the value of the time series at various times. On the other hand, a random walk is stationary. It does not matter when you observe it. It should look much the same at any point in time.

The main rule of thumb is that you cannot make any assumptions about the stationary time series in a moment of time. For example, say we have the following time series model $5 + 2t + E_t$: . What can we say about this time series at the point t = 10, well, it is highly likely that $T_{10} > 0$ and $T_{10} < T_{20}$ because it is an upward trend.

In *figure 1.10*, the stationary time series is shown:

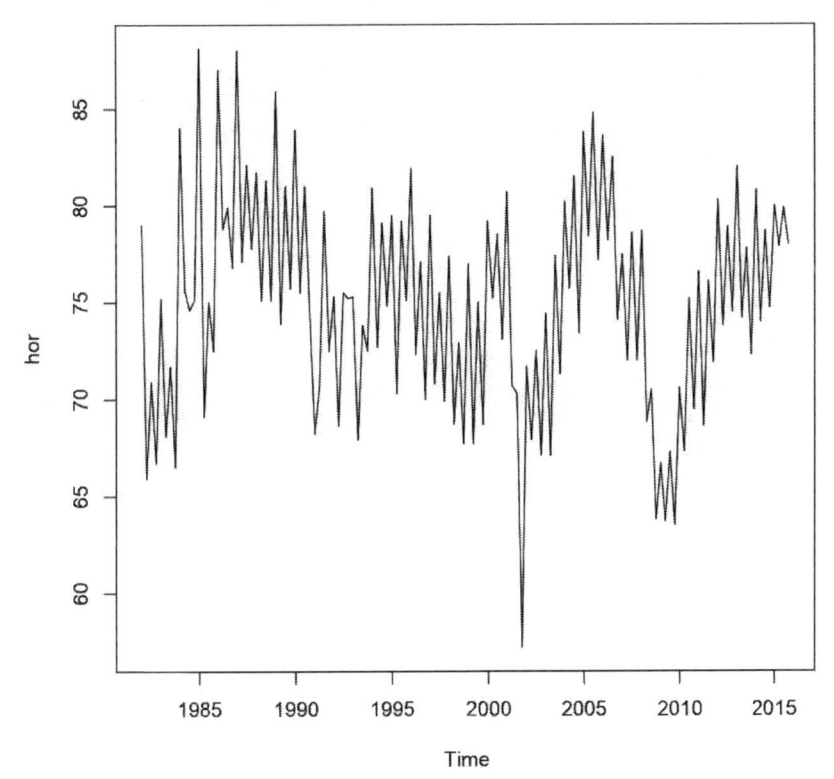

*Figure 1.10: Quarterly Hawaiian hotel occupancy rate (percent of rooms occupied) from 1982 to 2015 ('hor' dataset is presented in astsa package: **https://cran.r-project.org/web/packages/astsa/astsa.pdf**)*

Stationary processes usually do not have any obvious patterns.

Time series common problems

Globally, time series analysis problems can be divided into:

- Forecasting
- Modelling
- Anomaly detection

These tasks are closely related, and the solution of one task implies the solution of another.

Forecasting

As the name suggests, time series **forecasting** tries to find the most likely time series values in the future. This task has a global practical application and is used in many areas of human activity: economy, stock trading, medicine, etc. As a rule, the forecasting task does not imply an exact solution but the suggestion of a certain interval in which the time series future values will be located. Because every natural time series has a random component E_t and it is impossible to predict future value with 100% probability:

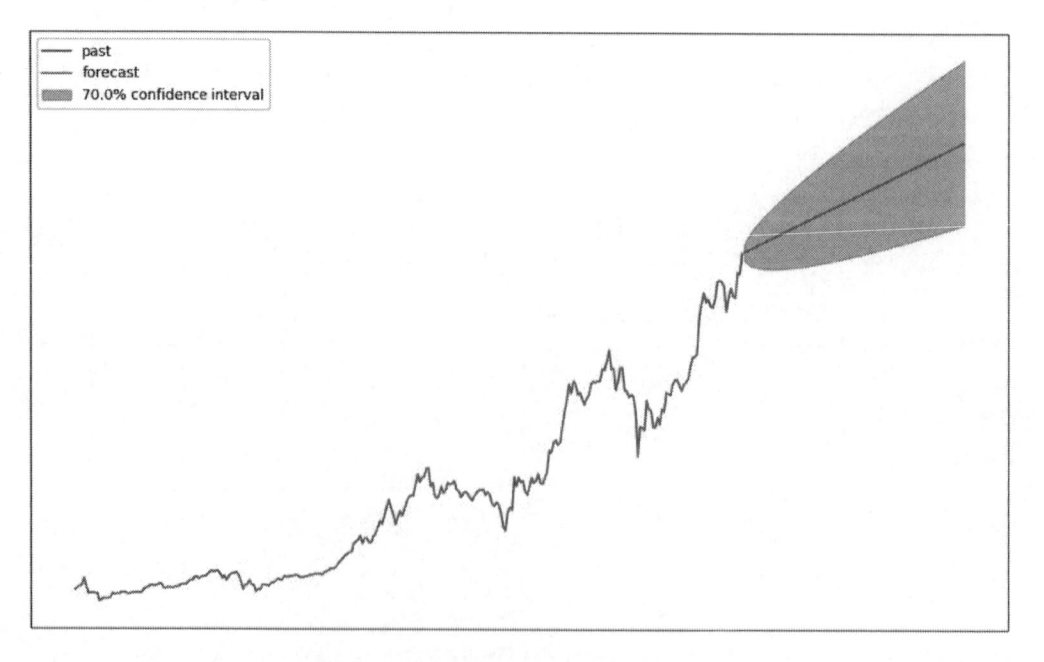

Figure 1.11: Time series forecasting problem

Modelling

Modelling task implies the construction of a model that would describe a certain process over the observed time series. The main goal is to understand the nature and logical form of the process, which hides behind the time series. For example: finding cycles and sub-cycles of astronomical objects movements, structural heart characteristics according to a cardiogram, studying customer preferences, and so on.

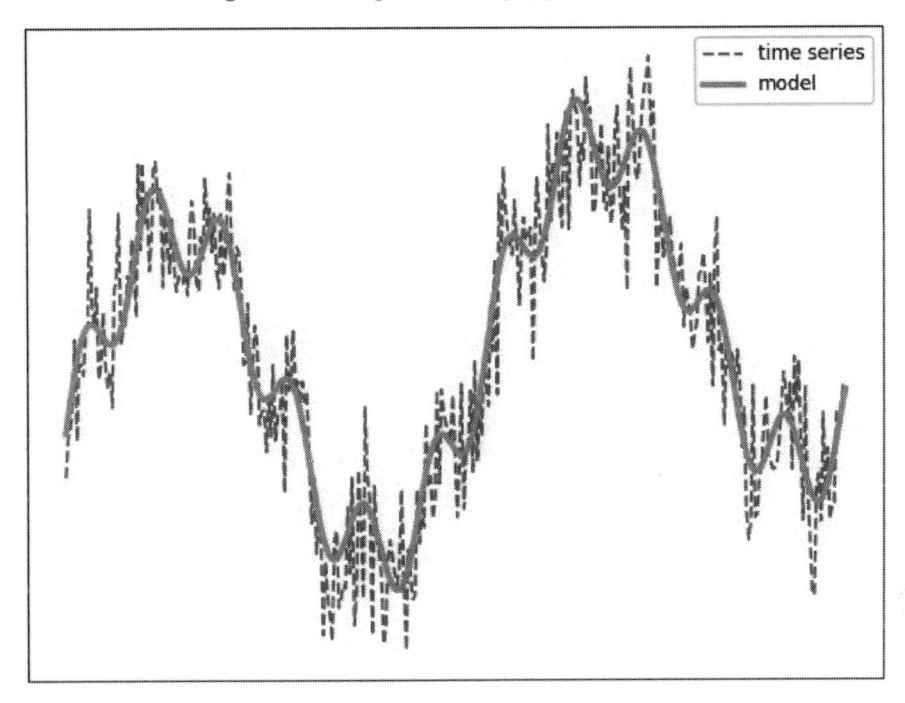

Figure 1.12: Time series modelling problem

Anomaly detection

Anomaly detection is a method used to recognize exceptional patterns that do not correspond to expected behaviour in time series. It has many business applications, unexpected engine temperature changes, fraud detection (atypical withdrawal activity), and heartbeat behaviour shifts:

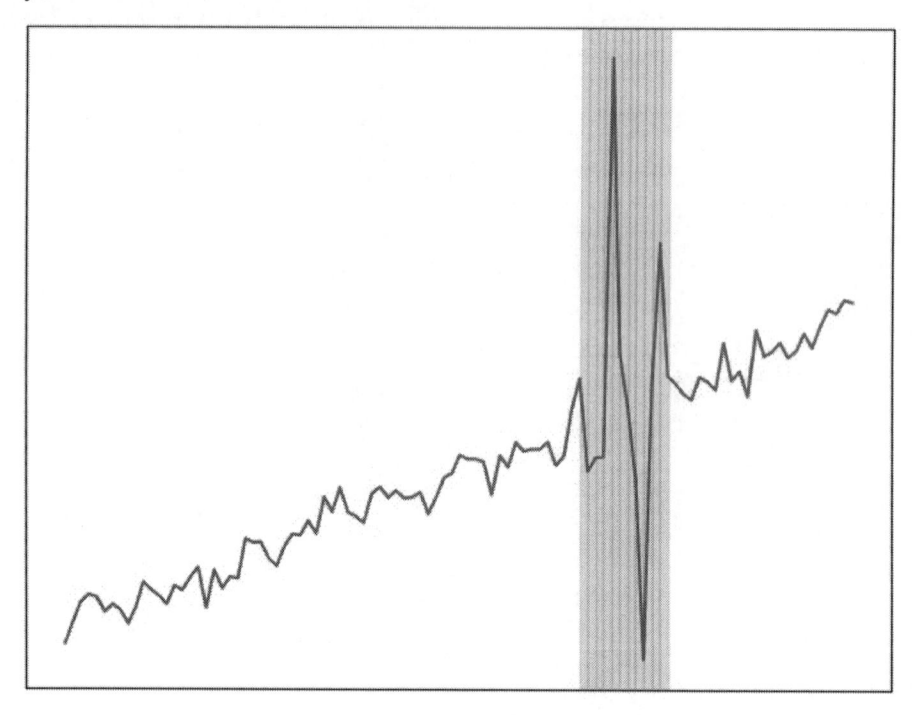

Figure 1.13: Anomaly detection

Classical approaches

In this topic, we will go through the main classical approaches to time series analysis. The theoretical basis of these approaches is outside the scope of this book. But in the next chapters, to measure deep learning models' effectiveness, we will need to compare them with the classical ones. So at least, we need to be able to construct classical models and evaluate them. The next sections will introduce some classical techniques to time series forecasting and their implementation to the Facebook stock price prediction problem. In further examples, we will try to predict tomorrow's close price by analyzing current close prices.

> **Caution:** In this book, we will use economic and stock datasets. The problems that we will investigate are of purely theoretical interest. Please remember that stock trading is a high-risk activity. Be very careful when you apply any approach in practice.

Autoregressive model (AR)

The main goal of autoregressive (AR) method is to find some model of the form:

$$T_t = a_0 + a_1 T_{t-1} + a_2 T_{t-2} + a_n T_{t-n}$$

which most likely describes a time series. The notation AR(p) means that the autoregressive model uses *p* history lag to make a prediction.

Let us create AR(2) model for Facebook quotes time series **ch1/classical_ar.py**:

```
from statsmodels.tsa.ar_model import AutoReg
import yfinance as yf
quotes = yf.download('FB', start = '2011-1-1', end = '2021-1-1')
model = AutoReg(quotes['Close'], lags = 2)
model_fit = model.fit()
print(model_fit.params)
```

Result

Intercept	0. 140215
Close.L1	0. 930913
Close.L2	0. 068906

That means that tomorrow's Close price is calculated as:

$$Fb_{tomorrow\ price} = 0.140215 + 0.930913 \times Fb_{today\ price} + 0.068906 \times Fb_{yesterday\ price}$$

Autoregressive integrated moving average model

Autoregressive integrated moving average (ARIMA) model is the advanced form of AR model, which includes the dependency between an observation and a residual error from a moving average model applied to lagged observations.

Let us predict the Facebook stock price using the ARIMA model **ch1/classical_arima.py**:

```
from statsmodels.tsa.arima.model import ARIMA
import yfinance as yf
from_date = '2015-1-1'
to_date = '2020-10-1'
quotes = yf.download('FB', start = from_date, end = to_date)
```

```
closes = quotes['Close'].values
train, test = closes[:-1], closes[-1]
model = ARIMA(train, order = (5, 2, 3))
results = model.fit()
forecast = results.forecast()
predicted = forecast[0]
print(f'Predicted Price on {to_date}: {round(predicted, 2)}$')
print(f'Actual Price on {to_date}: {round(test, 2)}$')
```

Result

Predicted Price on 2020-10-1	260.56$
Actual Price on 2020-10-1	261.9$

Seasonal autoregressive integrated moving average

Seasonal autoregressive integrated moving average (SARIMA) is an extension of the ARIMA model that also includes the impact of seasonality. This is one of the most advanced models from statistics and random process theory. It combines the ARIMA model with the seasonally adjusted predictions.

Below we provide the same example of the Facebook stock price prediction problem with the SARIMA model usage `ch1/classical_sarima.py`:

```
from statsmodels.tsa.statespace.sarimax import SARIMAX
import yfinance as yf
from_date = '2015-1-1'
to_date = '2020-10-1'
quotes = yf.download('FB', start = from_date, end = to_date)
closes = quotes['Close'].values
train, test = closes[:-1], closes[-1]
model = SARIMAX(train, order = (3, 1, 1), seasonal_order = (0, 0, 0, 0))
results = model.fit(disp = 0)
forecast = results.forecast()
predicted = forecast[0]
print(f'Predicted Price on {to_date}: {round(predicted, 2)}$')
print(f'Actual Price on {to_date}: {round(test, 2)}$')
```

Result

Predicted Price on 2020-10-1	261.3$
Actual Price on 2020-10-1	261.9$

Holt Winter's exponential smoothing

Holt-Winters exponential smoothing (HWES) is a way to model and forecast a time series's behaviour. HWES is a way to model three aspects of the time series: an average of a typical value, a trend, and a seasonality. HWES uses exponential smoothing to remember lots of data from the past and predict future values. So this method is suitable for time series with trend and seasonal components.

The implementation of HWES to the Facebook stock price prediction problem **ch1/classical_hwes.py**:

```
from statsmodels.tsa.holtwinters import ExponentialSmoothing
import yfinance as yf
from_date = '2015-1-1'
to_date = '2020-10-1'
quotes = yf.download('FB', start = from_date, end = to_date)
closes = quotes['Close'].values
train, test = closes[:-1], closes[-1]
model = ExponentialSmoothing(train)
results = model.fit()
forecast = results.forecast()
predicted = forecast[0]
print(f'Predicted Price on {to_date}: {round(predicted, 2)}$')
print(f'Actual Price on {to_date}: {round(test, 2)}$')
```

Result

Predicted Price on 2020-10-1	261.48$
Actual Price on 2020-10-1	261.9$

Classical approaches: Pros and cons

Linear methods like ARIMA, SARIMA, HWES are popular classical techniques for time series forecasting. But these traditional approaches also have some constraints:

- Focus on linear relationships and inability to find complex nonlinear ones
- Fixed lag observations and incapacity to make feature pre-processing

- Missing data are not supported
- Working with univariate time series only, but common real-world problems have multiple input variables
- One-step predictions: many real-world problems require predictions with a long time horizon

Promise of Deep Learning

Machine Learning and Deep Learning algorithms have obtained a lot of attention in recent years due to their applicability to many real-life problems, such as fraud detection, spam email filtering, finance, and medical diagnosis.

Deep Learning models can automatically detect arbitrary complex mappings from inputs to outputs and support multiple inputs and outputs. Time series forecasting is challenging. Unlike the more straightforward classification and regression problems, time series problems add the complexity of order dependence between observations.

Deep Learning models have several essential capabilities:

- Ability to learn from arbitrary mappings from inputs to outputs
- Multiple inputs and outputs support
- They can automatically detect patterns in a dataset that spread over long series

Simple **Multilayer Perceptron Neural Networks** or **MLP**s approximate a mapping function from input data to output targets. This capability is important for time series for several reasons:

- Robust to noise. Neural networks can even support learning and prediction in the presence of missing inputs, and they are robust to random noise (which we denoted as E_t in our time series models).
- Nonlinear. Neural networks do not make strict rules about the mapping function and readily learn linear, nonlinear, and fuzzy relationships.

Convolutional Neural Networks or **CNN**s are designed to handle image, audio, and video data efficiently. The CNN model learns how to extract the useful features for the problem automatically. The ability of CNNs to detect and automatically extract features from the input dataset can be applied to time series forecasting problems. Time series can be handled like a one-dimensional image that a CNN model can analyze. CNN models get Multilayer Perceptrons' advantages for time series forecasting, namely support for multivariate input, multivariate output, and learning arbitrary complex patterns. Still, they do not require that the model learn directly from the strict lag observations, which means that the CNN model will choose what history time series observations to select and how to process them. The CNN model can learn a representation from an arbitrary extended input sequence suitable for the forecast problem.

Recurrent neural networks or **RNNs** like the **Long Short-Term Memory networks** or **LSTMs** add the explicit treatment of order between time series data when learning a mapping function from inputs to outputs. RNNs add native support for input data comprised of observations' sequences. MLPs or CNNs do not offer this feature. The addition of sequence is a new dimension to the learning process. Instead of learning mapping inputs to outputs alone, the RNN model can learn a mapping function for the inputs over time to output.

Python for time series analysis

The Python environment is a powerful tool for applied mathematics, statistics, machine learning, and deep learning tasks. Python is simple, robust, and can be used for theoretical researches and practical tasks. It is easy to learn and use. Python is a dynamic language and very adapted to interactive development and quick prototyping. Python has excellent mathematical, machine learning, and deep-learning libraries. Here we'll make a short overview of the libraries we will use in this book.

Pandas

Pandas is a library that is incredibly useful for any operations with datasets. Since we're working with data constantly, we need a tool for that, and Pandas is the excellent one. Pandas has many killer features: loading dataframes, joining and merging, built-in analysis functions, time series data post processing, and so on.

Numpy

NumPy (short for Numerical Python) provides an efficient interface to operate with matrices. You can treat the NumPy library as a replacement for MATLAB in the python ecosystem. NumPy allows various mathematical operations on matrices like linear algebra procedures, statistical processing, Fourier transform, and so on.

Matplotlib

Matplotlib is a mighty plotting library useful for those working with any data visualizations. It is impossible to work with time series without the ability to plot them. It is better to see something once than to hear about it a thousand times. We will use this library for time series plotting, deep learning training process visualization, and the comparative analysis of effectiveness.

Statmodels

Statmodels library provides functionality for the estimation of many different statistical models. In this book, the modules regarded to time series models like ARIMA, SARIMA, HWES, and so on are the most useful for us. We will use this library for testing the results of deep learning model performance as well.

Scikit-learn

Scikit-learn gives a range of machine learning algorithms. It contains various scientific methods and functions. Scikit-learn is one of the most popular machine learning libraries. In this book, we will use this library for the implementation of specific auxiliary tasks.

PyTorch

PyTorch is an open-source deep-learning library for Python. It is developed by the Facebook artificial-intelligence research group. PyTorch has two main features:

- Tensor computation
- Function differentiation
- Neural networks construction and training

PyTorch will be our main tool in the construction of deep learning models.

Conclusion

In this chapter, we have made an introduction to time series analysis. We studied what a time series is and what characteristics they have. We have implemented some popular classical methods for time series analysis and forecasting. In the next chapter, we will start studying our primary deep learning tool, which will allow us to get a completely different approach to time series prediction.

Points to remember

- Many time series datasets have trends and seasonality.
- Deep learning models can automatically detect arbitrary complex mappings from inputs to outputs and support multiple inputs and outputs.
- Classical models are unable to deal with complex multivariate dependencies.

Multiple choice questions

1. Examine the time series below and choose its characteristics:

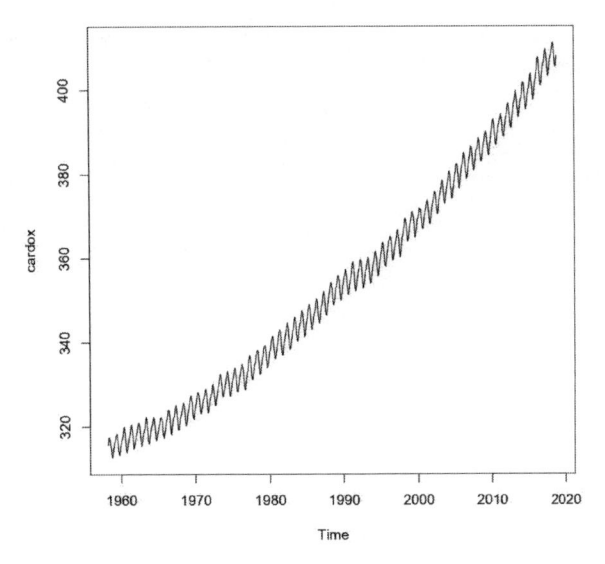

Figure 1.14: Monthly mean carbon dioxide (in ppm) measured at Mauna Loa Observatory, Hawaii.

   A. Trend, no seasonality
   B. No trend, seasonality
   C. Trend, seasonality

2. Examine the time series below and choose its characteristics:

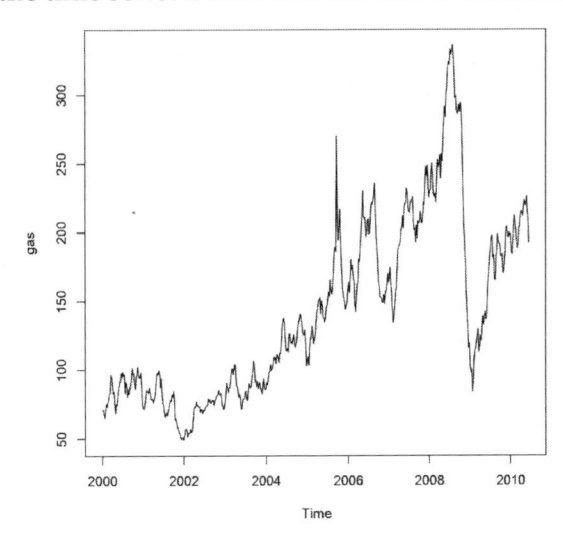

Figure 1.15: New York Harbor conventional regular gasoline weekly spot price FOB from 2000 to 2010.

A. Stationary

B. Non-stationary

3. In Classical Approaches section we have made some predictions to Facebook stock price on 2020-10-01. Let's make the same for 2020-10-01 (i.e. change the variable to_date to 2020-12-1 in scripts: ch1/classical_arima.py, ch1/classical_sarima.py, ch1/classical_hwes.py). Which model shows the closest prediction?

   A. ARIMA

   B. SARIMA

   C. HWES

Answers
1. C
2. B
3. B

Key terms

- *Time series:* Sequence of observations that depends on time
- *Random walk model:* $R_{t+1} = R_t + E_t$
- *Time series with linear trend model:* $T_t = A + Bt + E_t$
- *Time series with seasonality model:* $T_t = A + Bt + CS_t + E_t$
- *SARIMA:* Classical time series approach based on the concept of seasonal trends and autoregressive models.
- *HWES:* Classical technique with exponential smoothing.

CHAPTER 2
Deep Learning with PyTorch

In the first chapter, we highlighted the perspectives of deep learning in time series forecasting problems. And, of course, we need a tool to implement deep learning approaches. As the book's title suggests, we will be using PyTorch as the main framework to study the time series analysis. This chapter aims to explain the main concepts of deep learning with PyTorch. For more information on PyTorch, you can visit the official site : **https://pytorch.org/**.

Structure

In this chapter, we will discuss the following topics:

- Setting up PyTorch
- PyTorch as a derivative calculator
- PyTorch basics
- Deep Learning layers
- Neural network architecture
- Training
- Example of time series forecasting

Objectives

After studying this chapter, you should be able to install and set-up PyTorch. You will know the basic deep learning methods with PyTorch, and you will be able to design and implement a neural network. And as the final step, we will be able to create our first neural network for a time series forecasting problem.

Setting up PyTorch

PyTorch is available as a Python package, and you can install it in a traditional way:

```
$    pip install torch torchvision torchaudio
```

The full installation guide can be found on the official site: **https://pytorch.org/**.

In this book, we will use some additional PyTorch libraries:

```
$    pip install torchviz
```

Torchviz library requires **graphviz** package:

```
$    brew install graphviz
```

or

```
$    sudo apt install graphviz
```

It is optional, but I recommend using CUDA (Compute Unified Device Architecture) to speed up training and evaluate Deep Learning models. **CUDA** is a special API developed by NVIDIA, which allows the **Graphical Processing Unit (GPU)** to delegate tensor processing. Modern GPUs can increase the performance of deep learning models drastically.

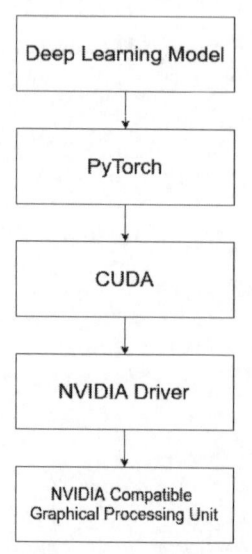

Figure 2.1: PyTorch + CUDA processing flow

To use CUDA your machine should have NVIDIA Compatible GPU. You can refer here for further details: https://developer.nvidia.com/cuda-zone.

Once CUDA is installed on your machine, you can check it with the following script:

```
import torch
print(torch.cuda.is_available())
```

Do not worry if you are experiencing some problems while installing or running CUDA, it will not block you from studying this book.

PyTorch as derivative calculator

All deep learning models perform basic operations from calculus to linear algebra. But we already have excellent tools in Python, like NumPy or SciPy. So why do we need another tool, especially for deep learning?

In the context of deep learning (and PyTorch), it is helpful to think about neural networks as computation graphs. One of the essential operations during neural network training is backpropagation. The backpropagation algorithm is based on the gradient descent concept, and it is impossible to perform gradient descent without the calculation of derivatives. The main feature of PyTorch is the ability to calculate derivatives of composite multivariable functions. This feature is crucial in neural network learning.

Let us consider how PyTorch operates with functions and calculates their derivatives. Say we have the following multivariate function:

$$f(x_1, x_2, x_3, x_4) = x_1^3 x_2 + x_3 x_4$$

Let us take a look at how this function can be implemented using PyTorch `ch2/dfdx/function.py`:

Function creation

```
import torch
def get_function(x1_val = 0, x2_val = 0, x3_val = 0, x4_val = 0):
    # variables
    x1 = torch.tensor(x1_val, requires_grad = True, dtype = torch.float32)
    x2 = torch.tensor(x2_val, requires_grad = True, dtype = torch.float32)
    x3 = torch.tensor(x3_val, requires_grad = True, dtype = torch.float32)
    x4 = torch.tensor(x4_val, requires_grad = True, dtype = torch.float32)
    # function
```

```
    p1 = x1.pow(3)
    m1 = p1 * x2
    m2 = x3 * x4
    f = m1 + m2
    vars = {'x1': x1, 'x2': x2, 'x3': x3, 'x4': x4}
    return f, vars
```

Computing function value

```
if __name__ == '__main__':
    f, _ = get_function(2, 4, 3, 5)
    print(f.item())
```

Result

```
47.0
```

We see here that the defined function **f** has the following value **f(2, 4, 3, 5) = 47**. Well, that is an absolutely trivial case and nothing special about it... yet.

Each neural network is a function. This function can be very complicated, it could be a complex composition of other functions, but anyway, a neural network is a function. Let us take a look at the fully connected neural network in *Figure 2.2*:

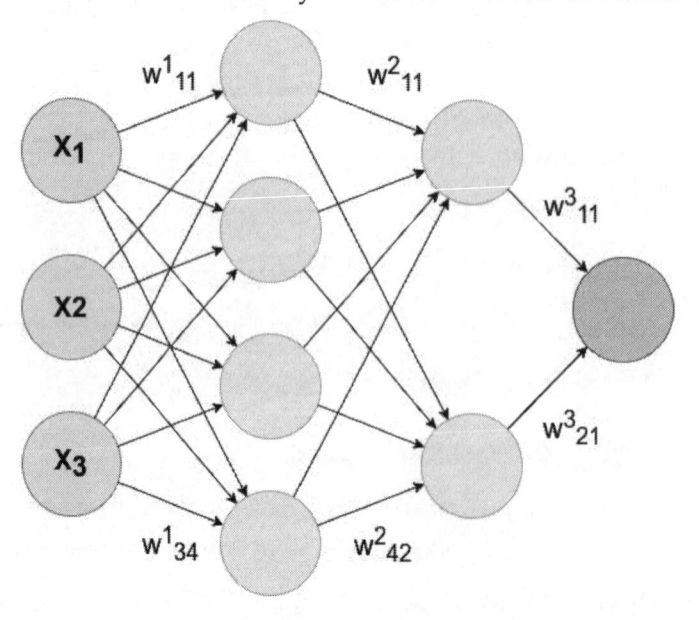

Figure 2.2: Neural network example

This trivial neural network can be presented as a function:

$F(x_1, x_2, x_3 ; w^1_{11}, ..., w^1_{34}, w^2_{11}, ..., w^2_{42}, w^3_{11}, w^3_{21})$

where x_1, x_2, x_3 is input and w^l_{ij} is neural network weights.

During the backpropagation process, we find derivative $\partial F/\partial w$ for each weight. And that is what PyTorch does. It computes partial derivatives of any multivariable function. As we know from the calculus the derivative of the composite function is calculated using the chain rule: $[f(g(x))]' = f'(g(x)) \cdot g'(x)$. To apply the chain rule to derivative calculation, we need to treat the neural network function as a computational graph. A computational graph is a directed graph where the nodes correspond to mathematical operations. In *figure 2.3*, we see the computational graph of function: $a \cdot sin(x) + b$:

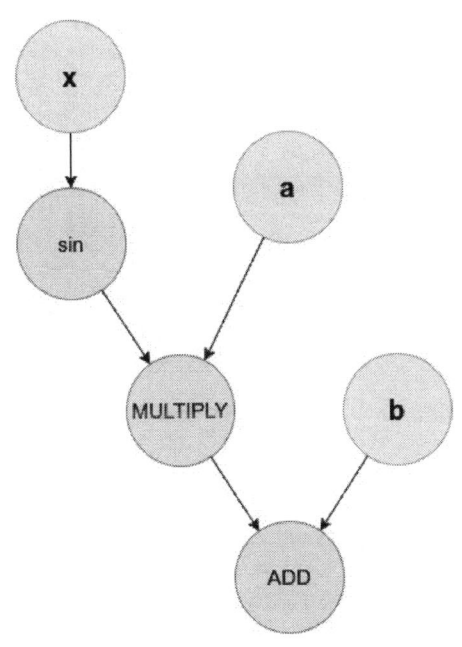

Figure 2.3: $a \cdot sin(x) + b$ as a computational graph

Let us examine how PyTorch creates computational graph **ch2/dfdx/ computational_graph.py**:

Import part

```
from ch2.dfdx.function import get_function
from torchviz import make_dot
import matplotlib.pyplot as plt
import matplotlib.image as mpimg
```

Create computational graph

```
f, params = get_function(2, 4, 3, 5)
make_dot(f, params).render("f_torchviz")
img = mpimg.imread('f_torchviz.png')
plt.xticks([])
plt.yticks([])
plt.imshow(img)
plt.show()
```

Result

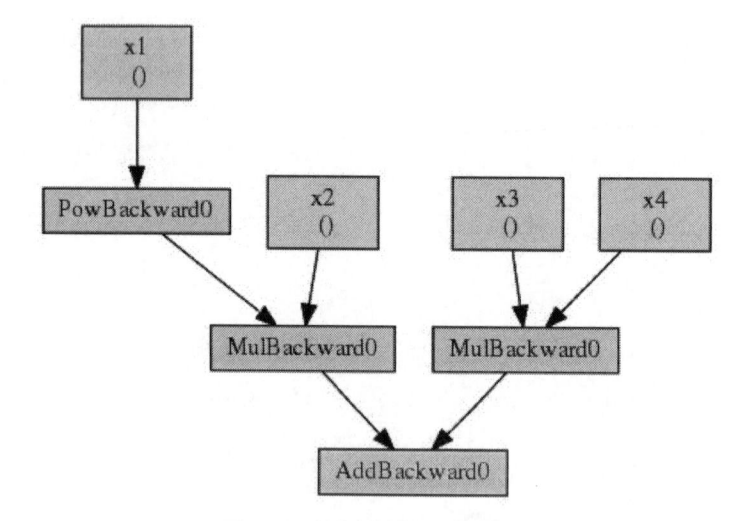

Figure 2.4: Computational graph

And we come to the main PyTorch feature, the ability of partial derivatives calculation. Let's find the partial derivative $\partial f/\partial x1$

$$f'_{x1}(x_1, x_2, x_3, x_4) = (x_1^3 x_2 + x_3 x_4)' = (x_1^3 x_2)' = 3x_1^2 x_2$$

then f'_{x1} at point (2, 4, 3, 5) is: $3 \cdot 2^2 \cdot 4 = 48$

Let us take a look how PyTorch calculates derivatives **ch2/dxdf/derivatives.py**:

```
from ch2.dfdx.function import get_function
from torch.autograd import grad
f, params = get_function(2, 4, 3, 5)
df_dx1 = grad(outputs = f, inputs = [params['x1']])
print(df_dx1)
```

Result

```
(tensor(48.),)
```

The result is the same as we calculated manually. As we know, partial derivatives are calculated to find the function gradient:

$$\nabla f = [\frac{\partial f}{\partial x1}, \frac{\partial f}{\partial x2}, \frac{\partial f}{\partial x3}, \frac{\partial f}{\partial 4}]$$

And PyTorch calculates the gradient in one line of code. Let's see how the value of $\nabla f(2, 4, 3, 5)$ is calculated **ch2/dfdx/gradient.py**:

```
from ch2.dfdx.function import get_function
from torch.autograd import grad
f, params = get_function(2, 4, 3, 5)
df_dx = grad(outputs = f, inputs = params.values())
print(df_dx)
```

Result

```
(tensor(48.), tensor(8.), tensor(5.), tensor(3.))
```

Creating a computational graph for a function and calculation of partial derivatives is crucial for neural network training, and PyTorch does it. Of course, this is not the only useful PyTorch feature. It provides an easy and seamless way of deep learning model construction.

PyTorch basics

PyTorch is a calculation tensor engine, and almost all its functionality aims to provide different mathematical operations. In this section, we will cover the basics of PyTorch.

Tensors

The main objects of PyTorch operations are **tensors**. Tensor is a multidimensional matrix. Usually, deep learning models are using tensors up to five dimensions.

Tensor creation

The creation of a tensor is a simple action. You can create a vector or 1-D tensor with a predefined list of values:

```python
import torch
x = torch.tensor(data = [1, 2, 3])
print(x)
>>>
tensor([1, 2, 3])
```

And the same can be done to create a matrix or 2-D tensor:

```python
import torch
x = torch.tensor(data = [[1, 2, 3], [4, 5, 6]])
print(x)
>>>
tensor([[1, 2, 3],
        [4, 5, 6]])
```

Usually, you must explicitly set the tensor type to make some mathematical operations available with the tensor you create:

```python
import torch
x = torch.tensor(data = [1.3, .5], dtype = torch.float32)
```

If you want to take derivatives of the tensor:

```python
import torch
x = torch.tensor(data=[1.3,.5], dtype=torch.float32, requires_grad=True)
```

Random tensor

Random tensors are an essential part of deep learning models. Usually, a deep learning model initiates with random sets of weights.

Random 3-D tensor where each tensor element is a random variable from zero to one:

```python
import torch
x = torch.rand((2, 2, 2))
print(x)
>>>
tensor([[[0.8553, 0.9385],
         [0.4108, 0.6903]],
        [[0.6604, 0.2956],
         [0.9576, 0.5071]]])
```

Reproducibility

Random tensors and random variables in common sense are an essential part of deep learning calculations. But of course, it is very convenient to get reproducible results for further investigation in some cases. Completely reproducible results are not guaranteed across PyTorch releases. Roughly speaking, there is no way to get a 100% guarantee that your script will get the same results in another environment. However, there is a measure you can take to limit the number of sources of nondeterministic behaviour:

```
import torch
torch.manual_seed(0)
```

Also, for custom random operators you might need to set python seed:

```
import random
random.seed(0)
```

To make the scripts reproducible we will often use the following snippet throughout this book:

```
import torch
import random
torch.manual_seed(0)
random.seed(0)
```

Common tensor types

Some of the tensor types below are commonly used in math computations:

zeros - Creates a tensor of zeros:

```
import torch
x = torch.zeros((2, 2))
print(x)
>>>
tensor([[0., 0.],
        [0., 0.]])
```

ones – Creates a tensor of ones:

```
import torch
x = torch.ones((2, 2)))
print(x)
```

```
>>>
tensor([[1., 1.],
        [1., 1.]])
```

eye – Creates an identity tensor:

```
import torch
x = torch.eye(3)
print(x)
>>>
tensor([[1., 0., 0.],
        [0., 1., 0.],
        [0., 0., 1.]])
```

Tensor methods and attributes

reshape - Changes a shape of a tensor:

```
import torch
x = torch.tensor([1, 2, 3, 4])
print(x)
y = x.reshape((2, 2))
print(y)
>>>
tensor([1, 2, 3, 4])
tensor([[1, 2],
        [3, 4]])
```

size - Returns a size of a tensor:

```
import torch
x = torch.tensor([[1, 2, 3], [4, 5, 6]])
x.size()
>>>
torch.Size([2, 3])
```

dim – Returns a tensor dimension:

```
import torch
x = torch.tensor([[1, 2, 3], [4, 5, 6]])
```

```
x.dim()
>>>
2
```

tolist – Returns a list of tensor values:

```
import torch
x = torch.tensor([[1, 2], [5, 6]])
x.tolist()
>>>
[[1, 2], [5, 6]]
```

backward – Calculates a gradient:

```
import torch
x = torch.tensor(data = [2], dtype = torch.float32, requires_grad = True)
f = x.pow(2)
f.backward()
x.grad.item()
>>>
4.0
```

Math functions

PyTorch provides a full set of mathematical functions:

- **abs** - Computes the absolute value of each element in a tensor
- **add** - Adds a scalar to each element of a tensor
- **ceil** - Returns a new tensor with the smallest integer greater than or equal to each element of a tensor
- **dist** - Returns the p-norm between two tensors. If p=2, then dist returns classical Euclidian norm.
- **div** - Divides each element of the tensor
- **eq** - Computes element-wise equality
- **floor** - Returns a new tensor with the largest integer less than or equal to each element of a tensor
- **mean** - Returns the mean value of all elements in the tensor
- **pow** - Takes the power of each element in the tensor

- **max** - Returns the maximum value of all elements in the tensor
- **min** - Returns the minimum value of all elements in the tensor
- **round** - Returns a new tensor with each of the elements of the tensor rounded to the closest integer
- **sign** - Returns a new tensor with the signs of the elements of input tensor
- **sum** - Return the sum of all elements in the input tensor

Deep Learning layers

Deep Learning neural networks have special layers that allow you to extract patterns and dependencies from datasets. The application of these layers gives Deep Learning models their power and strength.

Linear layer

Linear layer is the classical linear transformation based on matrix product:

$$f(x) = Ax + b$$

Linear layer is a function with the following parameters:

- weight – multiplication matrix
- bias

A linear layer is initialized with random weight and bias, and often it makes sense because weight and bias will be used in neural network training and will be adjusted after. Let us take a look:

```
import torch
torch.manual_seed(1)
l1 = torch.nn.Linear(3, 2)
print(l1.weight)
>>>
Parameter containing:
tensor([[ 0.2975, -0.2548, -0.1119],
        [ 0.2710, -0.5435,  0.3462]], requires_grad=True)
```

But if we want to set weight or bias manually to the linear layer (or any other PyTorch layer), we can do the following **ch2/layers/linear.py**:

```
import torch
```

```python
x = torch.tensor(data = [1, 2, 3]).float()
l1 = torch.nn.Linear(3, 2)
l1.weight = torch.nn.Parameter(torch.tensor([[0, 2, 5], [1, 0, 2]]).float())
l1.bias = torch.nn.Parameter(torch.tensor([1, 1]).float())
print(f'x: {x.tolist()}')
print(f'A: {l1.weight.tolist()}')
print(f'b: {l1.bias.tolist()}')
print(f'y = Ax + b: {l1(x).tolist()}')
```

Result

```
x: [1.0, 2.0, 3.0]
A: [[0.0, 2.0, 5.0], [1.0, 0.0, 2.0]]
b: [1.0, 1.0]
y = Ax + b: [20.0, 8.0]
```

Convolution

The **convolution** is a powerful technique aimed at extracting features and complex patterns from a dataset. The convolution layer is one of the most commonly used deep learning layers. The idea of convolutions was borrowed from nature. Different neurons in the brain respond to different features. The convolution layers show outstanding results in image classification, pattern detection, speech recognition, natural language processing, and so on. Also, convolution layers are very useful in sequential data processing, like time series.

There are three types of convolution layers:

- **1 D Convolution** – Is mainly used for sequential data, like time series or audio data streams.
- **2 D Convolution** – Is mainly used for image processing.
- **3 D Convolution** – Is mainly used for 3-D images of video streams.

Sometimes convolution is called as a *filter*. In this section, we will cover only 1 D and 2 D convolutions.

It is easier to understand the idea of the convolution action by an example. The convolution layer needs two tensors to calculate convolution: input tensor and *kernel tensor*. We are going to examine 2 D Convolution. Say we have 4×4 matrix as the input tensor:

Time Series Forecasting using Deep Learning

1	2	0	1
-1	0	3	2
1	3	0	1
2	-2	1	0

And 2×2 matrix as the kernel tensor:

1	-1
-1	1

The convolution result is the sum of element-wise multiplication of each "box" in the input tensor by the kernel tensor. First step: we take the upper right box in the input matrix and apply kernel to tensor to it: $1 \cdot 1 + 2 \cdot (-1) + (-1) \cdot (-1) + 0 \cdot 1 = 0$, like it is shown on *figure 2.5*:

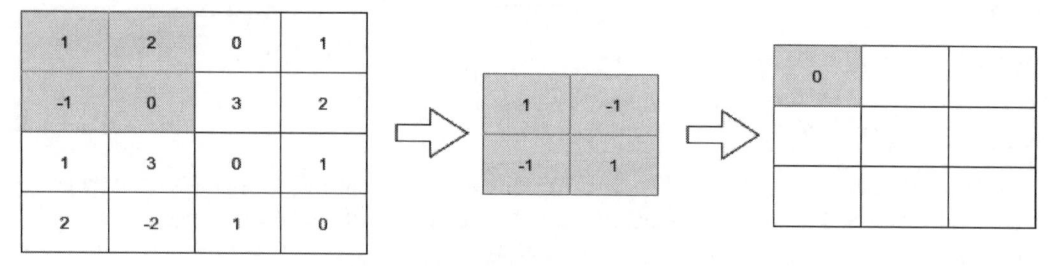

Figure 2.5: Convolution: 1st step

Then we move to another "box" and again calculate convolution:
$2 \cdot 1 + 0 \cdot (-1) + 0 \cdot (-1) + 3 \cdot 1 = 5$:

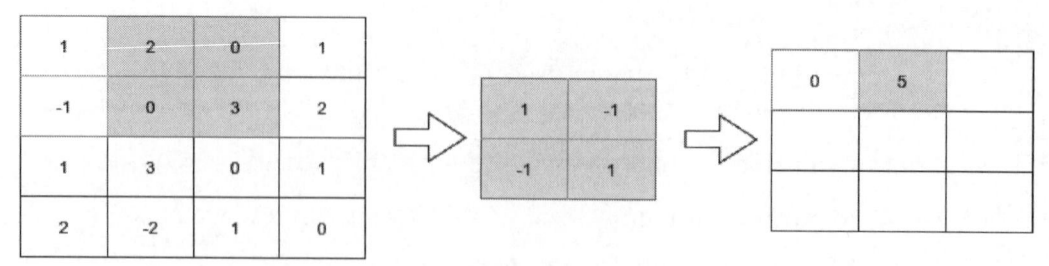

Figure 2.6: Convolution: 2nd step

And this operation takes place for each "box" in the input matrix. And at last, we have the following result:

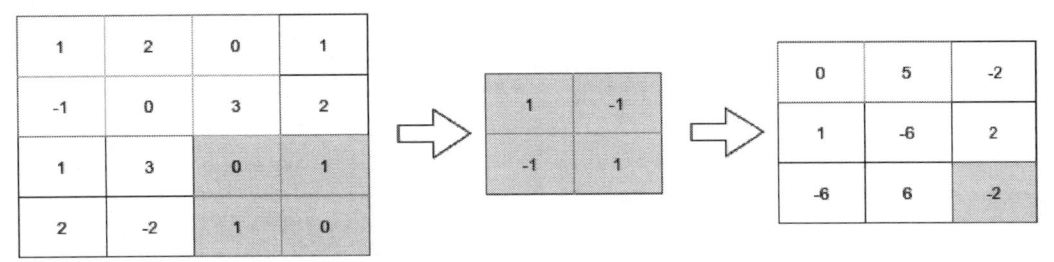

Figure 2.7: Convolution result

Let us do the same, but using PyTorch for 2-D convolution implementation **ch2/layers/conv2d.py**:

```
import torch
from torch.nn.parameter import Parameter
A = torch.tensor([[[[1, 2, 0, 1],
                   [-1, 0, 3, 2],
                   [1, 3, 0, 1],
                   [2, -2, 1, 0]]]]).float()
conv2d = torch.nn.Conv2d(1, 1, kernel_size = 2, bias = False)
conv2d.weight = Parameter(torch.tensor([[[[1, -1], [-1, 1]]]]).float())
output = conv2d(A)
print(output)
```

Result
```
tensor([[[[ 0.,  5., -2.],
          [ 1., -6.,  2.],
          [-6.,  6., -2.]]]], grad_fn=<MkldnnConvolutionBackward>)
```

Despite their simplicity, convolution layers allow to extract very complex patterns and dependencies from a dataset. In addition to 2 D convolutions, there are also 1

D and 3 D convolutions. These convolutions are calculated according to the same principle as the 2 D convolution:

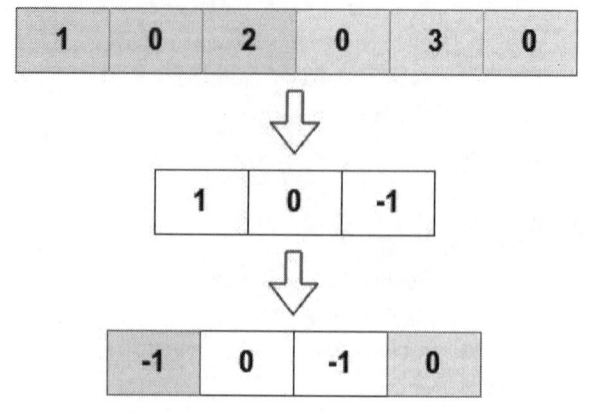

Figure 2.8: 1 D convolution example

The convolution layer can have multiple output channels, which means that multiple convolution tensors are applied to the input tensor:

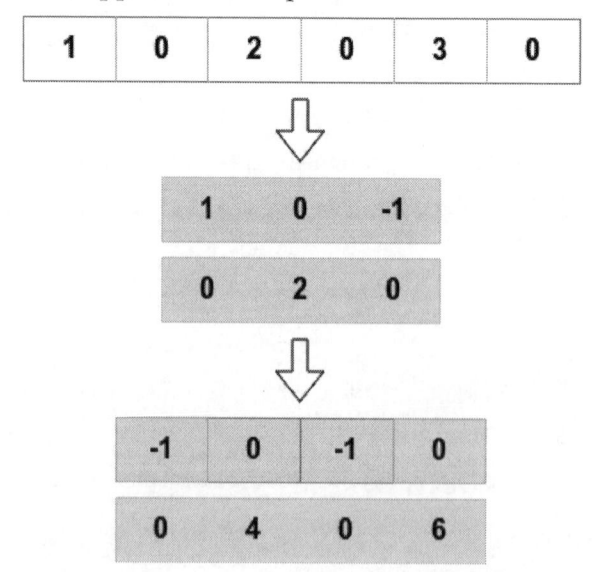

Figure 2.9: 1 D Convolution with two out channels

Let us have a look how the calculations shown in *Figure 2.9* are done by PyTorch **ch2/layers/conv1d.py**:

```
import torch
from torch.nn.parameter import Parameter
A = torch.tensor([[[1, 0, 2, 0, 3, 0]]]).float()
```

```
conv1d = torch.nn.Conv1d(1, out_channels = 2, kernel_size = 3, bias = False)
conv1d.weight = Parameter(torch.tensor([[[1, 0, -1]], [[0, 2, 0]]]).float())
output = conv1d(A)
print(output)
```

Result

```
tensor([[[-1.,  0., -1.,  0.],
         [ 0.,  4.,  0.,  6.]]], grad_fn=<SqueezeBackward1>)
```

The convolution layer has the following parameters:
- kernel
- weight
- padding
- stride

Kernel

Kernel is the size of a kernel tensor. Usually, kernel value is from 3 to 5. For 1-D Convolution `kernel=3` defines a vector with 3 elements as a kernel; for 2 D Convolution `kernel=3` defines a 3×3 matrix as a kernel, for 3-D Convolution `kernel=3` defines 3×3×3 tensor as a kernel:

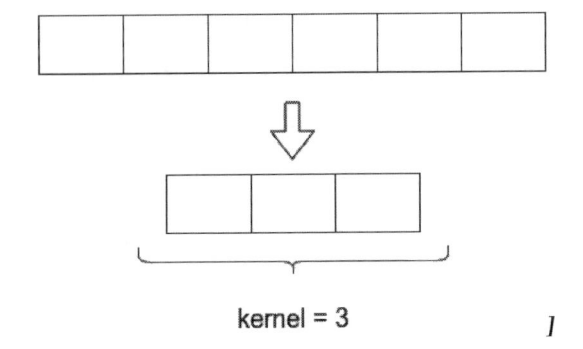

Figure 2.10: Convolution kernel

Weight

Weight is the actual kernel tensor. In the examples above, we have set weights manually, but it was done only to provide some examples of calculations. Convolution weights are being adjusted during neural network training, so normally you do not have to set these values by yourself.

Padding

Padding is a number of cells an input tensor can be extended by zeros. This technique is being used to obtain more information about the borders of the input tensor. An example of the convolution with padding is shown in *Figure 2.11*:

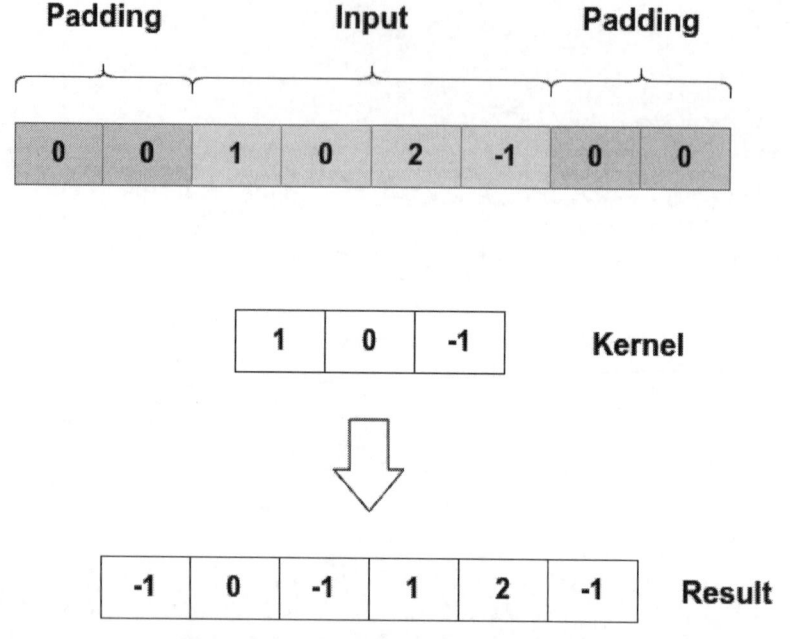

Figure 2.11: 1 D Convolution with padding=2

And below we provide the example of convolution shown in *Figure 2.11* with PyTorch ch2/layers/conv1d_padding.py:

```
import torch
from torch.nn.parameter import Parameter
A = torch.tensor([[[1, 0, 2, -1]]]).float()
conv1d = torch.nn.Conv1d(1, 1, kernel_size = 3, bias = False, padding = 2)
conv1d.weight = Parameter(torch.tensor([[[1, 0, -1]]]).float())
output = conv1d(A)
print(output.tolist())
```

Result

[[[-1.0, 0.0, -1.0, 1.0, 2.0, -1.0]]]

Stride

Stride is a size of step by which kernel tensor "slides" across the input tensor. *Figure 2.12* shows the example of 1 D Convolution with `stride=2`:

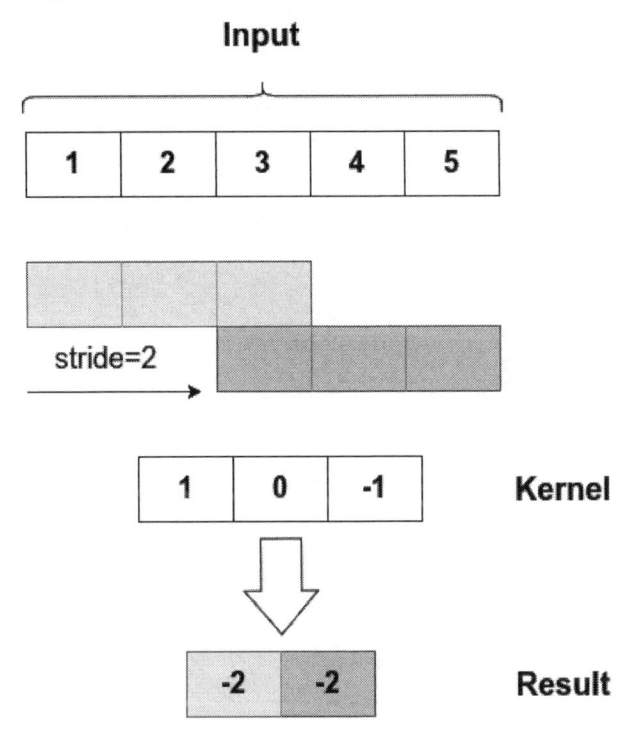

Figure 2.12: 1 D Convolution with stride=2

And here is the example of convolution with stride=2 in PyTorch `ch2/layers/conv1d_stride.py`:

```
import torch
from torch.nn.parameter import Parameter
A = torch.tensor([[[1, 2, 3, 4, 5]]]).float()
conv1d = torch.nn.Conv1d(1, 1, kernel_size = 3, bias = False, stride = 2)
conv1d.weight = Parameter(torch.tensor([[[1, 0, -1]]]).float())
output = conv1d(A)
print(output.tolist())
```

Result

```
[[[-2.0, -2.0]]]
```

Pooling

Pooling is an aggregation technique, which aims to reduce the size of the input tensor. The pooling layer tries to extract main tensor "features" and to reduce the computation costs.

The most popular pooling layers are Max Pooling and Average Pooling. The pooling layer has the kernel size. Regarding this kernel size, the aggregation action is taken. The most common kernel size of the pooling layer is 2.

Let us consider an example of 2 D Max Pooling layer in action in *Figure 2.13*:

Figure 2.13: 2 D Max Pooling with kernel size=2

And here is the same operation using PyTorch **ch2/layers/max_pool_2d.py**:

```
import torch
A = torch.tensor([[
    [1, 2, -1, 1],
    [0, 1, -2, -1],
    [3, 0, 5, 0],
    [0, 1, 4, -3]
]]).float()
max_pool = torch.nn.MaxPool2d(2)
out = max_pool(A)
```

```
print(out.tolist())
```
Result

[[
[2.0, 1.0],
[3.0, 5.0]
]]

Average pooling acts by the same principle but uses an average aggregation function instead of max:

Figure 2.14: *2 D Average Pooling with kernel size=2*

And here the example of 2-D Average Pooling with PyTorch `ch2/layers/avg_pool_2d.py`:

```
import torch
A = torch.tensor([[
    [1, 2, -1, 1],
    [0, 1, -2, -1],
    [3, 0, 5, 0],
    [0, 1, 4, -3]
]]).float()
avg_pool = torch.nn.AvgPool2d(2)
out = avg_pool(A)
print(out.tolist())
```

Result

[[

[1.0, -0.75],

[1.0, 1.5]

]]

Dropout

Dropout is an excellent regularization technique. A neural network is prone to overfitting. Overfitting leads to the problem when a model is trained, and it works so well on training data that it negatively affects the performance of the model on unobserved data. To overcome the problem of overfitting, a dropout layer can be used. The dropout layer is based on a straightforward principle: in the training mode, this layer drops out random elements of the input tensor with probability p. The left tensor elements are multiplied by $\frac{1}{1-p}$. In the evaluation mode, the dropout layer does not affect the input tensor untouched. Here is the example of dropout layer in action **ch2/layers/dropout.py**:

```
import torch
from torch.nn import Dropout
torch.manual_seed(1)
t = torch.randint(10, (5,)).float()
print(f'Initial Tensor: {t}')
dropout = Dropout(p = .5)
dropout.train()
r = dropout(t)
print(f'Dropout Train: {r}')
dropout.eval()
r = dropout(t)
print(f'Dropout Eval: {r}')
```

Result

Initial Tensor: tensor([5., 9., 4., 8., 3.])

Dropout Train: tensor([10., 18., 0., 16., 0.])

Dropout Eval: tensor([5., 9., 4., 8., 3.])

Activations

An **activation function** is a function that is added to a neural network to help the network learn complex nonlinear dependencies. A typical activation function should be differentiable and continuous everywhere. Below we provide some classic examples of activation functions in PyTorch.

ReLU

ReLU or Rectified linear function performs simple operation: `ReLU(x) = max(0,x)`. Here we provide an example of ReLU usage in PyTorch `ch2/layers/activation_relu.py`:

```
import torch
import matplotlib.pyplot as plt
x = torch.linspace(-10, 10)
relu = torch.nn.ReLU()
y = relu(x)
plt.title('ReLU')
plt.plot(x.tolist(), y.tolist())
plt.show()
```

Result

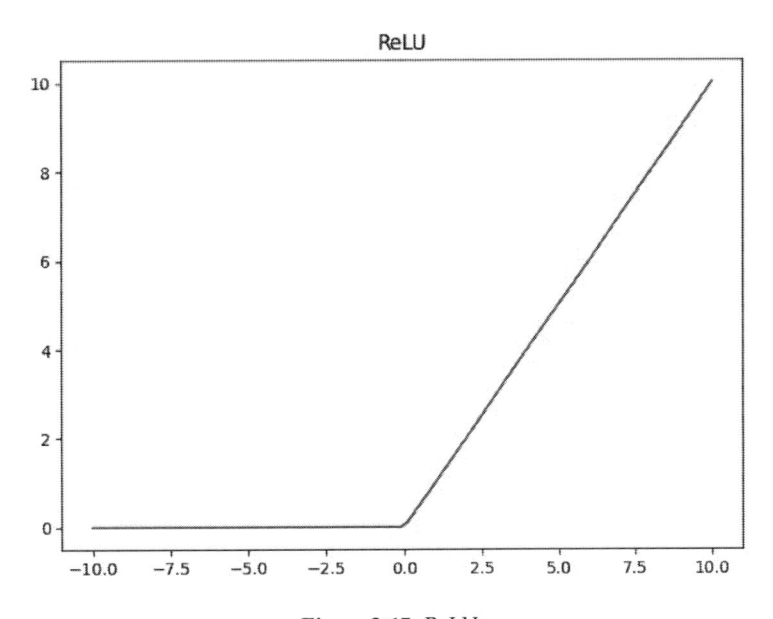

Figure 2.15: ReLU

Sigmoid

Sigmoid is one of the most common nonlinear activation functions. The sigmoid function is mathematically represented as:

$$sigmoid(x) = \frac{1}{(1+e^{-x})}$$

Like ReLU, the sigmoid function can be simply built using PyTorch **ch2/layers/activation_sigmoid.py**:

```
import torch
import matplotlib.pyplot as plt
x = torch.linspace(-10, 10)
relu = torch.nn.Sigmoid()
y = relu(x)
plt.title('Sigmoid')
plt.plot(x.tolist(), y.tolist())
plt.show()
```

Result

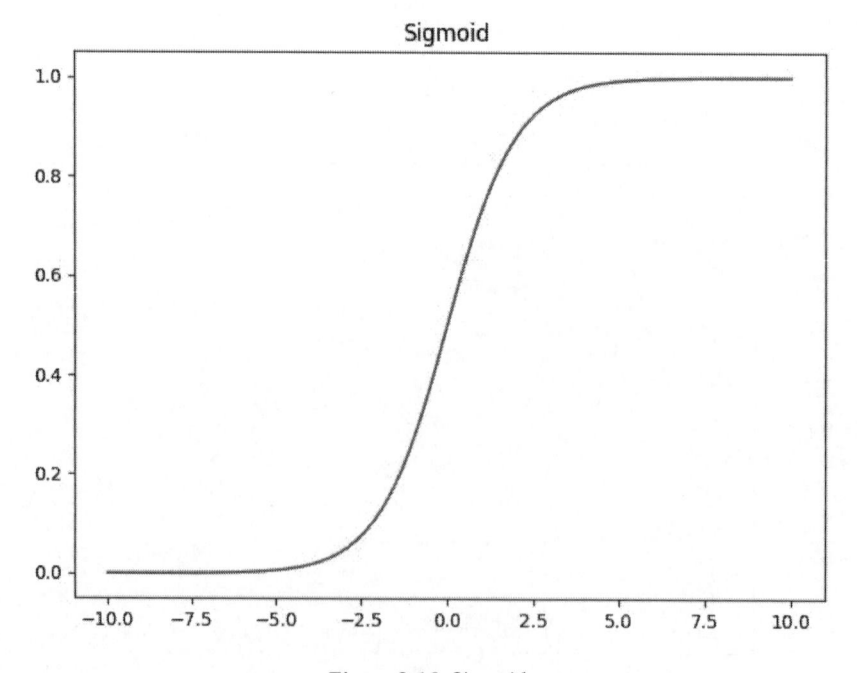

Figure 2.16: Sigmoid

Tanh

Tanh or **hyperbolic tangent function** is similar to the sigmoid function, but it returns values in the range (–1, 1). The benefit of tanh over sigmoid is that the negative inputs will be mapped strictly to negative, and the positive inputs will be mapped strictly to positive:

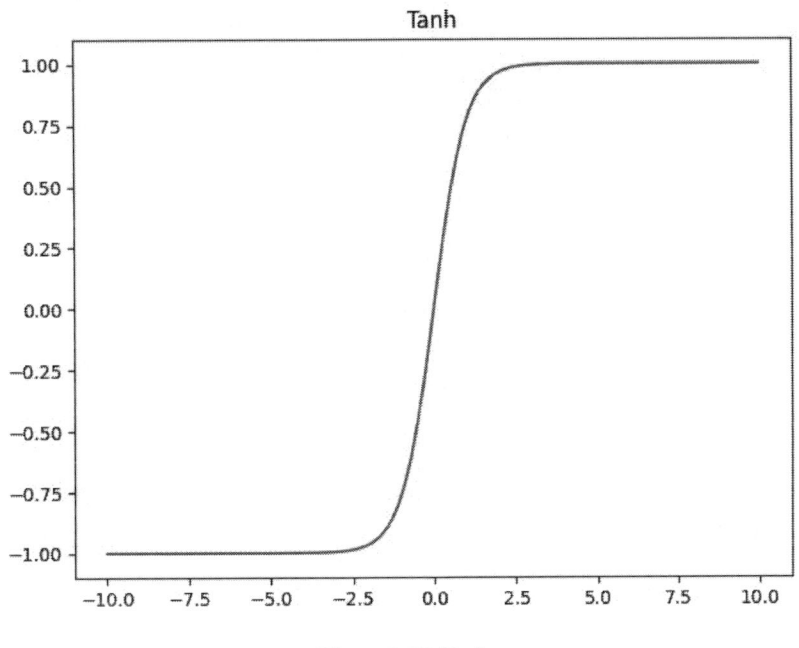

Figure 2.17: Tanh

Nonlinear activation functions, like sigmoid and tanh, suffer from a big computational problem called the vanishing gradient problem. Vanishing gradient makes it very difficult to train and adjust the initial layers' parameters in the network. This problem worsens as the number of layers in the network increases. The vanishing gradient is the main cause that makes sigmoid or tanh activations unsuitable for deep learning models. ReLU activation function does not suffer from vanishing gradient because the derivative is always 1 for positive inputs. So always consider using ReLU as the activation function at the first drafts of your model design.

Neural network architecture

To design neural network architecture, we need to create a computational graph. A computational graph is a directed graph of Deep Learning layers and activations.

Below we provide an example of visualization of neural network architecture for a common handwritten digit classification problem:

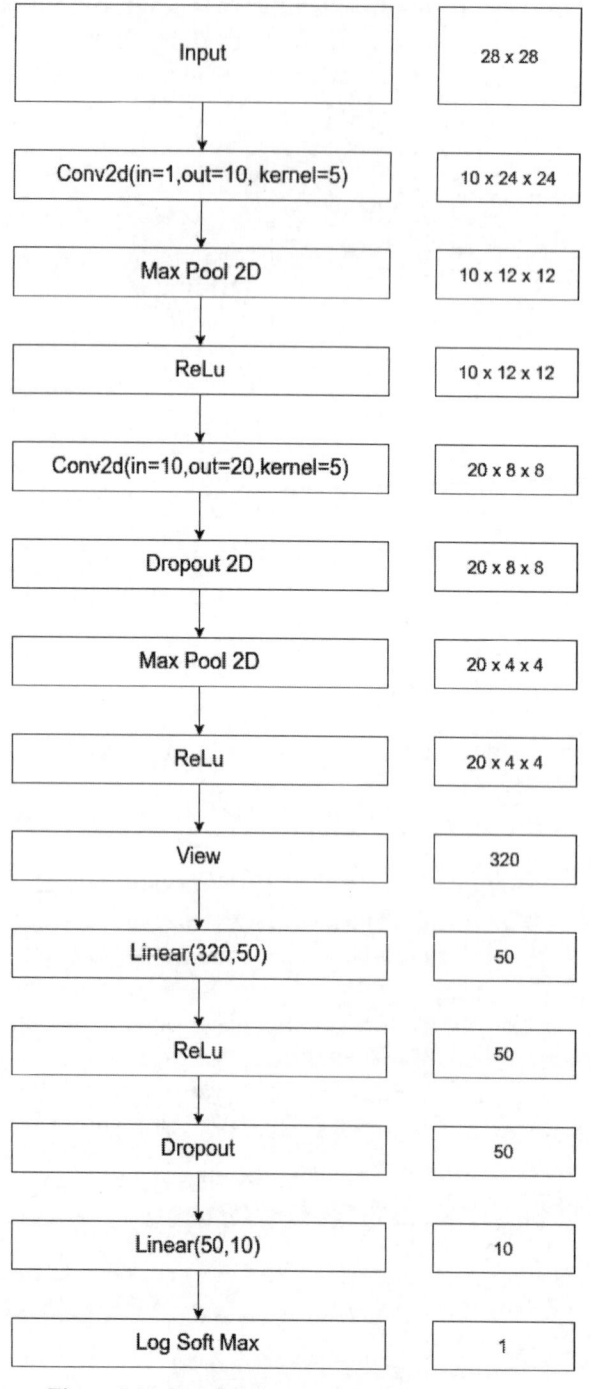

Layer	Shape
Input	28 x 28
Conv2d(in=1,out=10, kernel=5)	10 x 24 x 24
Max Pool 2D	10 x 12 x 12
ReLu	10 x 12 x 12
Conv2d(in=10,out=20,kernel=5)	20 x 8 x 8
Dropout 2D	20 x 8 x 8
Max Pool 2D	20 x 4 x 4
ReLu	20 x 4 x 4
View	320
Linear(320,50)	50
ReLu	50
Dropout	50
Linear(50,10)	10
Log Soft Max	1

Figure 2.18: Hand digit recognition NN architecture

Sometimes, we will add the size of tensors returned by each layer in the right column for convenience. The graphical representation of neural network architecture is very important for the intuitive understanding of its work and performance.

To create neural network architecture in PyTorch, we have to bind layers to the model and define a forward method **ch2/nn_architecture/mnist.py**:

```python
import torch.nn as nn
import torch.nn.functional as F
class MnistModel(nn.Module):
    def __init__(self):
        super(MnistModel, self).__init__()
        self.conv1 = nn.Conv2d(1, 10, kernel_size = 5)
        self.conv2 = nn.Conv2d(10, 20, kernel_size = 5)
        self.conv2_drop = nn.Dropout2d()
        self.fc1 = nn.Linear(320, 50)
        self.fc2 = nn.Linear(50, 10)
    def forward(self, x):
        x = self.conv1(x)
        x = F.max_pool2d(x, 2)
        x = F.relu(x)
        x = self.conv2(x)
        x = self.conv2_drop(x)
        x = F.max_pool2d(x, 2)
        x = F.relu(x)
        x = x.view(-1, 320)
        x = F.relu(self.fc1(x))
        x = F.dropout(x, training = self.training)
        x = self.fc2(x)
        return F.log_softmax(x)
```

As we see, each model is a subclass of **torch.nn.Module**, so it inherits special logic and methods. It useful sometimes to list all layers of a model using the **named_children()** method **ch2/nn_architecture/named_children.py**:

```python
from ch2.nn_architecture.mnist import MnistModel
net = MnistModel()
for name, layer in net.named_children():
    print(f'{name}: {layer}')
```

Result

```
conv1: Conv2d(1, 10, kernel_size=(5, 5), stride=(1, 1))
conv2: Conv2d(10, 20, kernel_size=(5, 5), stride=(1, 1))
conv2_drop: Dropout2d(p=0.5, inplace=False)
fc1: Linear(in_features=320, out_features=50, bias=True)
fc2: Linear(in_features=50, out_features=10, bias=True)
```

Some of the model layers, like the dropout layer, behave differently in training mode and in evaluation mode. As well, a deep learning model has two main modes: training and evaluation. Method `train()` is used to set training mode and method `eval()` to set evaluation one. Here is an example of how these methods are being used `ch2/nn_architecture/train_eval.py`:

```
from ch2.nn_architecture.mnist import MnistModel
net = MnistModel()
print(f'Training mode enabled: {net.training}')
net.eval()
print(f'Training mode enabled: {net.training}')
net.train()
print(f'Training mode enabled: {net.training}')
```

Result

```
Training mode enabled: True
Training mode enabled: False
Training mode enabled: True
```

Another handy PyTorch methods for `torch.nn.Module`:
- `zero_grad()` - Sets all weight gradients to zero
- `parameters()` - Set of parameters of each layer
- `children()` - Iterator over children modules
- `float()` - Casts all floating-point parameters to float datatype
- `modules()` - Iterator over all modules in the network

Improving neural network performance

The creation of a neural network architecture that is best suited for a particular problem is an art. There is a separate study direction in deep learning named Neural

Architecture Search, which automates network architecture engineering: **https://lilianweng.github.io/lil-log/2020/08/06/neural-architecture-search.html**. But even these search engines cannot compete with human heuristic abilities in design yet. There are some techniques that raise the probability of neural network performance improvement. Of course, these techniques do not guarantee improvement in all cases. Sometimes they can even worsen the neural network performance. But you likely develop robust model architecture following these approaches.

Do not put two same layers in a row

Usually, the application of two same layer types in a row has no positive effect. Furthermore, it can even worsen the performance of your model. That is why avoid using designs where there are sequences like:

- … → Convolution Layer → Convolution Layer → …
- … → Pooling Layer → Pooling Layer → …
- … → Sigmoid Activation → ReLU Activation → …

Prefer ReLU activation at first

Non-linear activation functions like tanh or sigmoid are suffering the gradient vanishing problem. It can slow down the learning process of a model drastically. ReLU is a linear function, and its gradient is distributed uniformly to all layer weights. So in the first sketches of your model design, prefer using the ReLU activation function.

Start from fully connected network

It is better to start your experiments from the classical fully connected network. A fully connected network is a network that uses only linear layers and activation functions:

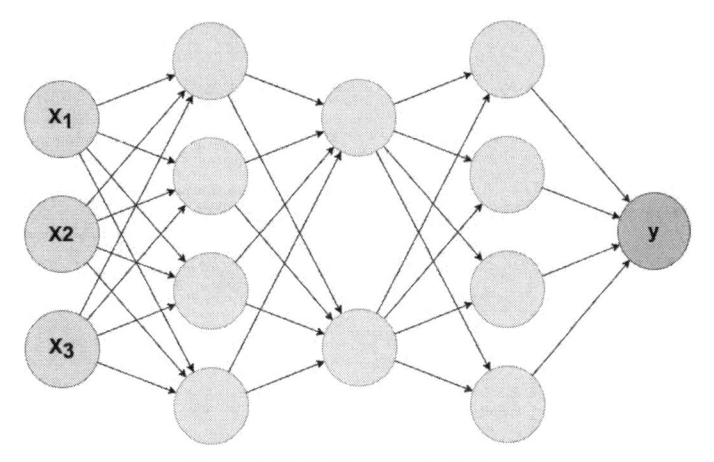

Figure 2.19: Fully connected network

> **Note:** The visualization used in *Figure 2.19* can be used only for fully connected networks. It is tough to create meaningful network visualization for a complex deep network using such style.

Below we provide a fully connected network representation using computational graph style:

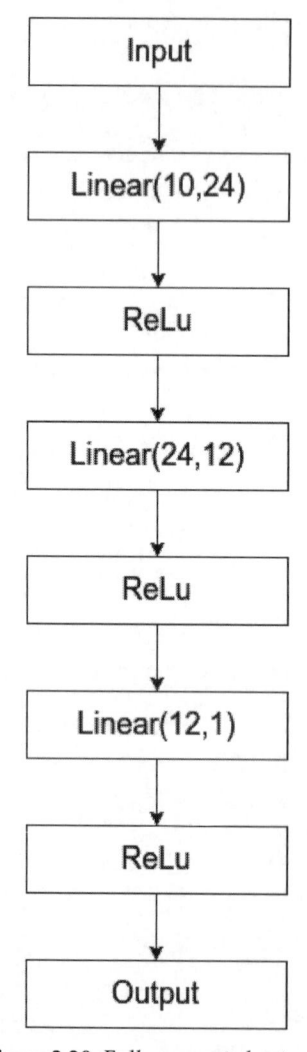

Figure 2.20: Fully connected network

More layers are better than more neurons

Usually, your model will get more effectiveness from adding more layers than adding more neurons in each layer. It means that if you are using a linear layer in your model, then is it better to add another linear layer instead of increasing the number of neurons in the existing one, like it is shown in *Figure 2.21*:

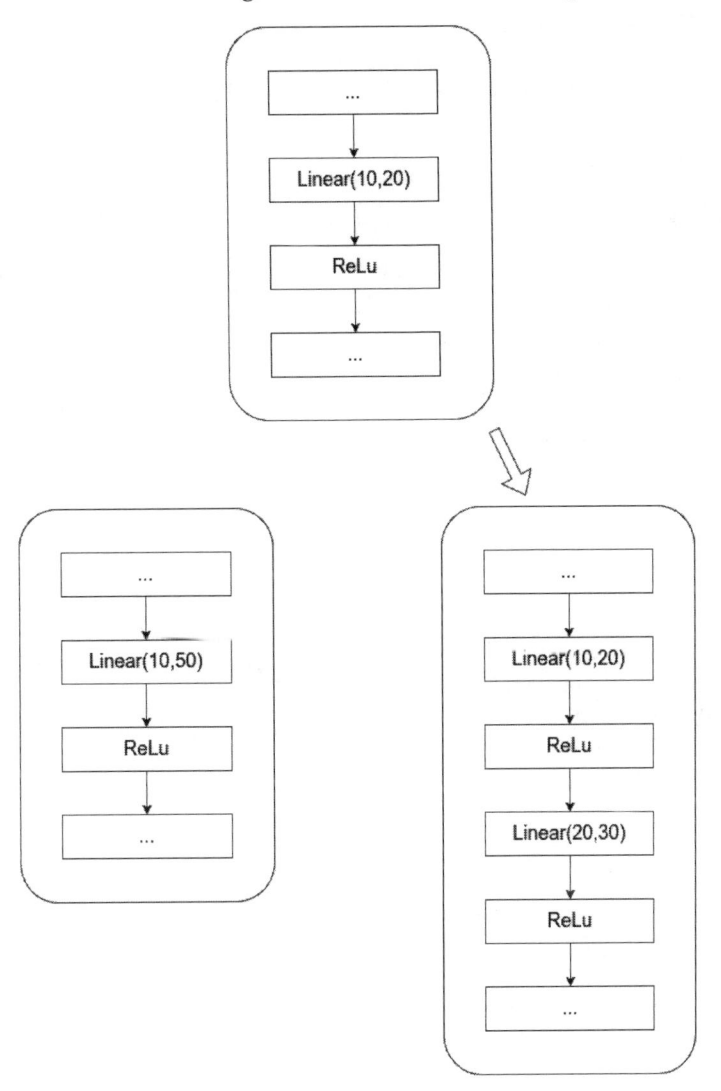

Figure 2.21: Linear Layer Improvement

Use dropout

Dropout is a fantastic regularization technique that improves the learning ability of your model drastically. Dropout makes the network more robust because it cannot rely on any particular set of input neurons for making predictions. Thus network tries to extract patterns from different places of a dataset. The knowledge is distributed amongst the whole network.

Put Deep Learning blocks in the beginning

Deep Learning layers like convolution, pooling, padding are best used for advanced, sophisticated feature extraction. They are not well suited for decision-making. So it is better to put these layers at the beginning of your model, like it is done in the architecture of the handwritten digit recognition model *Figure 2.18*.

Training

Roughly speaking, training is a weight adjustment by processing input examples and known "answers". During training, the model results are compared with the actual ones, and it is possible to understand how "*far*" current model weights are from being "*good*". The weight adjustment is realized through backward propagation of errors or shortly *backpropagation*. This method calculates the gradient of the error function concerning the neural network's weights:

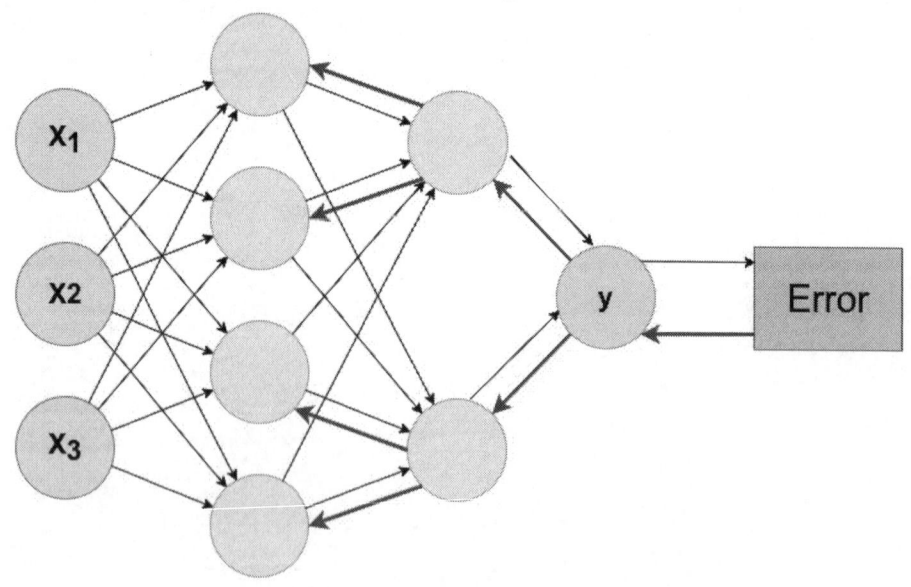

Figure 2.22: Backpropagation

Sometimes the concept of training is included in neural network architecture. It is better to distinguish these concepts. Same network architecture can be trained with different approaches and vice versa. The same training approach can be applied to different architectures.

To perform training in PyTorch, we have to define *loss* and *optimization* functions. The loss function will calculate a network error at each iteration, while the optimization function determines *"how and in what direction to shift weight parameters"*.

Loss functions

There are a various number of loss functions, each of them is meant for a particular task. For time series analysis there are three main loss functions: L1 loss or absolute loss, L2 loss or mean squared error, and smooth l1 loss.

Absolute loss

Absolute loss is the simplest metric of the distance between two vectors:

$$absolute\ loss = \frac{\sum |y_{actual} - y_{predicted}|}{n}$$

In PyTorch, the absolute loss function is implemented the following way:

```
import torch
a = torch.tensor([1, 2]).float()
b = torch.tensor([1, 5]).float()
abs_loss = torch.nn.L1Loss()
abs_error = abs_loss(a, b)
print(f'abs: {abs_error.item()}')
>>>
abs: 1.5
```

Mean squared error

Mean squared error, or simply MSE, is the most commonly used loss function for time series prediction problems:

$$mean\ squared\ error = \frac{\sum (y_{actual} - y_{predicted})^2}{n}$$

Smooth L1 loss

Smooth L1 loss is something intermediate between absolute and MSE loss functions. Smooth L1 loss is less sensitive to outliers than MSE:

$$smooth\_loss(y', y) = \frac{1}{n}\sum z_i$$

where y' is actual value, y is predicted value and z_i is defined as:

$$z_i = \begin{cases} \frac{0.5(y'_i - y_i)^2}{beta}, & if\ |y'_i - y_i| < beta \\ |y'_i - y_i| - 0.5 \cdot beta, & otherwise \end{cases}$$

Smooth L1 loss function has *beta* parameter, it equals 1 by default.

Optimizers

The main purpose of an **optimizer** is to shift the model's weight parameters to minimize the loss function. The selection of a suitable optimizer depends entirely on the architecture of the neural network and the data on which the training occurs.

Adagrad

Adagrad is a gradient-based optimization algorithm that adapts the learning rate to the parameters. It performs smaller updates for parameters associated with frequently occurring features and larger updates for parameters associated with rare features.

Adadelta

Adadelta is the advanced version of the Adagrad algorithm. Adadelta seeks to minimize its aggressive, monotonically decreasing learning rate. Instead of accumulating all past gradients, Adadelta limits the window of accumulated past gradients to some fixed size.

Adam

Adaptive Moment Estimation or **Adam** is another optimization method that computes adaptive learning rates for each parameter. In addition to saving an exponentially decaying average of past squared gradients like Adadelta, Adam also keeps an exponentially declining average of previous gradients.

Stochastic Gradient Descent (SGD)

SGD randomly picks one data row from the whole input dataset at each training iteration to decrease computation time. It also samples a small number of data rows instead of just one row at each step. This approach is called "mini-batch" gradient descent. Mini-batch descent tries to place a balance between the goodness of gradient descent and the speed of SGD.

In general, the training process in PyTorch looks the following way:

```
net = FooModel()
optimizer = torch.optim.Adam(params = net.parameters())
loss_func = torch.nn.MSELoss()
for i in range(1000):
    y_predicted = net(x_train)
    loss = loss_func(y_predicted, y_train)
```

```
optimizer.zero_grad()
loss.backward()
optimizer.step()
```

Time series forecasting example

Let us consider an example of time series forecasting problem. Say we have the following combined time series model:

$$T_t = 300 + 0.2t + 5sin(\frac{t}{5}) + 20cos(\frac{t}{24}) + 100sin(\frac{t}{120}) + 20R_t$$

This time series model has a trend, random deviation, and three seasonable periods.

We can realize this time series model the following way **ch2/nn/time_series.py**:

```
import random
from math import sin, cos
import matplotlib.pyplot as plt
def get_time_series_data(length):
    a = .2
    b = 300
    c = 20
    ls = 5
    ms = 20
    gs = 100
    ts = []
    for i in range(length):
        ts.append(b + a * i + ls * sin(i / 5) + ms * cos(i / 24) + gs * sin(i / 120) + c * random.random())
    return ts
if __name__ == '__main__':
    data = get_time_series_data(3_000)
    plt.plot(data)
    plt.show()
```

Result

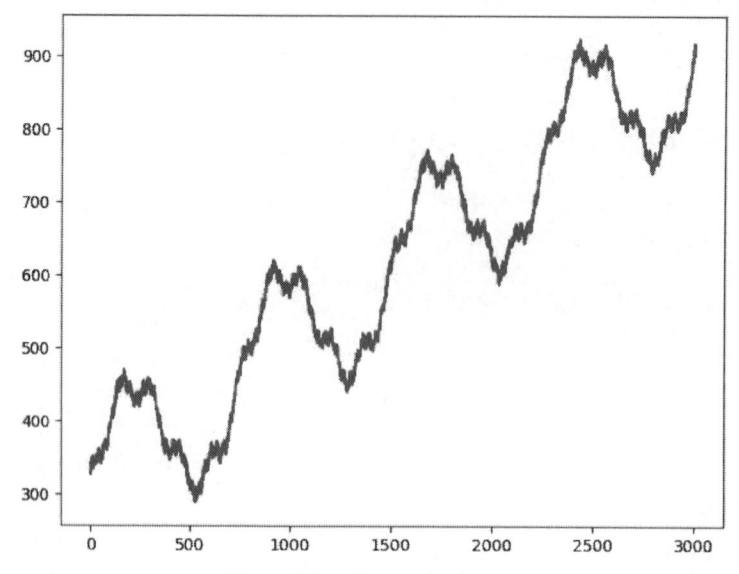

Figure 2.23: Time series dataset

Now we have to prepare a time series dataset as the series of inputs and outputs, and it is done using the *sliding window* technique. Sequences are grouped within a fixed-size window that slides across the data stream according to a specified interval. *Figure 2.24* visualizes this approach:

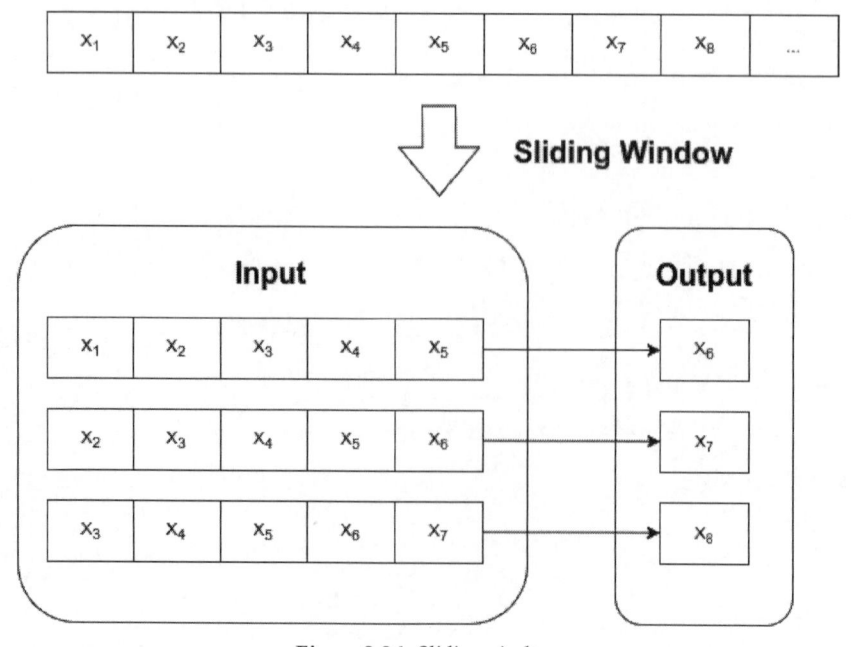

Figure 2.24: Sliding eindow

For supervised learning, we have to prepare train, validation and test datasets **ch2/nn/dataset.py**:

Import part

```
import torch
from ch2.nn.time_series import get_time_series_data
from sklearn.model_selection import train_test_split
```

Train, validation and test datasets

```
def get_time_series_datasets(features, ts_len):
    ts = get_time_series_data(ts_len)
    X = []
    Y = []
    for i in range(features + 1, ts_len):
        X.append(ts[i - (features + 1):i - 1])
        Y.append([ts[i]])
    X_train, X_test, Y_train, Y_test = train_test_split(X, Y, test_size = 0.3, shuffle = False)
    X_val, X_test, Y_val, Y_test = train_test_split(X_test, Y_test, test_size = 0.5, shuffle = False)
    x_train = torch.tensor(data = X_train)
    y_train = torch.tensor(data = Y_train)
    x_val = torch.tensor(data = X_val)
    y_val = torch.tensor(data = Y_val)
    x_test = torch.tensor(data = X_test)
    y_test = torch.tensor(data = Y_test)
    return x_train, x_val, x_test, y_train, y_val, y_test
```

We will use trivial Fully Connected Neural Network for this problem forecasting problem **ch2/nn/fcnn_model.py**:

```
import torch
import torch.nn.functional as F
class FCNN(torch.nn.Module):
    def __init__(self, n_inp, l_1, l_2, n_out):
        super(FCNN, self).__init__()
```

```python
        self.lin1 = torch.nn.Linear(n_inp, l_1)
        self.lin2 = torch.nn.Linear(l_1, l_2)
        self.lin3 = torch.nn.Linear(l_2, n_out)
    def forward(self, x):
        x1 = F.relu(self.lin1(x))
        x2 = F.relu(self.lin2(x1))
        y = self.lin3(x2)
        return y
```

It is always better to have another model for comparison to understand how effective the model we developed is. For this purpose, we will add another forecasting models to our study.

At first, we will add a straightforward model, which always predicts the last observed value. For example, if today's temperature is 20 degrees, tomorrow's prediction will be 20 degrees. Here is the implementation for this "dummy" predictor **ch2/nn/dummy_model.py**:

```python
import torch
class DummyPredictor(torch.nn.Module):
    def forward(self, x):
        last_values = []
        for r in x.tolist():
            last_values.append([r[-1]])
        return torch.tensor(data = last_values)
```

Another predictor will use linear interpolation for its forecast **ch2/nn/linear_interpolation_model.py**:

```python
from scipy import interpolate
import torch
import numpy as np
class InterpolationPredictor(torch.nn.Module):
    def forward(self, x):
        last_values = []
        values = x.tolist()
        for v in values:
            x = np.arange(0, len(v))
            y = interpolate.interp1d(x, v, fill_value = 'extrapolate')
```

```
            last_values.append([y(len(v)).tolist()])
        return torch.tensor(data = last_values)
```

And the last one is based on HWES classical method, which we covered in *Chapter 1* **ch2/nn/hwes_model.py**:

```
from statsmodels.tsa.holtwinters import ExponentialSmoothing
import torch
class HwesPredictor(torch.nn.Module):
    def forward(self, x):
        last_values = []
        for r in x.tolist():
            model = ExponentialSmoothing(r)
            results = model.fit()
            forecast = results.forecast()
            last_values.append([forecast[0]])
        return torch.tensor(data = last_values)
```

So now we are ready to start **ch2/nn/example.py**:

Import part

```
import copy
import torch
import torch.nn.functional as F
import matplotlib.pyplot as plt
from ch2.nn.dataset import get_time_series_datasets
from ch2.nn.dummy_model import DummyPredictor
from ch2.nn.fcnn_model import FCNN
from ch2.nn.hwes_model import HwesPredictor
from ch2.nn.linear_interpolation_model import InterpolationPredictor
```

Let us make this script reproducible:

```
random.seed(1)
torch.manual_seed(1)
```

We will use 256 as sliding window size and 3000 as time series length:

```
features = 256
ts_len = 3_000
```

Datasets for training, validation and testing:

```
x_train, x_val, x_test, y_train, y_val, y_test = get_time_series_
datasets(features, ts_len)
```

Next, we initialize prediction models:

```
net = FCNN(n_inp = features, l_1 = 64, l_2 = 32, n_out = 1)
net.train()
dummy_predictor = DummyPredictor()
interpolation_predictor = InterpolationPredictor()
hwes_predictor = HwesPredictor()
```

We will use Mean Squared Error as a loss function and Adam as the training optimization algorithm:

```
optimizer = torch.optim.Adam(params = net.parameters())
loss_func = torch.nn.MSELoss()
```

We will choose the model that has shown the best results on the validation set:

```
best_model = None
min_val_loss = 1_000_000
```

Let us start the training process of the FCNN model:

```
for t in range(10_000):
    prediction = net(x_train)
    loss = loss_func(prediction, y_train)
    optimizer.zero_grad()
    loss.backward()
    optimizer.step()
    val_prediction = net(x_val)
    val_loss = loss_func(val_prediction, y_val)
    training_loss.append(loss.item())
    validation_loss.append(val_loss.item())
    if val_loss.item() < min_val_loss:
        best_model = copy.deepcopy(net)
        min_val_loss = val_loss.item()
```

```
    if t % 1000 == 0:
        print(f'epoch {t}: train - {round(loss.item(), 4)}, val: -
{round(val_loss.item(), 4)}')
```

Next, we evaluate our models on the test set:

```
net.eval()
print('Testing')
print(f'FCNN Loss: {loss_func(best_model(x_test), y_test).item()}')
print(f'Dummy Loss: {loss_func(dummy_predictor(x_test), y_test).
item()}')
print(f'Linear Interpolation Loss: {loss_func(interpolation_predictor(x_
test), y_test).item()}')
print(f'HWES Loss: {loss_func(hwes_predictor(x_test), y_test).item()}')
>>>
Testing
FCNN Loss: 38.09475326538086
Dummy Loss: 75.77690887451172
Linear Interpolation Loss: 220.05862426757812
HWES Loss: 59.2370344161188
```

And here we have very promising results. Our trivial fully connected neural network has shown the best results from all models. Let us visualize the training process:

```
plt.title("Training progress")
plt.yscale("log")
plt.plot(training_loss, label = 'training loss')
plt.plot(validation_loss, label = 'validation loss')
plt.legend()
```

```
plt.show()
>>>
```

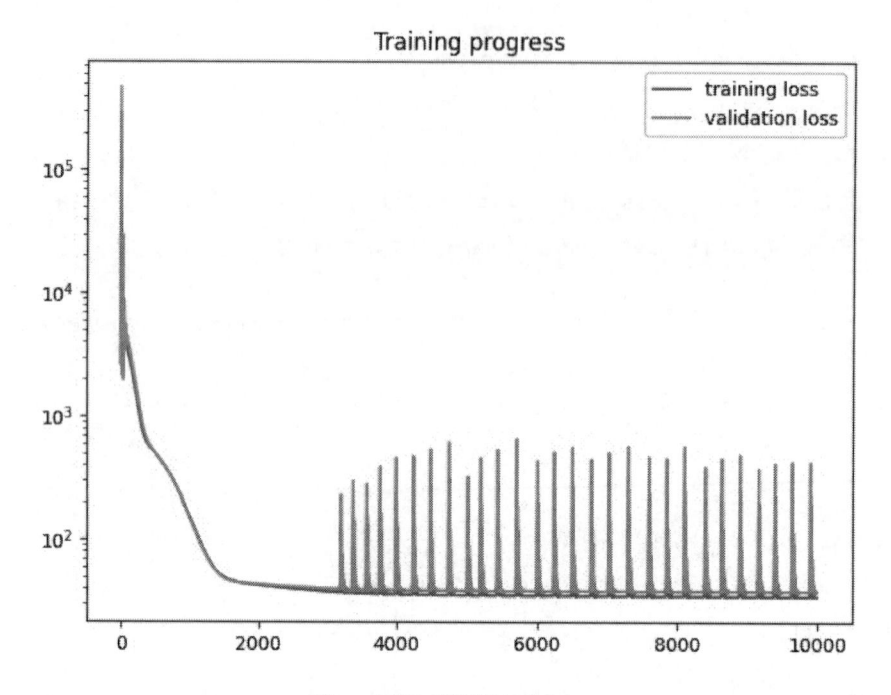

Figure 2.25: FCNN training

We can see that training and validation curves are very close, and we can conclude that our model has caught a behaviour of time series. Yes, the validation curve has some *"sharp spikes"*, but that is a normal training situation when the gradient *"slides"* too far and gets back in the next steps.

Let us see how the FCNN model performs on the training set:

```
plt.title("FCNN on Train Dataset")
plt.plot(y_train, label = 'actual')
plt.plot(best_model(x_train).tolist(), label = 'predicted')
plt.legend()
plt.show()
>>>
```

FCNN on Train Dataset

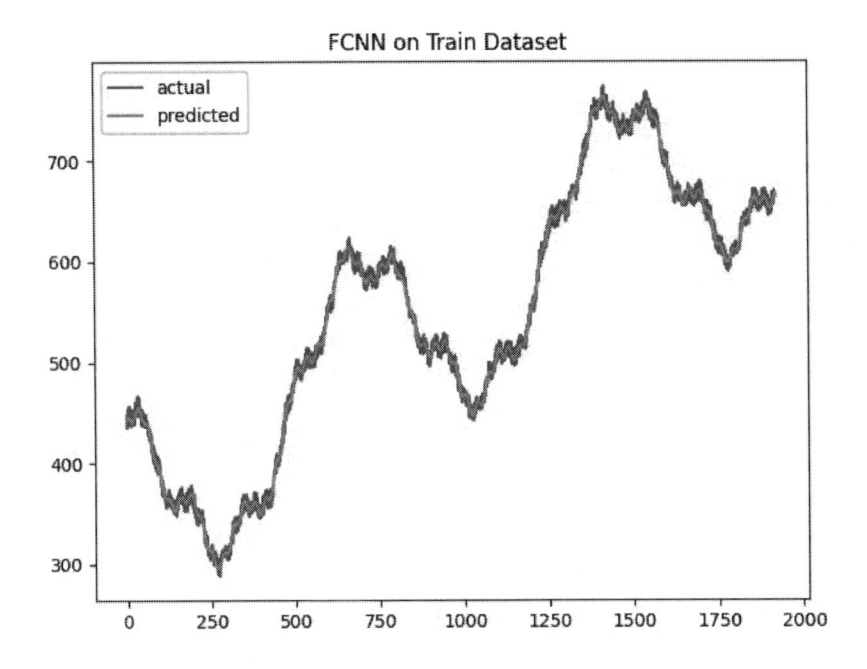

Figure 2.26: FCNN evaluation on the training set

It looks nice, but it is tough to understand how effective the model is. Let us try to compare the evaluation of FCNN and HWES on the test set:

```
plt.title('Test')
plt.plot(y_test, '--', label = 'actual')
plt.plot(best_model(x_test).tolist(), label = 'FCNN')
plt.plot(hwes_predictor(x_test).tolist(), label = 'HWES')
plt.legend()
```

```
plt.show()
>>>
```

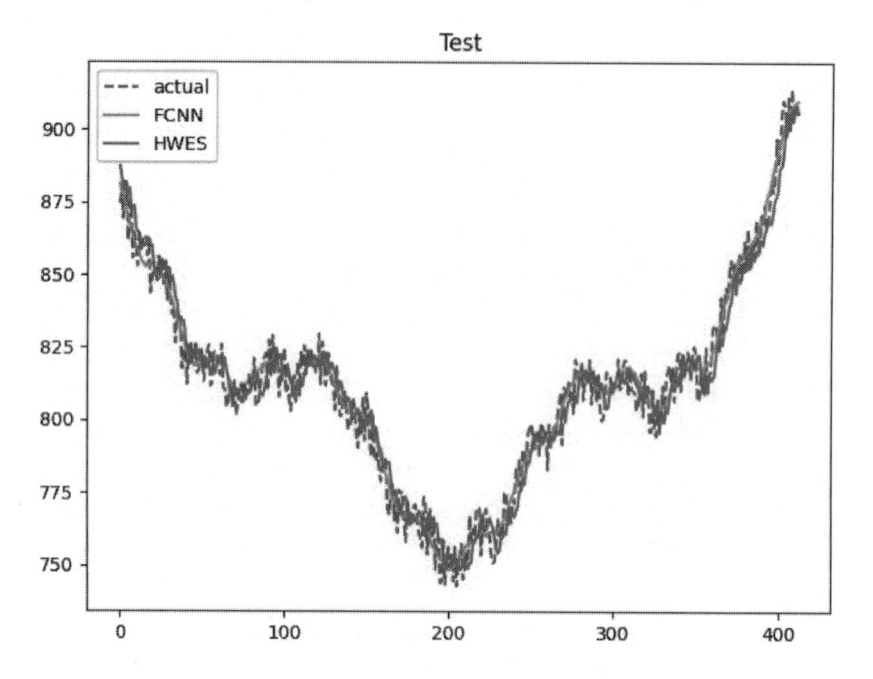

Figure 2.27: FCNN evaluation on the training set

Figure 2.26 still does not give an answer to which model performs better. And of course, we do not need any visual proof because we have already calculated FCNN and HWES loss on the test set. But there is one visualization that can help to understand the difference between the two prediction models:

```
test_n = len(y_test)
net_abs_dev = (best_model(x_test) - y_test).abs_()
hwes_abs_dev = (hwes_predictor(x_test) - y_test).abs_()
diff_pos = F.relu(hwes_abs_dev - net_abs_dev).reshape(test_n).tolist()
diff_min = (-F.relu(net_abs_dev - hwes_abs_dev)).reshape(test_n).tolist()
plt.title('HWES Predictor VS FCNN Predictor')
plt.hlines(0, xmin = 0, xmax = test_n, linestyles = 'dashed')
plt.bar(list(range(test_n)), diff_pos, color = 'g', label = 'FCNN Wins')
plt.bar(list(range(test_n)), diff_min, color = 'r', label = 'HWES Wins')
plt.legend()
plt.show()
>>>
```

HWES Predictor VS FCNN Predictor

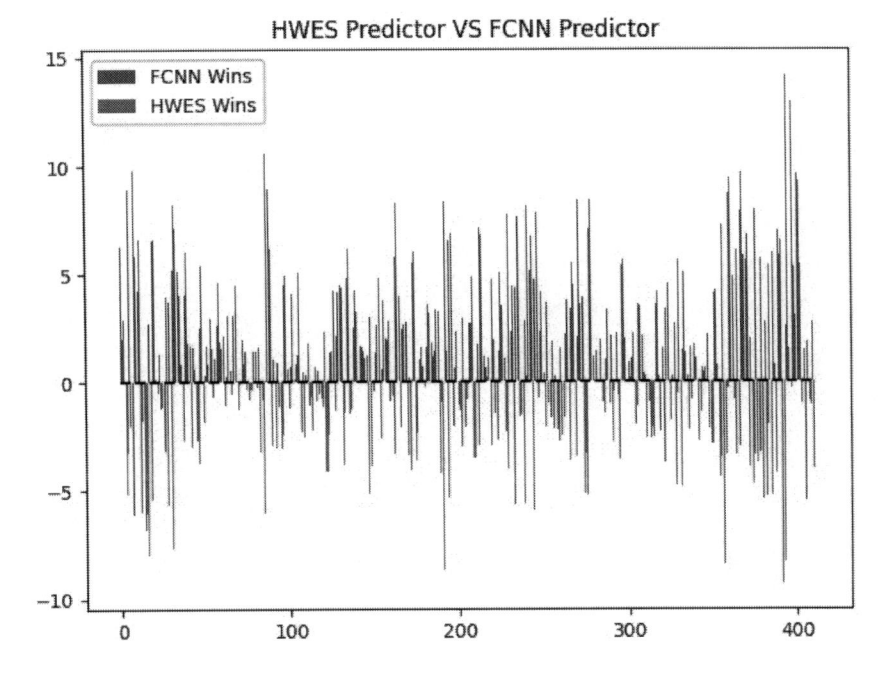

Figure 2.28: FCNN vs HWES

If the FCNN prediction is closer to the actual value than the HWES prediction, then we get a green bar. The green bar height shows how far HWES prediction is far from FCNN prediction. And if HWES prediction is closer to the actual value than FCNN prediction, then we get a red bar. This visualization is more obvious that FCNN predicts time series data more often and more precisely than HWES.

In this example, we have shown that neural networks have nice potential in time series prediction compared to classical models. We have designed a rather simple FCNN model with a trivial sequence of layers:

$$\text{Input} \to \text{Linear} \to \text{ReLU} \to \text{Linear} \to \text{ReLU} \to \text{Linear} \to \text{Output}$$

But even this architecture has won in this contest. In the next chapters, we will learn more sophisticated deep learning architectures and their application to real-world problems.

Conclusion

In this chapter, we have studied deep learning basics and their implementation in PyTorch. Now we know how to design and train deep networks. We also examined the simple implementation of a neural network to time series forecasting, and we have seen its strength. In the next chapter, we will study how to treat time series forecasting as a supervised machine learning problem.

Points to remember

- Tensor is the main object of PyTorch.
- Linear layers are best used at the final steps of network architecture.
- Convolution layers are used for feature extraction and are best used at the first steps of network architecture.
- Pooling layers are used for aggregation to improve network training performance.
- Dropout layers are used as a regularization technique in order not to fall into an overfitting problem.
- ReLU activation function does not suffer from vanishing gradient problem.

Multiple choice questions

1. **Say we have the following tensor:**

   [
   [1, 0, 0],
   [0, 1, 0],
   [0, 0, 1]
   ]

   What function could produce the tensor above?

   A. torch.ones(3)

   B. torch.eye(3,3)

   C. torch.eye(3)

2. **Say we have the following input tensor:**

   [2, 5, 5, 7]
   and the following output tensor:
   [0, 10, 0, 14]

   What layer could produce this result?

   A. Max Pooling

   B. Dropout with p = 0.2

   C. Linear

   D. Dropout with p = 0.5

3. Which activation function has a constant derivative? :

A. ReLU

B. Sigmoid

C. Tanh

Answers
1. C
2. D
3. B

Key terms

- *Linear layer:* Applies classical linear mapping of the input tensor.
- *Convolution layer:* Applies convolution kernel to extract features from the dataset.
- *Pooling layer:* Aggregates "cell" of the tensor to reduce the input tensor size.
- *Dropout layer:* Randomly *"drops out"* elements from the input tensor.
- *ReLU activation:* Linear activation.
- *Sigmoid activation:* Nonlinear activation in range (0, 1).
- *Tanh activation:* Nonlinear activation in range (-1, 1).
- *Absolute loss:* Sum of all absolute deviations between two tensors.
- *Mean squared error:* Average of the squares of the errors.

CHAPTER 3
Time Series as Deep Learning Problem

At the moment, we know what time series analysis is, and we have studied PyTorch as a tool for building deep learning models. The last chapter showed how a simple neural network could predict the next values in generated time series sequence. But still, we are far from getting down to work with the real-world problems of time series analysis. We must know how to formulate the problem and look for its solution correctly. In this chapter, we will study time series problems from a supervised learning view.

Structure

In this chapter, we will discuss the following topics:
- Problem statement
- Regression versus classification
- Univariate versus multivariate
- Single-step versus multi-step
- Datasets
- Sliding window

- Feature engineering
- Time series preprocessing and post-processing
- Effectiveness and loss function
- Static versus dynamic
- Architecture design
- Training, validating, and testing
- Alternative model
- Model optimization
- Example: UK monthly minimal temperature prediction problem

Objectives

This chapter's primary purpose is to describe the time series forecasting task as a supervised learning problem. After reading this chapter, the reader will know various types of prediction models and how to formulate a task correctly, prepare input and output data for neural networks training, and estimate their effectiveness.

Problem statement

Before we start preparing to develop a deep learning model, we must clearly understand what we want to achieve. Perhaps we want to predict the maximum temperature for the next day; maybe we want to classify human activity according to the sensors' data. A common mistake before developing a model is unclear requirements.

Regression versus classification

All supervised learning problems are divided into two parts: regression tasks and classification tasks. Regression models attempt to estimate the mapping function f from the inputs x to numerical or continuous outputs variable y. On the other hand, classification models try to estimate the mapping function f from the inputs x to categorical outputs variable y.

Time series regression problems

The most common regression problem for time series is a forecasting task. The forecasting task assumes the development of the model, that returns some number to predict future value. It is difficult to overestimate the practical significance of this task. 90% of all problems related to time series are reduced to the forecasting, expressed as a regression problem in a supervised learning context:

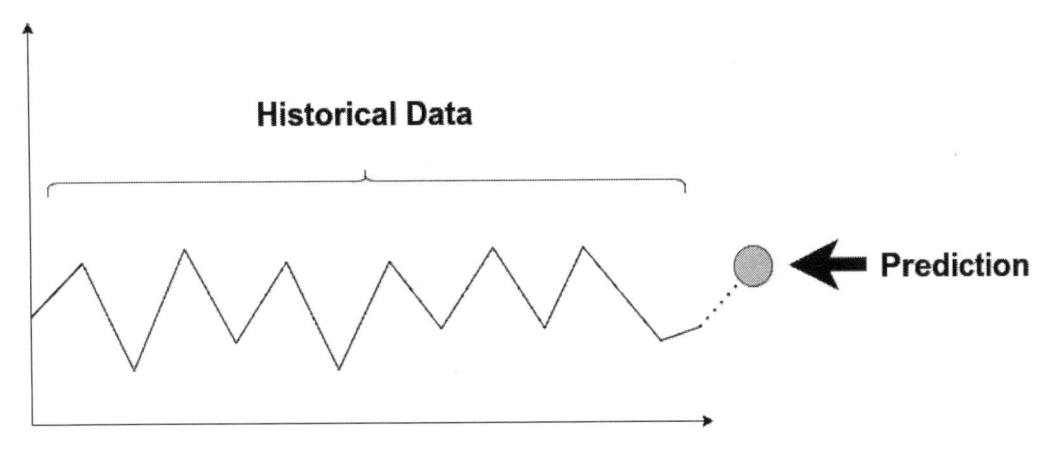

Figure 3.1: Time series forecasting as a regression problem

Time series classification problems

Forecasting tasks can also be formulated as classification problems. For example, if we need to determine tomorrow's weather type, which can belong to the following set: {Sunny, Cloudy, Rainy}:

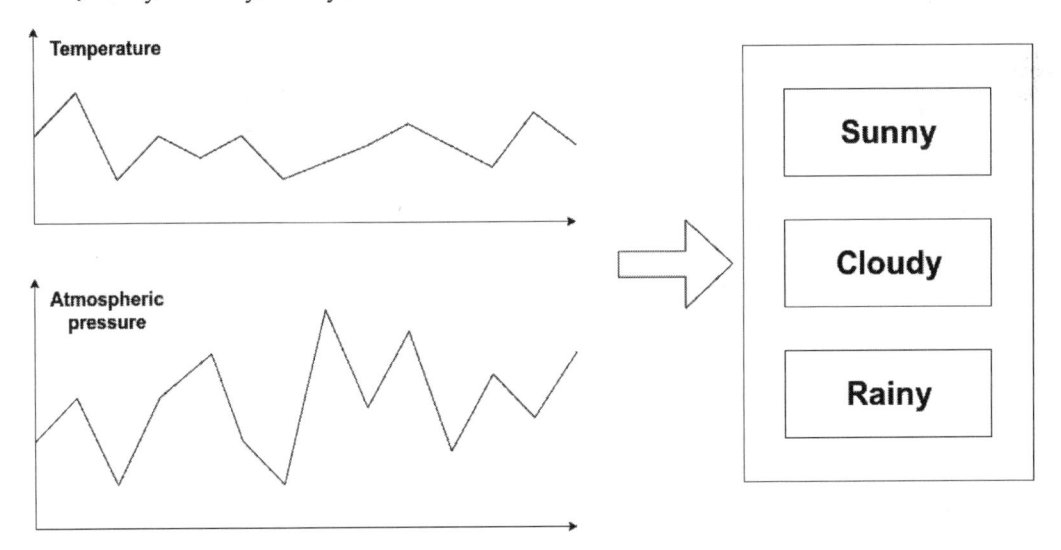

Figure 3.2: Time series forecasting as a classification problem

Another typical time series classification problem is pattern recognition. That is a common task for bank fraud activity identification, device sensor monitoring, and so on. This task assumes that the model highlights time series intervals and maps some classes to them:

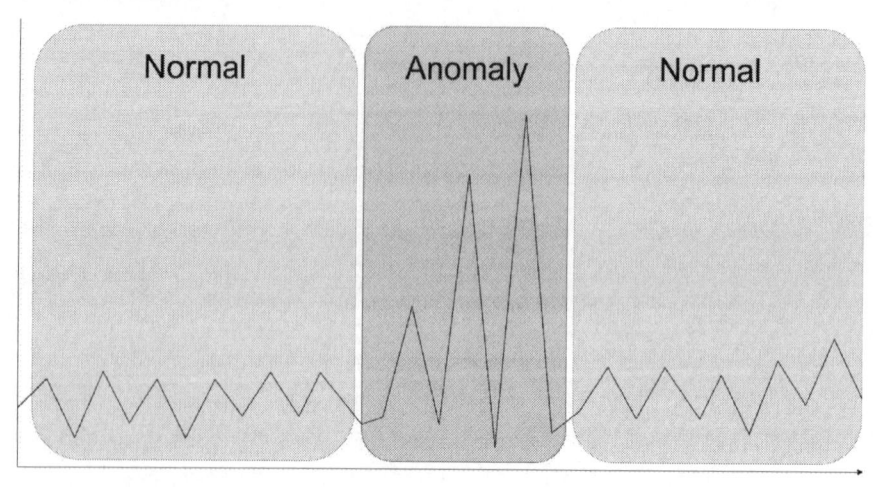

Figure 3.3: Time series pattern recognition as a classification problem

Univariate versus multivariate

The time series problems do not always assume operating with a single data series. There can be several data sequences that are scaled by the time axis.

Table 3.1 contains an example of multivariate time series:

Month	Max temperature, °C	Min temperature, °C	Rainfall, mm °C
January	6.4	2.1	118
February	8.8	2.9	10.8
March	10.1	5.2	94.1
April	11.5	6.4	84.
May	15.5	8.9	46.2
June	17.3	10.9	34.9
July	19.1	12.7	55.5
August	19.1	13	17.2
September	19.6	11.5	8.9
October	16.2	10.8	157.4
November	10.5	6.6	229
December	9.1	4.9	148.9

Table 3.1: Multivariate time series

In forecasting problems, the following types of time series inputs and outputs are met:

- univariate input - univariate output
- multivariate input - univariate output
- multivariate input - multivariate output

Univariate input - univariate output

Univariate input - univariate output is the classic and most straightforward forecasting problem. This task is usually solved by the traditional statistical methods mentioned in the first chapter, like SARIMA HWES, and so on. This type of problem assumes only one input time series and one output time series:

Figure 3.4: Time series forecasting: univariate input – univariate output

Multivariate input – univariate output

Multivariate input - univariate output is the most promising task for deep learning models. Deep neural networks can find complex predictive patterns in multivariate time series that classical methods fail to find. Usually, there is the primary time series sequence for a forecast and secondary ones. The secondary time series sequences contain auxiliary data that help determine the nature of a primary time series behaviour more accurately. *Figure 3.5* contains an example of a temperature prediction model with multivariate input – univariate output:

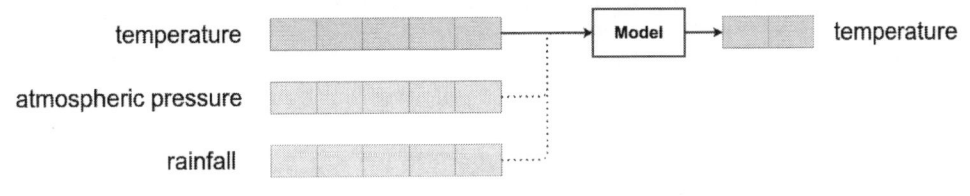

Figure 3.5: Time Series Forecasting: multivariate input – univariate output

Multivariate input – multivariate output

This type of task is the most difficult to develop. There are two approaches to this type of problem.

Many-to-many

We are developing only one predictive model that makes predictions for each of the time series sequences:

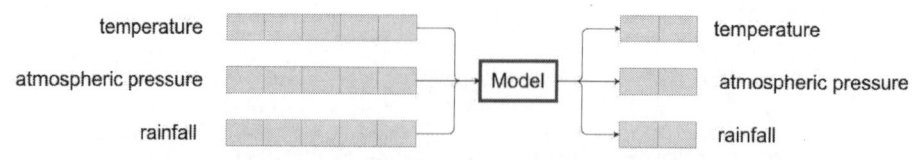

Figure 3.6: Multivariate input – multivariate output: many-to-many

Many-to-one

Another approach is to reduce the task to several multivariate input - univariate output problems. And to develop n different models for each time series:

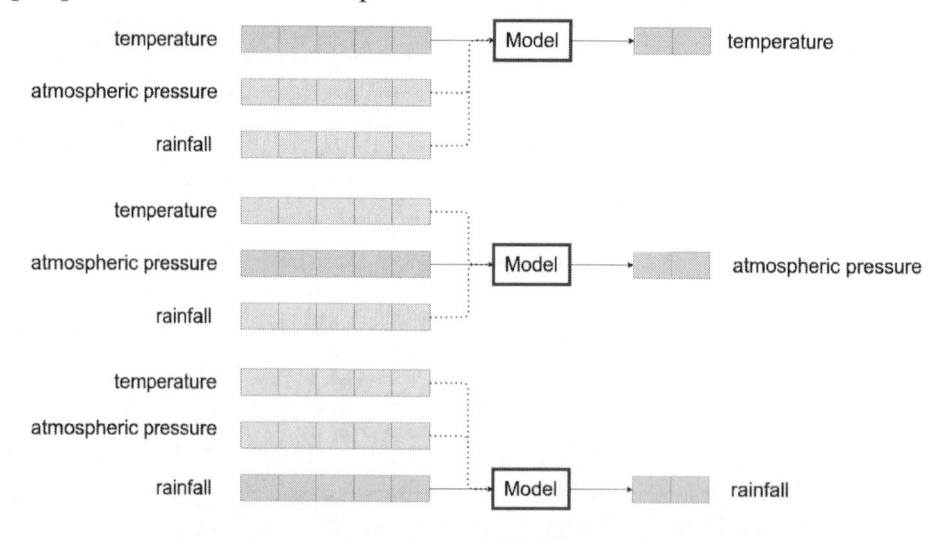

Figure 3.7: Multivariate input – multivariate output: many-to-one

> **Note:** The reader might notice another type of problem: "univariate input - multivariate output". But in practice, when constructing such predictive models, the multivariate output time series has a clear correlation with each other. So such task is reduced to the task univariate input - univariate output.

Single-step versus multi-step

Each task implies its forecasting horizon. Sometimes we only need one step forecast. In weather prediction problems, we have a much longer forecasting horizon. It is already essential for us to know the weather for tomorrow and in the week after.

There are two types of forecasts: single-step and multi-step.

Single-step

This model implies forecasting only the next value of the time series:

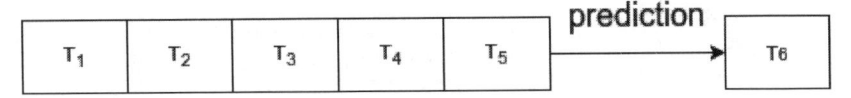

Figure 3.8: Single-step forecasting

Multi-step

As the name suggests, this model implies a forecast several steps ahead. Such models' development is much more difficult because, with each step forward, the model's forecast accuracy decreases:

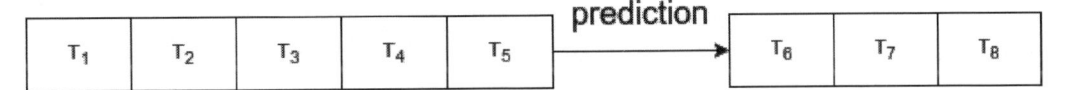

Figure 3.9: Multi-step forecasting

There are three approaches to multi-step model development:

- Single multi-step model
- Multiple single-step model
- Recurrent single-step model

Single multi-step model

This approach assumes the development of one model that returns the forecast sequence for the next steps. These models are easier to maintain and deploy but harder to train and customize. The complexity of such models lies in the fact that the neural network performs better for regression tasks when its training is focused on returning one single value. Multivalued optimization can take more time, and usually, it does not achieve acceptable results:

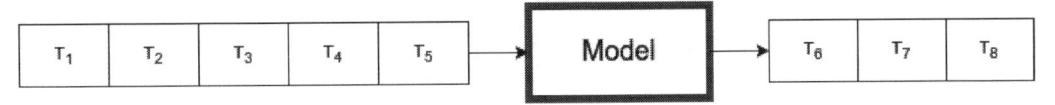

Figure 3.10: Single multi-step model

Multiple single-step model

This approach assumes the existence of its own model for each prediction step. This technique is more flexible than the single multi-step model and allows you to customize the models for each step and use various architectures for different forecasting steps:

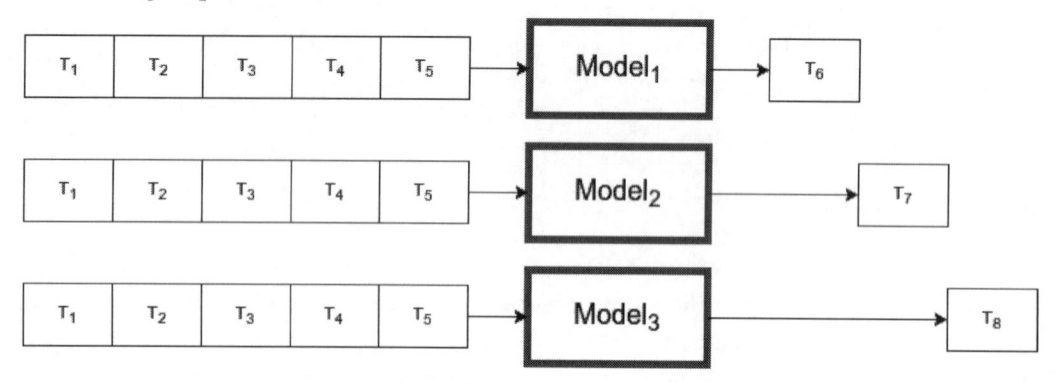

Figure 3.11: Multiple single-step models

Recurrent single-step model

This method implies a complete reduction of the multi-step forecasting task to the single-step forecasting. In this case, to obtain a forecast for several steps ahead, the model recursively uses its own forecast as an input. It is the simplest way to develop multi-step prediction models:

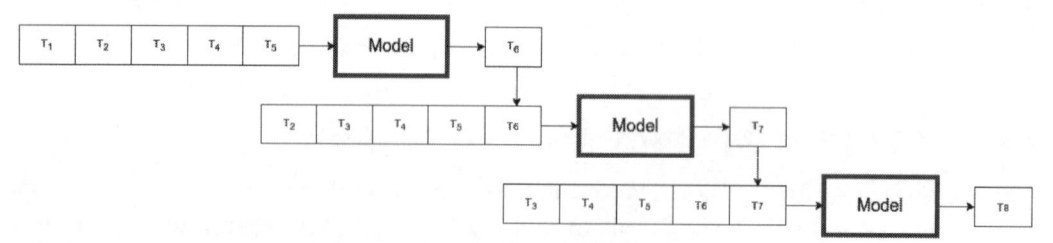

Figure 3.12: Recurrent single-step model

Datasets

For any supervised learning task, data selection is a critical step for developing a robust model. The first thing to do is collect the historical time series data for the forecast we are about to make. This task is not always as easy as it seems. Sometimes you have to work with different sources to get a consistent historical time series.

In some cases, the data may be missing, and it is necessary to fill in *n/a* values somehow. There are several approaches to solve the problem of missing values:

- Insert last known value (equivalent to pandas **bfill** method):

  | 1 | 2 | 3 | 3 | 5 | 6 |

- Insert the next known value (equivalent to pandas **ffill** method): |

  | 1 | 2 | 3 | 5 | 5 | 6 |

- Fill the values with zeros (equivalent to pandas **fillna(0)** method):

  | 1 | 2 | 3 | 0 | 5 | 6 |

- Fill the values with the time series mean value (equivalent to pandas **df.fillna(df.mean())**):

  | 1 | 2 | 3 | 3,5 | 5 | 6 |

- Linear interpolation (equivalent to pandas **df.interpolate()** method):

  | 1 | 2 | 3 | 4 | 5 | 6 |

The power of human intuition and heuristics should never be underestimated. Therefore, before starting a research, it is necessary to observe the time series visually. This will help you choose the right approach and neural network architecture. Therefore, after collecting data, it is recommended to plot a time series graph and try to make some assumptions and hypotheses about the nature of the process you are investigating.

Another problem is the actual lack of a large amount of data for training. The investigation process may be new, and there is simply no large historical sample data for it. In this case, you can find a very similar process to the process you study and use its historical data for training.

Feature engineering

The main advantage of deep learning models is automatic feature extraction. But if we can help our model learn better, then we must do it. The neural network perceives a time series as a simple sequence of numbers and usually does not see the dependencies that a human sees.

Let us consider the time series of clothes retail sales:

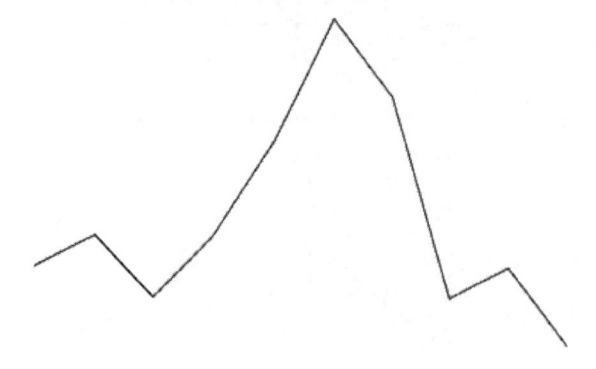

| Sales, K$ | 7 | 8 | 6 | 8 | 11 | 15 | 13 | 6 | 7 | 5 | ? | ? | ? | ? |

Figure 3.13: Retail sales

We see a simple time series in *figure 3.13*. But look how the nature of this time series becomes more evident if we add information about weekends:

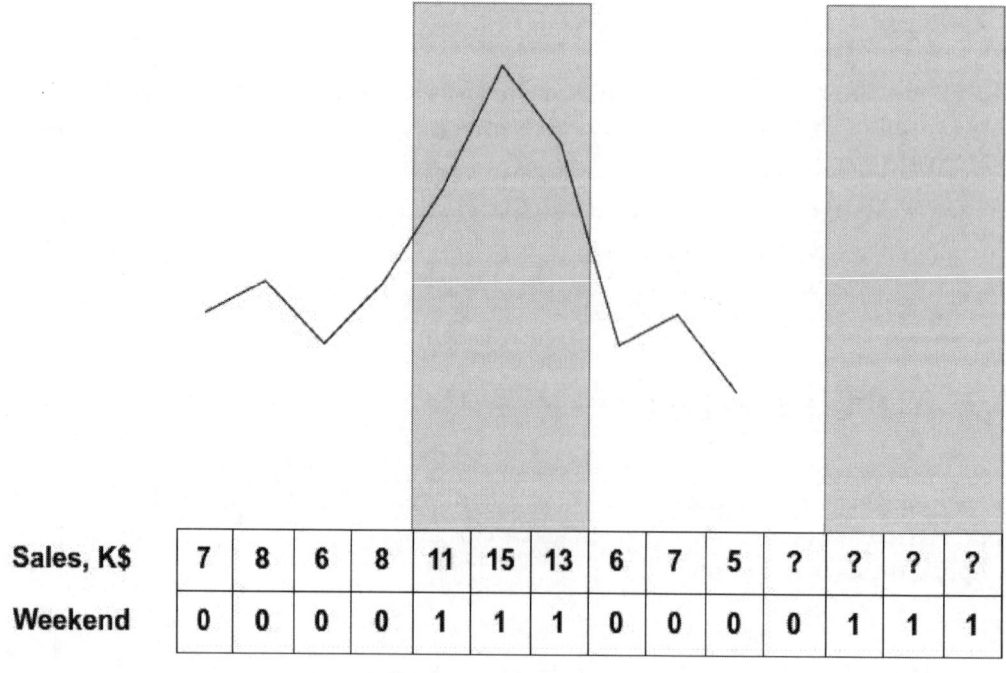

| Sales, K$ | 7 | 8 | 6 | 8 | 11 | 15 | 13 | 6 | 7 | 5 | ? | ? | ? | ? |
| Weekend | 0 | 0 | 0 | 0 | 1 | 1 | 1 | 0 | 0 | 0 | 0 | 1 | 1 | 1 |

Figure 3.14: Retail sales and weekend marks

From the preceding *figure 3.14*, we can conclude that retail sales increase on weekends, which is pretty obvious. Of course, now we can assume that the time series values will get higher on weekends.

It is evident that retail sales of clothes increase on weekends, but this is completely non-obvious to the neural network because the neural network does not know anything about weekends and the nature of human habits. The neural network gets only raw data as it is shown in *figure 3.13*. Information about weekends and holidays will be very useful for training and will significantly improve the accuracy of forecasting.

Figure 3.15 demonstrates the concept of feature engineering:

| Sales | 250 | 120 | 280 | 550 | 1100 | 960 | 310 | 220 | 1230 | 301 |

Feature Engineering

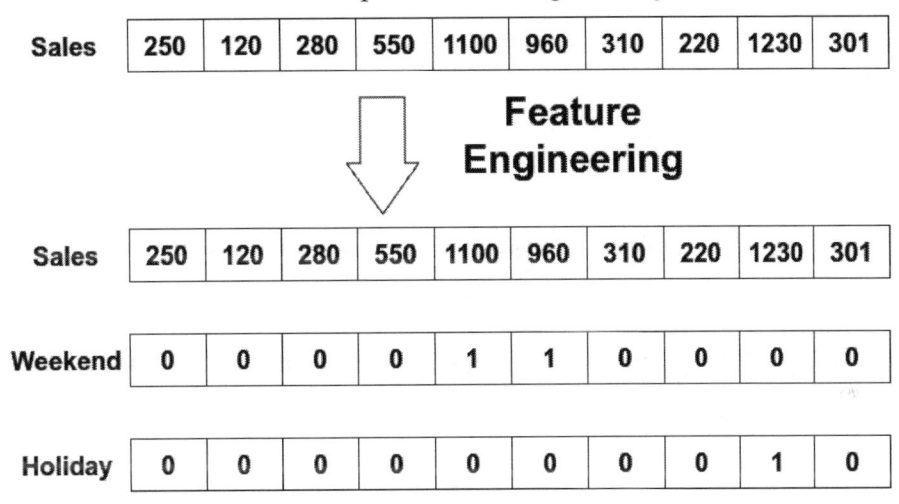

| Sales | 250 | 120 | 280 | 550 | 1100 | 960 | 310 | 220 | 1230 | 301 |

| Weekend | 0 | 0 | 0 | 0 | 1 | 1 | 0 | 0 | 0 | 0 |

| Holiday | 0 | 0 | 0 | 0 | 0 | 0 | 0 | 0 | 1 | 0 |

Figure 3.15: Feature engineering

The main idea of feature engineering and feature enrichment is to supply additional useful information to the model.

Another approach to feature engineering is to add time series, which are the result of mathematical transformations of the original time series. Sometimes, such additions can provide a lot of new information for the neural network.

For example, there are stock markets that are more likely to support the current trend. Knowing this feature, we can inform the neural network about it. We can add a new time series that will count the number of positive and negative changes in a row, as shown in *figure 3.16*:

| Close Price | 121 | 125 | 127 | 130 | 135 | 133 | 129 | 120 | 117 | 120 |

⇩ **Feature Engineering**

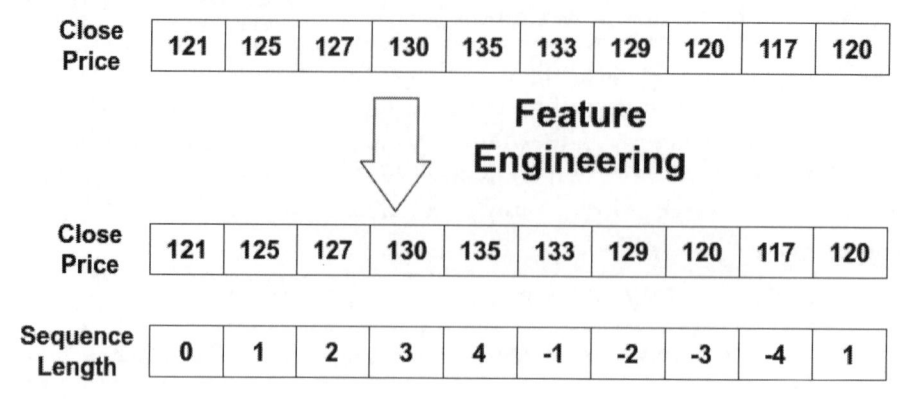

| Close Price | 121 | 125 | 127 | 130 | 135 | 133 | 129 | 120 | 117 | 120 |
| Sequence Length | 0 | 1 | 2 | 3 | 4 | -1 | -2 | -3 | -4 | 1 |

Figure 3.16: Feature engineering

A feature engineering approach automatically changes the problem from univariate input to multivariate input. Feature engineering is a powerful technique for increasing prediction accuracy and creating hybrid architectures based on classical statistical and deep learning methods.

Time series pre-processing and post-processing

This approach is often confused with feature engineering. The time series pre-processing and post-processing's primary goal is to bring the dataset to the canonical form, which will be more convenient for training a neural network. The most common ways to transform time series are normalization, trend removal, and differencing. The main requirement for applying pre-processing operation to a time series is the possibility of converting it back to the original one. With this approach, we need a pre-process time series as an input of a neural network and post-process its output, as shown in *figure 3.17*:

Time seires → Normalize → Input → Model → Output → Denormalize → Prediction

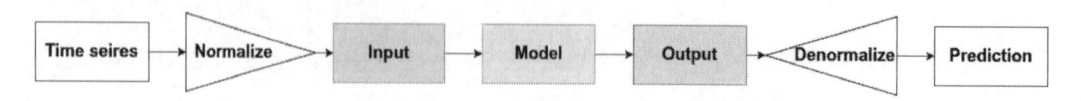

Figure 3.17: Preprocessing and post-processing flow

In the examples below, we will look at preprocessing techniques that can significantly improve a neural network's trainability:

Normalization

This operation's result is the casting of all values of the time series in the [0, 1] or [-1 to 1] range. Here is an example of the time series normalization and denormalization process **ch3/preprocessing/normalize.py**:

```python
import random
from math import sin, cos
import matplotlib.pyplot as plt
def normalize(ts):
    max_ts = max(ts)
    min_ts = min(ts)
    normal_ts = [(v - min_ts) / (max_ts - min_ts) for v in ts]
    return normal_ts, max_ts, min_ts
def denormalize(ts, max_ts, min_ts):
    denormal_ts = [v * (max_ts - min_ts) + min_ts for v in ts]
    return denormal_ts
if __name__ == '__main__':
    random.seed(1)
    ts = [10 * sin(i) * cos(i) * cos(i) for i in range(20)]
    normal_ts, max_ts, min_ts = normalize(ts)
    denormal_ts = denormalize(normal_ts, max_ts, min_ts)
    fig = plt.figure()
    ax1 = fig.add_subplot(311)
    ax2 = fig.add_subplot(312)
    ax3 = fig.add_subplot(313)
    ax1.set_title("Raw Time Series")
    ax1.plot(ts)
    ax2.set_title("Normalized Time Series")
    ax2.plot(normal_ts)
    ax3.set_title("Denormalized Time Series")
    ax3.plot(denormal_ts)
    plt.show()
```

Result

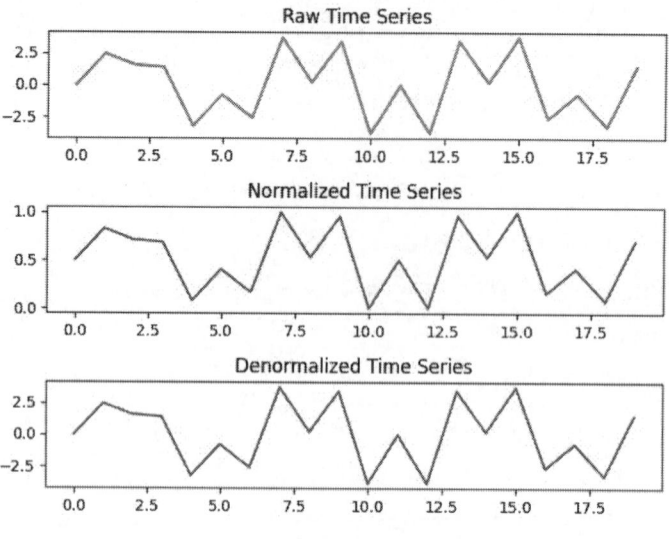

Figure 3.18: Normalization

Sometimes, normalization can significantly affect the performance of the model. Usually, neural networks quickly adjust their weights to the time series's threshold values. But anyway, I recommend using normalization in all your forecasting problems.

Trend removal

Some time series have a clear constant trend. Usually, a trend removal in a time series helps the neural network learn better **ch3/preprocessing/detrend.py**:

```python
import random
from math import sin
import matplotlib.pyplot as plt
from sklearn.linear_model import LinearRegression
import numpy as np
def detrend(ts):
    X = [[i] for i in range(len(ts))]
    y = np.array(ts).reshape(-1, 1)
    reg = LinearRegression().fit(X, y)
    a = reg.coef_[0][0]
    b = reg.intercept_[0]
    detrend_ts = [(ts[i] - a * i - b) for i in range(len(ts))]
    return detrend_ts, a, b
```

```python
def retrend(ts, a, b):
    return [(ts[i] + a * i + b) for i in range(len(ts))]
if __name__ == '__main__':
    random.seed(1)
    ts = [10 + .8 * i + sin(i) + 3 * random.random() for i in range(20)]
    detrend_ts, a, b = detrend(ts)
    retrend_ts = retrend(detrend_ts, a, b)
    fig = plt.figure()
    ax1 = fig.add_subplot(311)
    ax2 = fig.add_subplot(312)
    ax3 = fig.add_subplot(313)
    ax1.set_title("Trended Time Series")
    ax1.plot(ts)
    ax2.set_title("Detrended Time Series")
    ax2.plot(detrend_ts)
    ax3.set_title("Retrended Time Series")
    ax3.plot(retrend_ts)
    plt.show()
```

Result

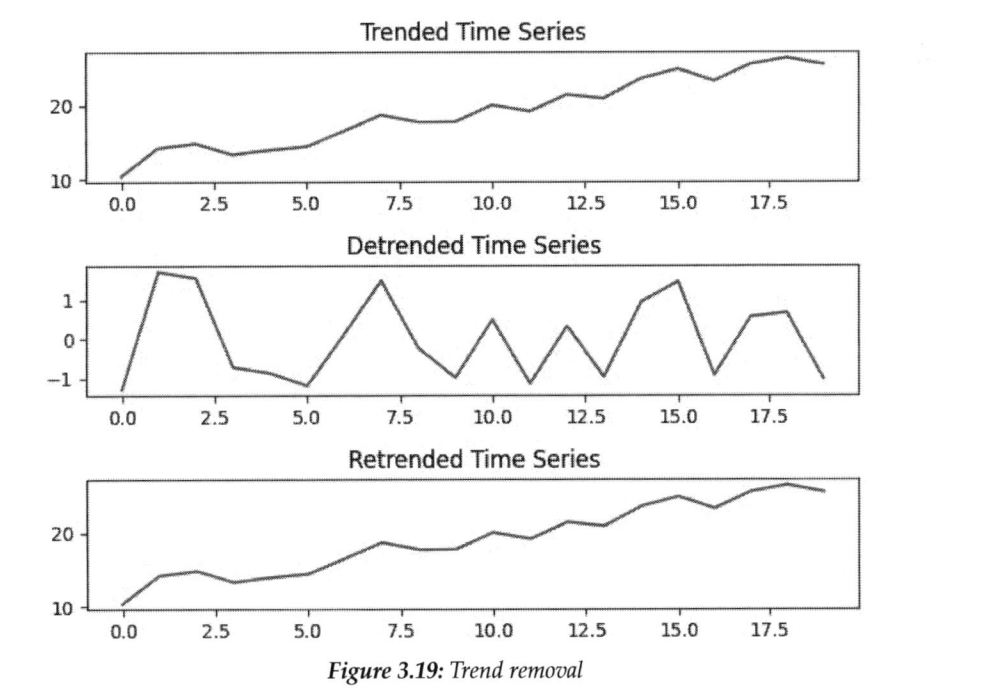

Figure 3.19: Trend removal

Removing the trend from the time series can help the neural network concentrate on looking for other patterns, and usually, this preprocessing method improves the model's performance. It is much easier even for a human to find dependencies in a detrended time series.

Differencing

Another way to remove permanent or temporal trends in a time series is differencing. Differencing builds the following time series:

$$D_t = T_t - T_{t-1}$$

Therefore, time series forecasting is reduced to predicting its changes relative to previous values **ch3/preprocessing/differencing.py**:

```
import random
from math import sin
import matplotlib.pyplot as plt
def differencing(ts):
    diff_ts = [(ts[i + 1] - ts[i]) for i in range(len(ts) - 1)]
    return diff_ts, ts[0]
def integration(ts, b):
    int_ts = [b]
    for i in range(len(ts)):
        int_ts.append(ts[i] + int_ts[i])
    return int_ts
if __name__ == '__main__':
    random.seed(1)
    ts = [50 + .8 * i + 3 * sin(i) + 5 * random.random() for i in range(20)]
    diff_ts, b = differencing(ts)
    int_ts = integration(diff_ts, b)
    fig = plt.figure()
    ax1 = fig.add_subplot(311)
    ax2 = fig.add_subplot(312)
    ax3 = fig.add_subplot(313)
    ax1.set_title("Raw Time Series")
    ax1.plot(ts)
```

```
ax2.set_title("Differenced Time Series")
ax2.plot(diff_ts)
ax3.set_title("Integrated Time Series")
ax3.plot(int_ts)
plt.show()
```

Result

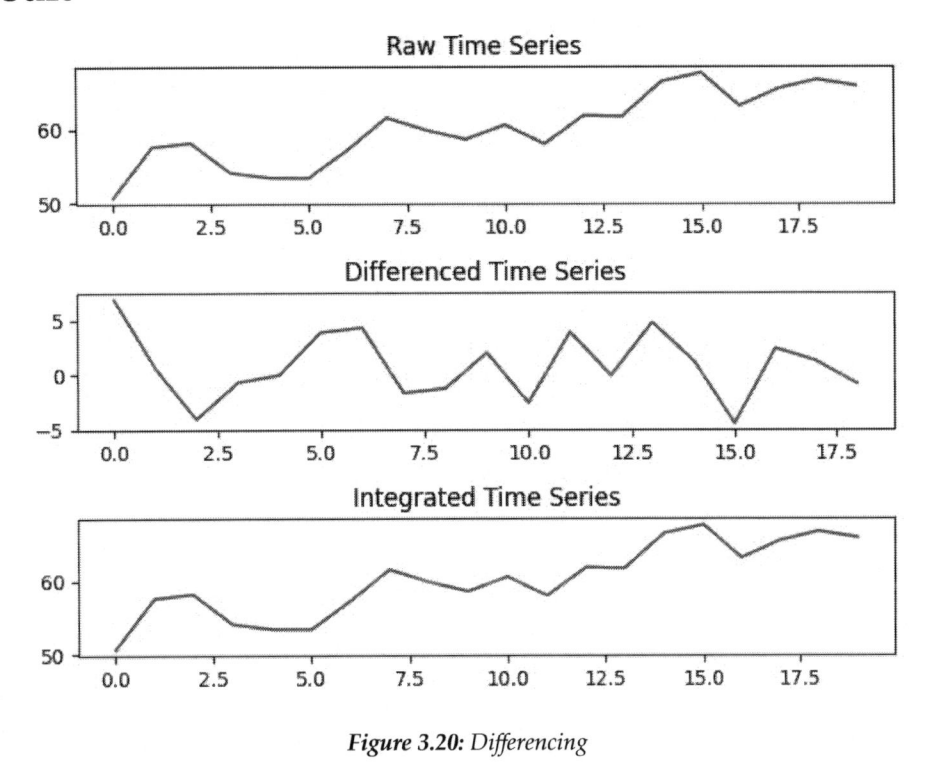

Figure 3.20: Differencing

Differencing is one of the most powerful techniques for improving the model accuracy.

Sliding window

We can start preparing the dataset for neural network training when we have collected and preprocessed historical data. The sliding window is the basis for turning any time series dataset into a supervised learning problem. We slide the window through the time series, collecting data in input and output datasets. The best way to understand the concept of a sliding window is to look a *Figure 3.21*:

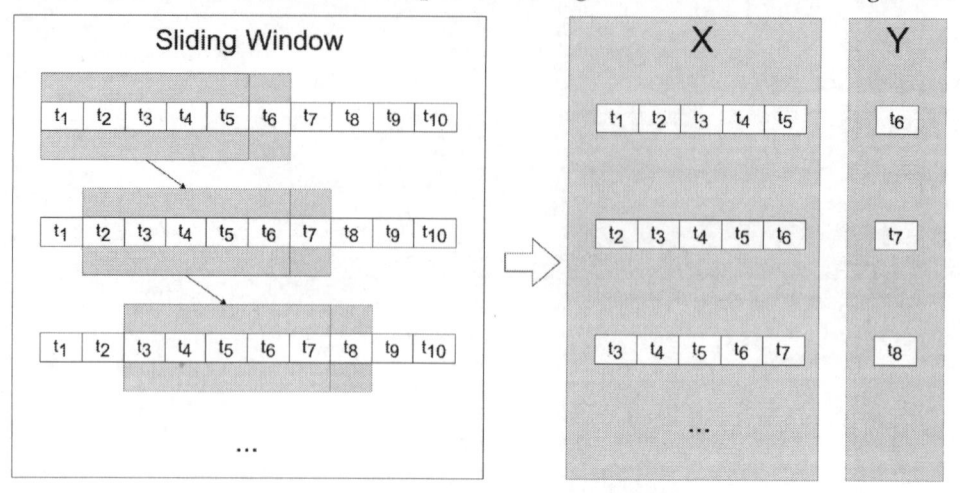

Figure 3.21: Sliding window

Here, we provide an implementation of the sliding window technique `ch3/dataset/sliding_window.py`:

```python
def sliding_window(ts, features):
    X = []
    Y = []
    for i in range(features + 1, len(ts) + 1):
        X.append(ts[i - (features + 1):i - 1])
        Y.append([ts[i - 1]])
    return X, Y
if __name__ == '__main__':
    ts = list(range(6))
    X, Y = sliding_window(ts, 3)
    print(f'Time series: {ts}')
    print(f'X: {X}')
    print(f'Y: {Y}')
```

Result

```
Time series: [0, 1, 2, 3, 4, 5]
X: [[0, 1, 2], [1, 2, 3], [2, 3, 4]]
Y: [[3], [4], [5]]
```

Effectiveness and loss function

It is important to determine how exactly the forecast accuracy will be estimated. One of the following loss functions is usually chosen as an estimate of the regression model's accuracy: *absolute loss* or *mean squared error*. The final choice depends solely on problem requirements.

Let us consider two examples that lead to different choices of the loss function. Suppose we are building a model for predicting the movement of stock quotes, and our trading strategy gives the following profit from a trade:

$$100 \times (10 - |Price_{real} - Price_{predicted}|) \$$$

So, we earn:

- 1000$ if the forecast is completely accurate;
- 500$ if the forecast differs by 5 points from the actual future price;
- 0 if the forecast differs by 10 points;
- And we lose 1000$ if the forecast differs by 20 points.

The main thing for us in this task is making a profit. And we calculate the profit from each trade according to a linear function. This means that the model, which in 19 cases gives an absolutely accurate forecast, and in one case, 100 points mistake, is acceptable for us. This model will allow us to earn anyway:

Total profit: 19×1000$ - 1×9000$ = 10 000$

If our model's efficiency is calculated using a linear function and we can afford rare high mistakes in forecasts, that is why we should choose the *absolute loss* function.

But let us look at another example. Let us say our model predicts the number of cases of some virus infection. Based on this model, a vaccine development plan is made, hospital bed allocation is created, and so on. In this complex and important task, we cannot afford high forecast deviation. Any high deviation can lead to a shortage of medicine, a lack of medical personnel, and fatal consequences. Such models are often allowed to make minor deviations, but they are strictly forbidden to make high deviations. For such problems, it is necessary to use *mean squared error* loss.

Static versus dynamic

There are two types of prediction models, depending on the process's nature, that generate the time series we are trying to predict.

Static processes change their characteristics quite rarely. Therefore, once having trained a neural network, you can use its predictions for a long time without the need to retrain it. These tasks include astronomical, natural, and biological processes. Of course, there is nothing permanent in our world, but nevertheless, such models can work effectively for a long time. We call a predictive model static if it doesn't need to be retrained based on new data.

On the other hand, some processes constantly change their nature and establish new patterns of behaviour. To effectively capture these patterns, the model needs to be retrained after a certain time. Such models are called **dynamic**.

Architecture design

And here we come to the most challenging and exciting part. Designing the architecture of a neural network is a difficult creative task. In general, there is no clear guide for all cases on how to make an effective forecasting model. We will look at the main ways of building such neural networks in *Chapter 4, Recurrent Neural Networks,* and *Chapter 5, Advanced Forecasting Models.* Remember that each process and time series has its own architecture. Do not try to find an architecture that works equally well for absolutely all kinds of forecasting problems.

Training, validating and testing

Separately, it is worth paying attention to the process of training a neural network in the context of the time series forecasting problem. In forecasting problems, we use the classical approach of training a neural network by dividing the entire chronologically ordered dataset into three subsets: train set, validation set, and test set. The validation set is allocated for choosing the best model, that is, we prefer a model with parameters that showed the best result on the validation set.

In machine learning, there is another approach for training and choosing the best model called **cross-validation**. In the case of time series forecasting problems, this approach's application does not always give positive results. The fact is that in the case of forecasting problems, the most important thing for us is to find out the performance of our candidate model on the most recent data. In a cross-validation approach, the chronological order of validation is violated, which does not allow choosing the most relevant model:

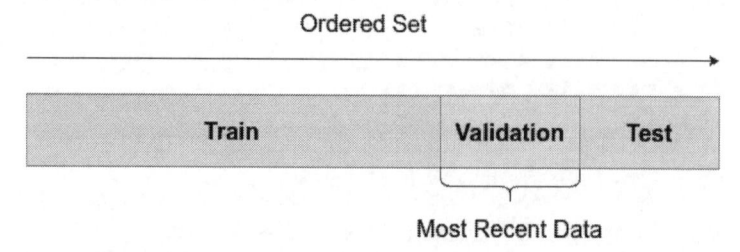

Figure 3.22: Dataset split

Here is the function that prepares datasets for the training **ch3/uk_temperature_prediction/training_datasets.py**:

```
import torch
from ch3.dataset.sliding_window import sliding_window
from ch3.uk_temperature_prediction.interpolated_time_series import interpolated_time_series
def get_training_datasets(features, test_len):
    ts = interpolated_time_series()
    X, Y = sliding_window(ts, features)
    X_train, Y_train, X_test, Y_test = X[0:-test_len], \
                                       Y[0:-test_len], \
                                       X[-test_len:], \
                                       Y[-test_len:]
    train_len = round(len(ts) * 0.7)
    X_train, X_val, Y_train, Y_val = X_train[0:train_len],\
                                     X_train[train_len:],\
                                     Y_train[0:train_len],\
                                     Y_train[train_len:]
    x_train = torch.tensor(data = X_train)
    y_train = torch.tensor(data = Y_train)
    x_val = torch.tensor(data = X_val)
    y_val = torch.tensor(data = Y_val)
    x_test = torch.tensor(data = X_test)
    y_test = torch.tensor(data = Y_test)
    return x_train, x_val, x_test, y_train, y_val, y_test
```

Alternative model

In this topic, we will study the most common mistake. If the predictive model we are developing does not give 100% accuracy, then we need to compare it with some other methods. On the Internet, you can find many examples of applications of Deep Learning models for forecasting problems. But very few articles compare the performance of these models with other classical methods. Without creating an alternative forecasting model, we cannot objectively estimate the quality of the model we developed. Deep learning methods do not always work well on specific datasets, and there is nothing special about it. According to the *No Free Lunch*

Theorem, there is no optimal method for all datasets in any problem class. Very often, classical statistical forecasting methods like ARIMA, GARCH, and others show excellent results. And in this case, there is no need to use deep learning methods. Throughout this book, we will always make comparisons of deep learning methods with classical ones. This approach will allow you to estimate the effectiveness better.

Model optimization

If we have established that our deep learning architecture shows good results compared to classical methods, we can optimize the chosen architecture. As we already mentioned, there is a separate direction that studies the search of optimal neural network architectures for a specific type of task (*neural architecture search* - https://en.wikipedia.org/wiki/Neural_architecture_search). We will learn more about the architecture optimization process in *Chapter 6, PyTorch Model Tuning with Neural Network Intelligence*.

Summary

Let us summarize all stages of forecasting model development:

- Identify the problem you will be working on
- Determine if it will be a *regression or classification* problem
- Determine the dimension of the time series you are working with: *univariate or multivariate*
- Define the forecasting horizon of the model: *single-step or multi-step*
- Analyze the dataset and explore the possibility of using *feature engineering* to enrich input data for a neural network
- Preprocess the time series (*normalization, trend removal, differentiation*)
- Prepare data for the training the neural network using the *sliding window* method
- Choose the correct *loss function*
- Decide how often your model will be retrained: *static or dynamic*
- Design the model *architecture*
- *Train* the model
- *Compare* results with alternative classical forecasting methods
- *Optimize* the model

Example: UK minimal temperature prediction problem

We will accompany this chapter with a real-life example. We try to find a solution for the UK monthly minimal temperature prediction problem. It should be said right away that this task is one of the most difficult to predict. Everything related to the weather is difficult to forecast. But this is much more interesting than taking artificial time series examples.

Here, we have a classical *regression task*. We will analyze only one-time series sequence: minimal temperature history. So here we have *univariate input – univariate output* problem. We are focusing on predicting the next value only, thus we'll get the *single-step model*.

Dataset

We will use Kaggle dataset: https://www.kaggle.com/josephw20/uk-met-office-weather-data, it contains measurements of various weather metrics from different points in the UK. The dataset is located here: `ch3/uk_rainfall_prediction/data/MET_Office_Weather_Data.csv`:

Year	Month	tmax	tmin	af	Rain	Sun	Station
...							
1929	1	3.8	0.3	12	40.5	23.7	armagh
1929	2	2.6	−2.5	17	32.5	170.4	armagh
1929	3	12.1	2.4	6	3.3	NA	armagh
...							

Table 3.2: MET Office Weather Dataset

This dataset contains measurements from different stations. We will pick only one station as the primary source: *Sheffield*.

`ch3/uk_temperature_prediction/raw_time_series.py`:

```
import pandas as pd
import os
def raw_time_series():
    dir_path = os.path.dirname(os.path.realpath(__file__))
    ts_df = pd.read_csv(f'{dir_path}/data/MET_Office_Weather_Data.csv')
    ts = ts_df.loc[ts_df['station'] == 'sheffield']['tmin'].tolist()
    return ts
```

Let us analyze this **dataset ch3/dataset/analyze.py**:

```
import numpy as np
from ch3.uk_temperature_prediction.raw_time_series import raw_time_series
ts = raw_time_series()
print(f'Count: {len(ts)}')
print(f'Max: {np.nanmax(ts)}')
print(f'Min: {np.nanmin(ts)}')
print(f'Avg: {round(np.nanmean(ts), 2)}')
print(f'Median: {round(np.nanmedian(ts), 2)}')
print(f'Std: {round(np.nanstd(ts), 2)}')
print(f'NA values: {np.count_nonzero(np.isnan(ts))}')
```

Result

Count	1650
Max	14.5
Min	–4.2
Avg	6.22
Median	5.7
Std	4.04
NA values	27

This time series contains *n/a* values. We use the linear interpolation method to fill them **ch3/uk_temperature_prediction/interpolated_time_series.py**:

```
import os
import pandas as pd
import matplotlib.pyplot as plt
def interpolated_time_series():
    dir_path = os.path.dirname(os.path.realpath(__file__))
    ts_df = pd.read_csv(f'{dir_path}/data/MET_Office_Weather_Data.csv')
    ts = ts_df.loc[ts_df['station'] == 'sheffield']['tmin']\
        .interpolate().dropna().tolist()
    return ts
if __name__ == '__main__':
```

```
ts = interpolated_time_series()
plt.plot(ts[-120:])
plt.show()
```

Result

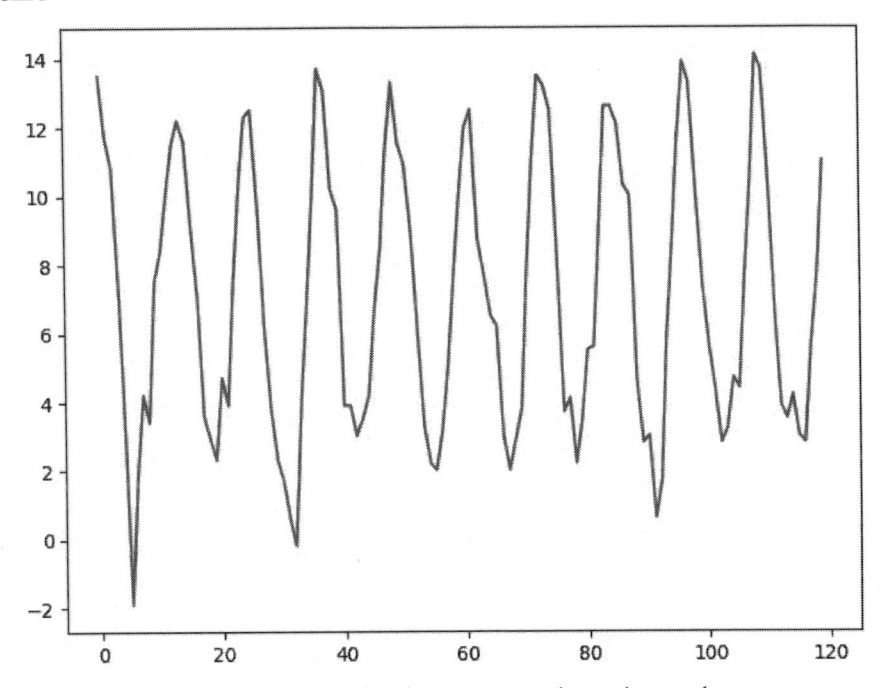

Figure 3.23: Monthly min temperature time series sample

As expected, we see a clear seasonality in this time series. We can suppose that classical forecasting methods such as SARIMA and HWES will perform well on this dataset.

Architecture

In *Chapter 2, Deep Learning with PyTorch*, we already used the Fully Connected network as an example of neural network architecture. Let's look at a more interesting architecture that uses deep learning techniques.

Our model will have two global layers: *feature extraction* and *decision-making*. The feature extraction layer will be based on convolution operations, and the decision-

98 ■ *Time Series Forecasting using Deep Learning*

making layer will be based on a fully connected neural network. The entire architecture of the neural network is shown in *Figure 3.24*:

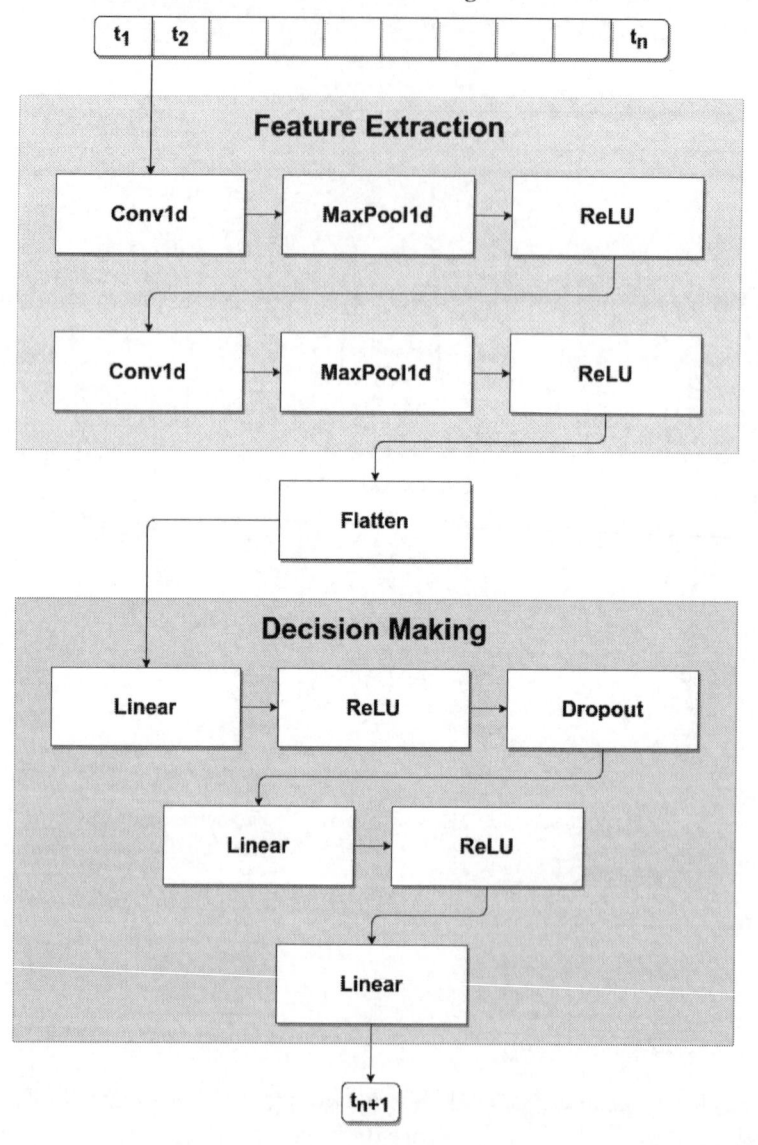

Figure 3.24: NN architecture for UK monthly minimal temperature prediction problem

Let us look at the implementation of this architecture **ch3/uk_temperature_prediction/model/dl_model.py**:

```
import torch
import torch.nn.functional as F
class DL(torch.nn.Module):
```

```python
    def __init__(self, n_inp, l_1, l_2, conv1_out, conv1_kernel, conv2_kernel, drop1 = 0, n_out = 1):
        super(DL, self).__init__()
        conv1_out_ch = conv1_out
        conv2_out_ch = conv1_out * 2
        conv1_kernel = conv1_kernel
        conv2_kernel = conv2_kernel
        self.dropout_lin1 = drop1
        self.pool = torch.nn.MaxPool1d(kernel_size = 2)
        self.conv1 = torch.nn.Conv1d(in_channels = 1, out_channels = conv1_out_ch, kernel_size = conv1_kernel,
                                    padding = conv1_kernel - 1)
        self.conv2 = torch.nn.Conv1d(in_channels = conv1_out_ch, out_channels = conv2_out_ch,
                                    kernel_size = conv2_kernel,
                                    padding = conv2_kernel - 1)
        feature_tensor = self.feature_stack(torch.Tensor([[0] * n_inp]))
        self.lin1 = torch.nn.Linear(feature_tensor.size()[1], l_1)
        self.lin2 = torch.nn.Linear(l_1, l_2)
        self.lin3 = torch.nn.Linear(l_2, n_out)
    def feature_stack(self, x):
        x = x.unsqueeze(1)
        x = F.relu(self.pool(self.conv1(x)))
        x = F.relu(self.pool(self.conv2(x)))
        x = x.flatten(start_dim = 1)
        return x
    def fc_stack(self, x):
        x1 = F.dropout(F.relu(self.lin1(x)), p = self.dropout_lin1)
        x2 = F.relu(self.lin2(x1))
        y = self.lin3(x2)
        return y
    def forward(self, x):
        x = self.feature_stack(x)
        y = self.fc_stack(x)
        return y
```

As we see, this model has the following hyper-parameters:
- **n_inp** – The number of features or the length of the sliding window
- **conv1_out** – Output channels of the first convolution layer
- **conv1_kernel** – Kernel of the first convolution layer
- **conv2_kernel** – Kernel of the second convolution layer
- **drop1** – Probability of dropout layer
- **l_1** – Output for first linear layer
- **l_2** – Output for second linear layer

We will use the following ones:

```
net = DL(
    n_inp = 120,
    l_1 = 400,
    l_2 = 48,
    conv1_out = 6,
    conv1_kernel = 36,
    conv2_kernel = 12,
    drop1 = .1
)
```

Alternative model

For this problem, we will use two classic alternative forecasting methods that usually suites well for natural time series with seasonality HWES and SARIMA. For convenience, we use the same interface as for deep learning models.

For SARIMA, we will use 12 as the seasonable parameter **ch3/uk_temperature_prediction/model/sarima_model.py**:

```
from statsmodels.tsa.statespace.sarimax import SARIMAX
import torch
class SarimaxPredictor(torch.nn.Module):
    def forward(self, x):
        last_values = []
        l = x.tolist()
        counter = 0
```

```
            for r in l:
                model = SARIMAX(r,
                                order = (1, 1, 1),
                                seasonal_order = (1, 1, 1, 12))
                results = model.fit(disp = 0)
                forecast = results.forecast()
                last_values.append([forecast[0]])
                counter = counter + 1
                print(f'debug: SARIMA calculation {counter} / {len(l)}')
            return torch.tensor(data = last_values)
```

For HWES, we will use 12 as seasonable parameter too and no trend-setting ch3/uk_temperature_prediction/model/hwes_model.py:

```
from statsmodels.tsa.holtwinters import ExponentialSmoothing
import torch
class HwesPredictor(torch.nn.Module):
    def forward(self, x):
        last_values = []
        for r in x.tolist():
            model = ExponentialSmoothing(r,
                                         trend = None,
                                         seasonal = "add",
                                         seasonal_periods = 12
                                         )
            results = model.fit()
            forecast = results.forecast()
            last_values.append([forecast[0]])
        return torch.tensor(data = last_values)
```

Testing

Finally, we are ready to put everything together and build our prediction model ch3/uk_temperature_prediction/example.py:

Import part

```
import copy
import random
import sys
import torch
import matplotlib.pyplot as plt
from ch3.uk_temperature_prediction.model.dl_model import DL
from ch3.uk_temperature_prediction.model.hwes_model import HwesPredictor
from ch3.uk_temperature_prediction.model.sarima_model import SarimaxPredictor
from ch3.uk_temperature_prediction.training_datasets import get_training_datasets
```

Making script reproducible

```
random.seed(1)
torch.manual_seed(1)
```

Number of features

Each model will take a 10-year observation history as input:

```
features = 120
```

Preparing datasets

For test, we will use a 5-year interval:

```
x_train, x_val, x_test, y_train, y_val, y_test =\
    get_training_datasets(features, 60)
```

Initializing models

```
net = DL(
    n_inp = features,
    l_1 = 400,
    l_2 = 48,
    conv1_out = 6,
    conv1_kernel = 36,
    conv2_kernel = 12,
```

```
        drop1 = .1
)
net.train()
sarima_predictor = SarimaxPredictor()
hwes_predictor = HwesPredictor()
```

Loss function and optimization algorithm

```
optimizer = torch.optim.Adam(params = net.parameters())
abs_loss = torch.nn.L1Loss()
```

Training process

As said earlier, we will pick the model which shows the best performance on the validation set:

```
best_model = None
min_val_loss = sys.maxsize
training_loss = []
validation_loss = []
for t in range(150):
    prediction = net(x_train)
    loss = abs_loss(prediction, y_train)
    optimizer.zero_grad()
    loss.backward()
    optimizer.step()
    val_prediction = net(x_val)
    val_loss = abs_loss(val_prediction, y_val)
    training_loss.append(loss.item())
    validation_loss.append(val_loss.item())
    if val_loss.item() < min_val_loss:
        best_model = copy.deepcopy(net)
        min_val_loss = val_loss.item()
    if t % 10 == 0:
        print(f'epoch {t}: train - {round(loss.item(), 4)}, '
              f'val: - {round(val_loss.item(), 4)}')
```

Evaluation on test set

```
net.eval()
dl_prediction = best_model(x_test)
sarima_prediction = sarima_predictor(x_test)
hwes_prediction = hwes_predictor(x_test)
dl_abs_loss = round(abs_loss(dl_prediction, y_test).item(), 4)
sarima_abs_loss = round(abs_loss(sarima_prediction, y_test).item(), 4)
hwes_abs_loss = round(abs_loss(hwes_prediction, y_test).item(), 4)
```

Getting results

```
print('===')
print('Results on Test Dataset')
print(f'DL Loss: {dl_abs_loss}')
print(f'SARIMA Loss: {sarima_abs_loss}')
print(f'HWES Loss: {hwes_abs_loss}')
```

Results on Test Dataset	
DL Loss	0.8678
SARIMA Loss	0.9227
HWES Loss	1.0615

Finally, we can observe the results of three different models. Our Deep Neural Network has shown the best performance.

Let us examine the training progress:

```
plt.title("Training progress")
plt.plot(training_loss, label = 'training loss')
plt.plot(validation_loss, label = 'validation loss')
plt.legend()
plt.show()
```

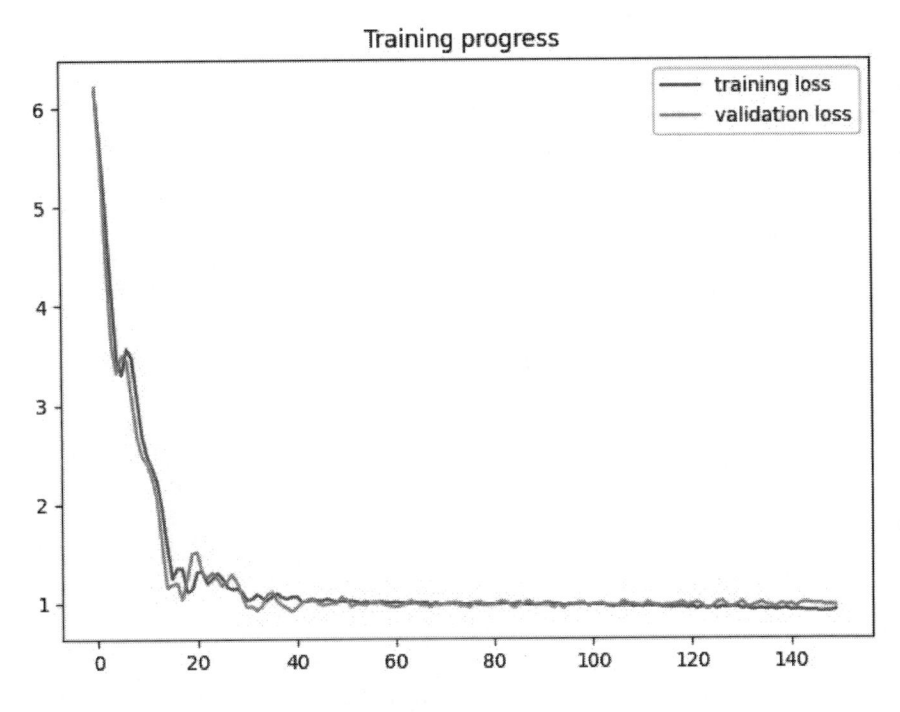

Figure 3.25: Training progress

Training progress looks nice. There is no significant gap between performance on the train set and the validation set. So we can conclude that the deep learning model really captures time series behaviour without great overfitting.

Let us check how the predictions are mapped on the actual test dataset:

```
plt.title('Test Dataset')
plt.plot(y_test, '--', label = 'actual', linewidth = 3)
plt.plot(best_model(x_test).tolist(), label = 'DL', color = 'g')
plt.plot(sarima_prediction.tolist(), label = 'SARIMA', color = 'r')
plt.plot(hwes_prediction.tolist(), label = 'HWES', color = 'brown')
```

```
plt.legend()
plt.show()
```

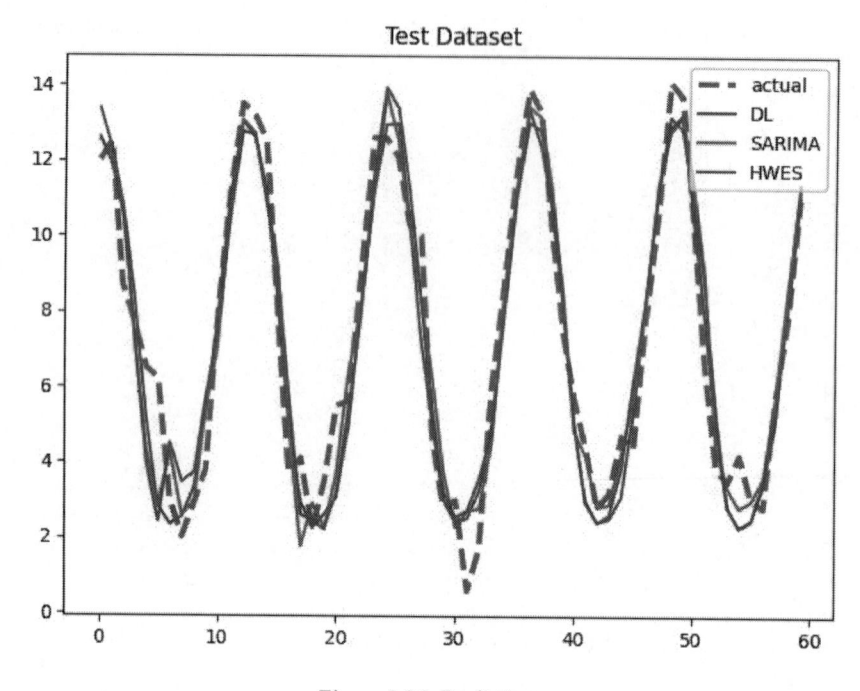

Figure 3.26: Predictions

Well, it is impossible to make any assumptions looking at *Figure 3.26*. All of them are pretty close to the actual data.

Another way to check deviations of the predictions is to construct the *"actual – predicted"* graph:

```
test_n = len(y_test)
dl_abs_dev = (dl_prediction - y_test).abs_()
sarima_abs_dev = (sarima_prediction - y_test).abs_()
hwes_abs_dev = (hwes_prediction - y_test).abs_()
fig = plt.figure()
ax1 = fig.add_subplot(311)
ax2 = fig.add_subplot(312)
ax3 = fig.add_subplot(313)
ax1.set_title(f'Deep Learning Model: {dl_abs_loss}')
ax1.bar(list(range(test_n)), dl_abs_dev.view(test_n).tolist(), color = 'g')
```

```
ax2.set_title(f'SARIMA Model: {sarima_abs_loss}')
ax2.bar(list(range(test_n)), sarima_abs_dev.view(test_n).tolist(), color
= 'r')
ax3.set_title(f'HWES Model: {hwes_abs_loss}')
ax3.bar(list(range(test_n)), hwes_abs_dev.view(test_n).tolist(), color =
'brown')
plt.show()
```

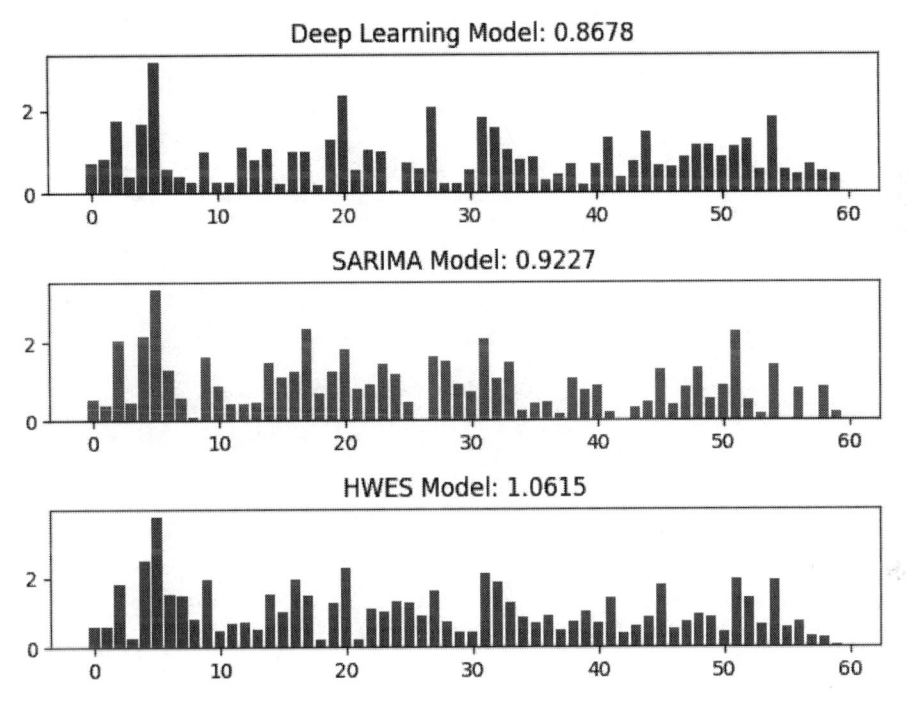

Figure 3.27: Actual vs predicted

In this graph, we can notice that the deep learning model's predictions are closer to the real ones. This is a very good result. We managed to build a very accurate weather prediction model, which is more precise than classical forecasting methods.

Conclusion

In this chapter, we have established the process of setting the forecasting problem. We now know how to declare a task correctly and how to estimate its solution. This chapter can be used as a ready-made guide for solving various time series forecasting issues. In the next chapter, we will consider the principles of building deep neural network architectures.

Points to remember

- Forecasting can be both regression and classification problems in the supervised learning context.

- In multivariate input - univariate output forecasting, we usually take a one-time series sequence as the primary and the other ones as the secondary.

- There are two ways to construct models for multivariate input - multivariate output problems: many-to-many model and many-to-one models.

- There are three approaches to multi-step model development: single multi-step model, multiple single-step models, recurrent single-step model.

- Ways to fill *n/a* values in the dataset: linear interpolation, time series mean value, fill with zeros, fill the next known, fill the last known.

- Main time series preprocessing methods are: normalization, trend removal, and differencing.

- There are two main loss functions for forecasting regression problems: absolute loss and mean squared error.

- Cross-validation technique does not perform well for time series forecasting problems.

- Always compare the performance of the model you've developed with alternative ones.

Multiple choice questions

1. Say we want to predict the number of sunny days in a new month. We will make our prediction based on the sunny days, temperature, and atmospheric pressure history. What type of forecasting problem is it?

    A. Univariate input – univariate output

    B. Multivariate input – univariate output

    C. Multivariate input – multivariate output

2. Say we have a single-step prediction model, and we need to get the prediction for two steps in a row. But we have no time to create another model. What can we do to get a forecast for two steps?

    A. That is impossible.

    B. We can construct multi-step model using the recurrent model approach.

3. **After long research, we could not find a deep learning model that would show better performance than classical methods. What decision can we make?**

   A. If one of the classical methods shows high accuracy, then pick it as the solution.

   B. Continue searching because there is always a neural network architecture that will perform better than classical methods.

Answers
1. B
2. B

Key terms

- *Univariate input:* Time series problem, which assumes one sequence as the input data.
- *Multivariate input:* Time series problem, which assumes several sequences as the input data.
- *Univariate output:* Time series problem, which assumes one sequence as the input data.
- *Multivariate output:* Time series problem, which assumes several sequences as the output data.
- *Single-step:* Predicting the next value only.
- *Multiple-step:* Predicting several next values.
- *Feature engineering:* enriching the input dataset with additional information.
- *Sliding window:* method that prepares data for training a forecasting model.

CHAPTER 4
Recurrent Neural Networks

In this chapter, we will begin by exploring some of the most efficient neural network architectures for time series forecasting. This chapter focuses on the theory and implementation of **recurrent neural networks (RNN)**, **gated recurrent units (GRU)**, long short-term memory (LSTM) networks. Understanding the basic principles of RNNs will be a good basis for their direct application and mastering other similar architectures. This chapter covers the logic and core of each architecture, its practical application, and pros and cons.

After this chapter, the reader will have a very powerful tool and deep knowledge of time series forecasting.

Structure

In this chapter, we will discuss the following topics:

- Recurrent neural network
- Gated recurrent unit network
- Long short-term memory network
- Objectives

After completing this chapter, the reader will have comprehended the basic theory of recurrent neural networks (RNN) and will be able to construct efficient predictive models based on RNN, GRU, and LSTM architectures.

Recurrent neural network

Before starting, I would like to introduce several terminological clarifications. The term *RNN* is used in two senses:

- **General** - Means any neural network whose architecture is built using a recurrent computational graph.

- **Special** - Means a concrete architecture of a neural network, which is covered in this section.

The *RNN* in the general meaning includes such architectures: **RNN** in a special sense, *gated recurrent unit* (**GRU**), *long short-term memory* (**LSTM**), and so on. Usually, the meaning of the term RNN is understood from the context of reading.

Let us go back to the basis of a fully connected neural network that we already used as a time series forecasting model:

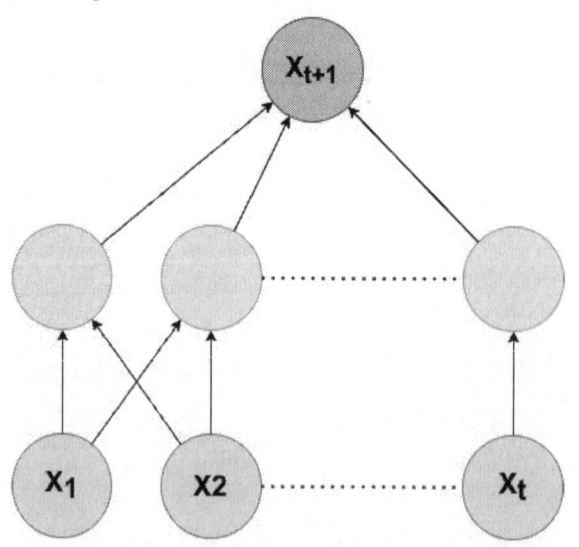

Figure 4.1: Fully connected neural network as single-step prediction model

We have already seen that this type of model can perform well, but it has two major disadvantages:

- *Fixed input*. The fully connected neural network can only accept an input sequence of fixed length. If some input vector values are missed, then it would be impossible to use this model.

- *Does not perceive the vector as an ordered sequence.* For a fully connected neural network, the input vector is just a set of numbers. The fully connected neural network does not attempt to extract patterns that characterize the behavior of a sequence. Such models often tend to overfit, and the gradient descent algorithm for parameters of this neural network finds a local minimum that poorly reproduces the behavior of the sequence.

RNN can solve both of these problems. It has a concept of a hidden state. A hidden state can be treated as internal memory. The hidden state does not try to remember all past values of the sequence but only their effect. Because of internal memory, RNNs can remember important things about their input, which allows them to be very accurate in predicting future values.

Let us look at the RNN in action by example. Say we have the following forecasting problem:

To predict the amount of John Smith's job bonus at the end of the month.

We have some events as an input sequence. RNN takes the internal memory (hidden state), combines it with an event, and returns the new updated internal memory (hidden state). The internal memory (hidden state) contains a summary of previous events.

Say we have the following events in the current month:

- John Smith demonstrates an excellent presentation
- Company capitalization rises by 2%
- John Smith gets late on an important conversation

Each of these events, in some way, affects the size of the monthly bonus. Let us say we have some scoring system that registers scores. The prediction of the future bonus is made based on the collected points.

Events	Effect	Scoring system
<Start>		• Personal score: 0 • Company score: 0
John Smith introduces excellent presentation	+90 Personal Score	• Personal score: 90 • Company score: 0
Company capitalization rises by 2%	+25 Company Score	• Personal score: 90 • Company score: 25
John Smith gets late on important conversation	-50 Personal Score	• Personal score: 40 • Company score: 25

Table 4.1: Monthly Bonus Scoring System

At the last prediction step, the points are summed according to a certain system of weights:

$$Personal\ Score \times 10\$ + Company\ Score \times 2\$ = 450\$$$

As described above, RNN works on the same principle. RNN has some a scoring system (hidden state). It learns how to update this scoring system according to the input sequence of values. And map the collected scores to some prediction.

In a simplified form, the activity of RNN can be demonstrated as it is shown in *figure 4.2*:

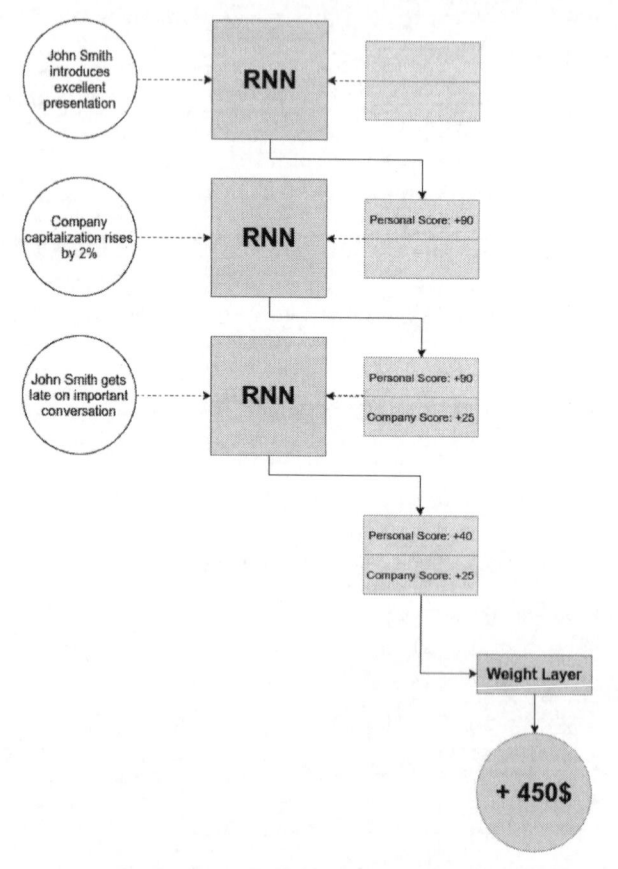

Figure 4.2: RNN in action with 3 events

That is why a RNN is called that. Processing each new value in the sequence recalculates the hidden state recurrently. This principle underlies all recurrent architectures: RNN, GRU, and LSTM.

We have some understanding of how RNN acts, so let us study the RNN theory in a more formal way. In RNN, the input sequence cycles through a loop. When it makes a decision, it considers the current input and also what it has learned from the inputs it received previously. RNN's computational graph can be presented the following way:

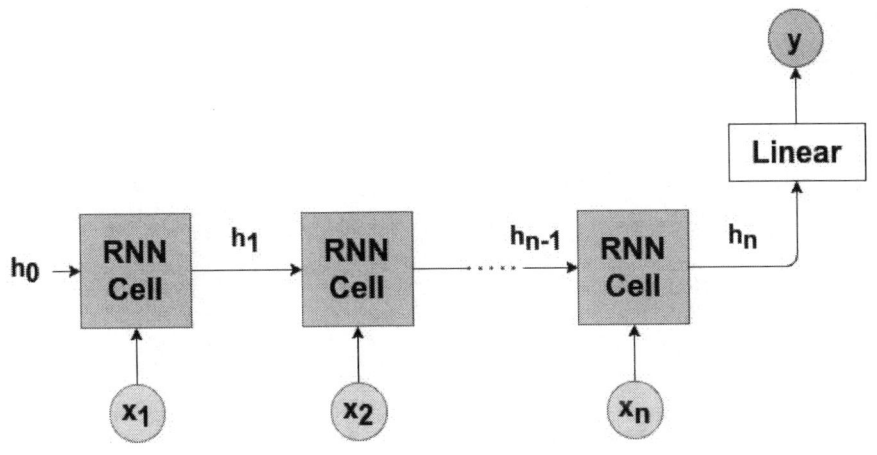

Figure 4.3: RNN computational graph

where,

- $x_1, x_2, ..., x_n$ – input sequence.
- h_i – hidden state. h_i – is a vector of length h.
- *RNN Cell* – represents neural network layer that computes the following function: $h_t = \tanh(W_{ih}x_t + b_{ih} + W_{hh}h_{(t-1)} + b_{hh})$

Figure 4.4 demonstrates construct the computational graph of the RNN Cell:

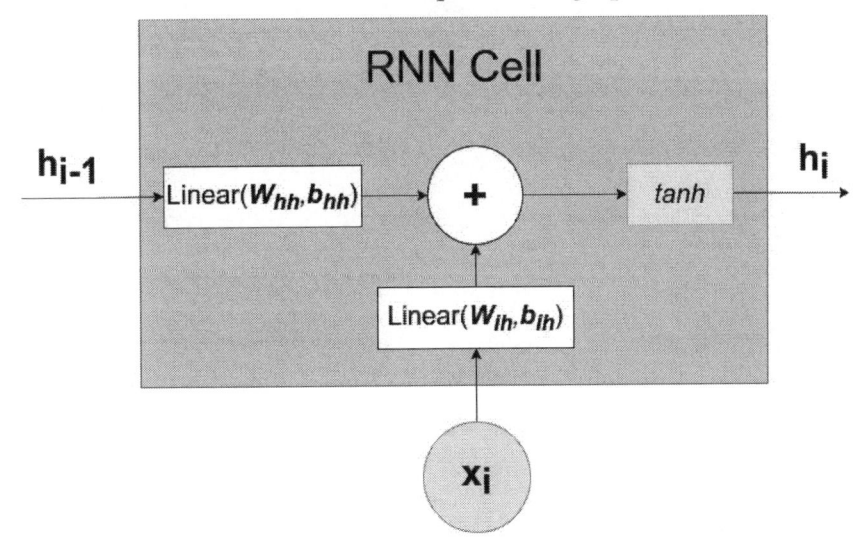

Figure 4.4: RNN cell computational graph: $\tanh(W_{ih}x_t + b_{ih} + W_{hh}h_{(t-1)} + b_{hh})$

RNN cell combines information about the current value of the sequence x_i and the previously hidden state h_{i-1}. RNN Cell returns an updated hidden state h_i after applying the activation function.

The RNN has the following parameters, which are adjusted during training:

- W_{ih} – input-hidden weights
- b_{ih} – input-hidden bias
- W_{hh} – hidden-hidden weights
- b_{hh} – hidden-hidden bias

> **Note:** A common mistake occurs when the subscripts in RNN parameters (W_{ih}, b_{ih}, W_{hh}, b_{hh}) are interpreted as an index or tensor dimension.
>
> No, they are just shorthand for input-hidden (i_h) and hidden-hidden (h_h).
>
> The same principle takes place for parameters of other models: GRU and LSTM.

Sometimes data scientists use the following depiction of RNNs:

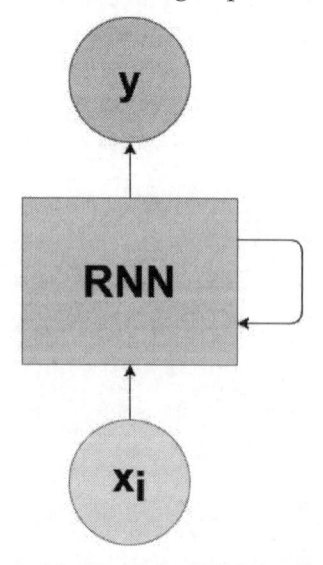

Figure 4.5: Alternative RNN visualization

The graph shown in *Figure 4.5* can lead to some misunderstanding, and I am trying to avoid this style. But if this type of graph suits your intuition, then use it without any doubt.

Now we are ready to examine PyTorch implementation of RNN **ch4/model/rnn.py**:

```python
import torch.nn as nn
class RNN(nn.Module):
    def __init__(self,
                    hidden_size,
                    in_size = 1,
                    out_size = 1):
        super(RNN, self).__init__()
        self.rnn = nn.RNN(
            input_size = in_size,
            hidden_size = hidden_size,
            batch_first = True)
        self.fc = nn.Linear(hidden_size, out_size)
    def forward(self, x, h = None):
        out, _ = self.rnn(x, h)
        last_hidden_states = out[:, -1]
        out = self.fc(last_hidden_states)
        return out, last_hidden_states
```

We see that **torch.nn.RNN** layer returns hidden states for each iteration. The last hidden state is passed to the linear layer. Our model returns two outputs: prediction and hidden state. It is crucial to reuse hidden states during RNN evaluation. We will consider this moment further.

In this chapter, we will use *Hourly Energy Consumption datasets* for research (**https://www.kaggle.com/robikscube/hourly-energy-consumption**). Let us examine one of them **ch4/aep_hourly_timeseries.py**:

```python
import matplotlib.pyplot as plt
from ch4.training_datasets import get_aep_timeseries
plt.title('AEP Hourly')
plt.plot(get_aep_timeseries()[:500])
plt.show()
```

Result

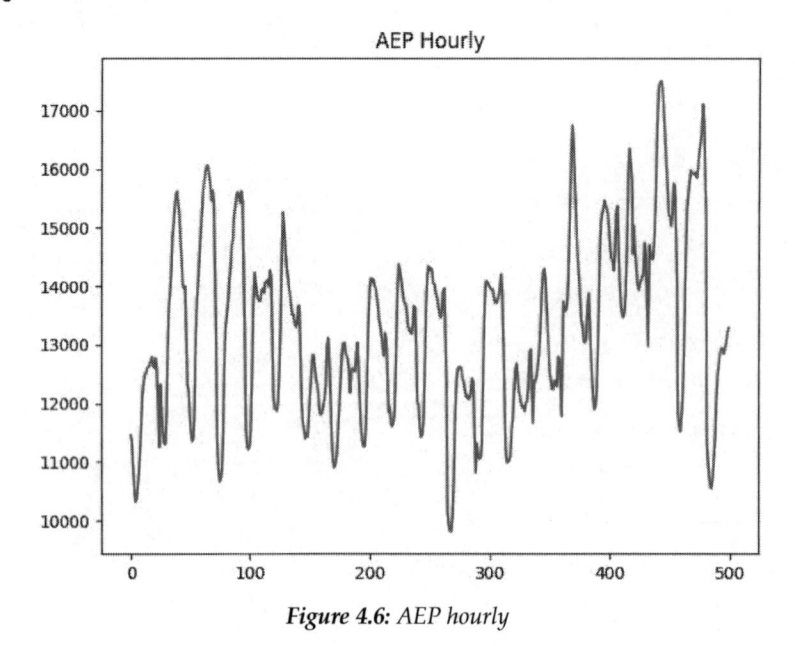

Figure 4.6: AEP hourly

We can see in *figure 4.6* that this is a really complicated time series. It has various seasonality factors with and hardly predictable spikes.

Let us show how RNN performs on AEP hourly time series **ch4/rnn_example.py**:

Import part

```
import copy
import random
import sys
import numpy as np
import matplotlib.pyplot as plt
import torch
from sklearn.preprocessing import MinMaxScaler
from ch4.model.rnn import RNN
from ch4.training_datasets import import get_training_datasets, get_aep_timeseries
```

Making this script reproducible

```
random.seed(1)
```

```
torch.manual_seed(1)
```

Parameters

Here is a set of global parameters:

```
# length of sliding window
features = 240
# length of test dataset
test_ts_len = 300
# size of RNN hidden state
rnn_hidden_size = 24
# Optimizer learning rate
learning_rate = 0.02
training_epochs = 500
```

Preparing datasets for training

We normalize time series in range [0, 1] and create a classical train, validation, test datasets:

```
ts = get_aep_timeseries()
scaler = MinMaxScaler()
scaled_ts = scaler.fit_transform(ts)
x_train, x_val, x_test, y_train, y_val, y_test =\
    get_training_datasets(scaled_ts, features, test_ts_len)
```

Initializing the model

```
model = RNN(hidden_size = rnn_hidden_size)
model.train()
```

Training

After we perform the training process:

```
optimizer = torch.optim.Adam(params = model.parameters(), lr = learning_rate)
mse_loss = torch.nn.MSELoss()
best_model = None
```

```
min_val_loss = sys.maxsize
training_loss = []
validation_loss = []
for t in range(training_epochs):
    prediction, _ = model(x_train)
    loss = mse_loss(prediction, y_train)
    optimizer.zero_grad()
    loss.backward()
    optimizer.step()
    val_prediction, _ = model(x_val)
    val_loss = mse_loss(val_prediction, y_val)
    training_loss.append(loss.item())
    validation_loss.append(val_loss.item())
    if val_loss.item() < min_val_loss:
        best_model = copy.deepcopy(model)
        min_val_loss = val_loss.item()
    if t % 50 == 0:
        print(f'epoch {t}: train - {round(loss.item(), 4)}, '
              f'val: - {round(val_loss.item(), 4)}')
```

Evaluation

And here we come to the trickiest place. You have to pass the 'warm' hidden state to the RNN model when you evaluate it. The simplest way to warm up the hidden state is to run the model on validation data once and pass warm hidden state through each iteration:

```
best_model.eval()
_, h_list = best_model(x_val)
# warm hidden state
h = (h_list[-1, :]).unsqueeze(-2)
predicted = []
for test_seq in x_test.tolist():
    x = torch.Tensor(data = [test_seq])
    # passing hidden state through each iteration
    y, h = best_model(x, h.unsqueeze(-2))
```

```
    unscaled = scaler.inverse_transform(np.array(y.item()).reshape(-1,
1))[0][0]
    predicted.append(unscaled)
```

Performance on test dataset

Let us evaluate the model we built on the test dataset:

```
real = scaler.inverse_transform(y_test.tolist())
plt.title("Test dataset")
plt.plot(real, label = 'real')
plt.plot(predicted, label = 'predicted')
plt.legend()
plt.show()
```

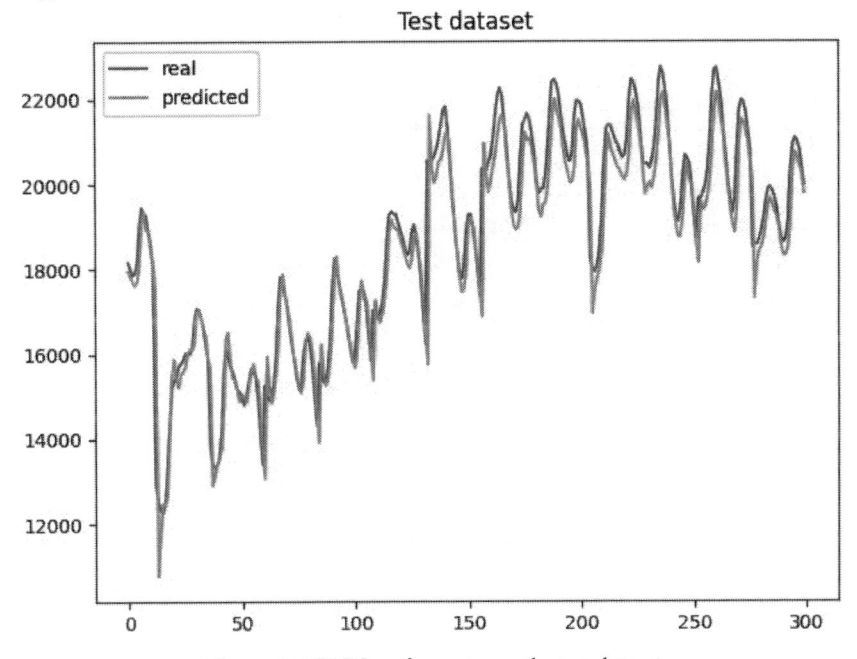

Figure 4.7: RNN performance on the test dataset

RNN shows great performance on the test dataset. The model we have trained predicts seasonable spikes very accurately.

Training progress

Finally, let us examine the training process itself.

```
plt.title('Training')
```

```
plt.yscale('log')
plt.plot(training_loss, label = 'training')
plt.plot(validation_loss, label = 'validation')
plt.ylabel('Loss')
plt.xlabel('Epoch')
plt.legend()
plt.show()
```

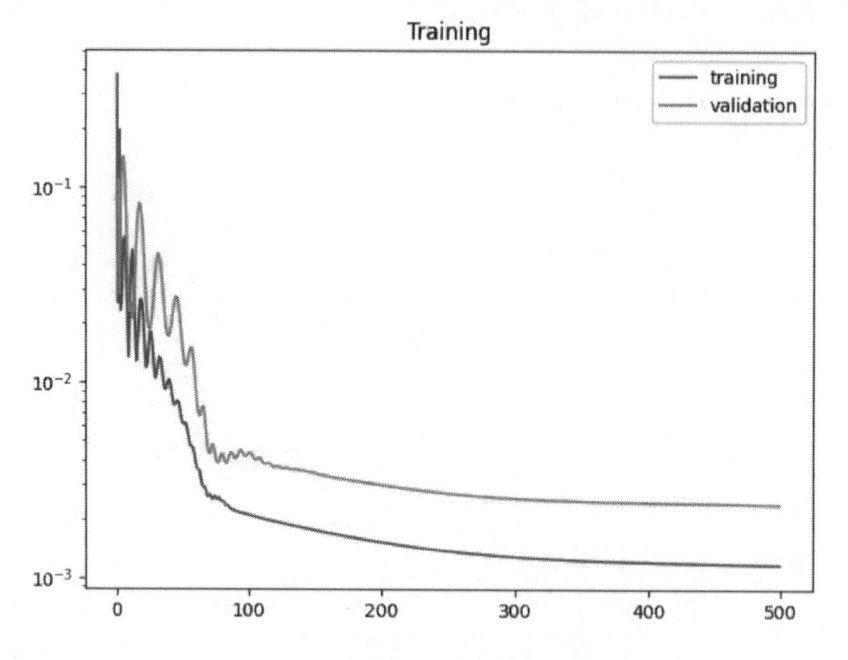

Figure 4.8: RNN training progress

Training progress is smooth without sharp and unpredictable spikes.

Now, we can confidently state the promise and effectiveness of the RNN's application to time series forecasting problems. RNNs can find obscure dependencies and patterns in sequences and produce accurate predictions.

Despite all the advantages of RNN, it has significant disadvantages:

- Due to computational complexity, they suffer from vanishing gradient problems. The training process becomes too slow. The vanishing gradient problem is a common problem to all RNNs.

- Hidden state is updated on each iteration what makes it difficult to store long-term information in RNN. GRU and LSTM architectures solve this issue. They have similar approaches how to store long-term information.

Gated recurrent unit

The **GRU** is an advanced version of the classical RNN. The primary purpose of GRU is to store long-term information. In this section, we will explore how GRU achieves this.

The easiest way to store long-term information in a hidden state is to restrict hidden state updates on each iteration. This approach will avoid overwriting important long-term information.

You can find the following definition of GRU on the internet:

$$r_t = \sigma(W_{ir} x_t + b_{ir} + W_{hr} h_{(t-1)} + b_{hr})$$
$$z_t = \sigma(W_{iz} x_t + b_{iz} + W_{hz} h_{(t-1)} + b_{hz})$$
$$n_t = \tanh(W_{in} x_t + b_{in} + r_t \circ (W_{hn} h_{(t-1)} + b_{hn}))$$
$$h_t = (1 - z_t) \circ n_t + z_t \circ h_{(t-1)}$$

where:

- σ is the *sigmoid* function
- $\circ$ is the Hadamard product, that is:

$$\begin{bmatrix} a_1 \\ a_2 \\ a_3 \end{bmatrix} \circ \begin{bmatrix} b_1 \\ b_2 \\ b_3 \end{bmatrix} = \begin{bmatrix} a_1 b_1 \\ a_2 b_2 \\ a_3 b_3 \end{bmatrix}$$

Looks nice. Do not panic. Everything is not so complicated as it seems!

Let us consider the first variable r_t:

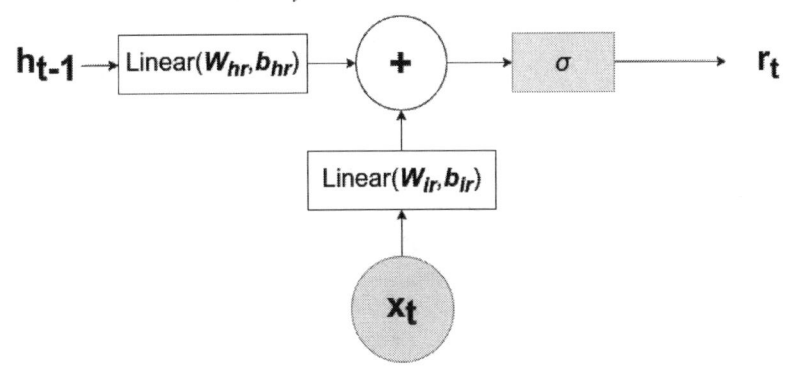

Figure 4.9: r_t variable computational graph

r_t is an output of a simple neural network on two input vectors: h_{t-1} and x_t. The variable r_t is responsible for forgetting unimportant parts in the hidden state of GRU.

Let us look at an example of the vector $r_t = [0.1, 0, 0.8, 1, \ldots]$:

- **0.1** - This value is close to zero, and highly likely corresponding hidden state value will be forgotten.
- **0** - This value is equal to zero, which means that the corresponding hidden state value will be forgotten.
- **0.8** - This value is close to one, and highly likely corresponding hidden state value will be passed to a further hidden state.
- **1** - This value is equal to one, which means that the corresponding hidden state value will be passed to a further hidden state.

This is how GRU controls the hidden state rewriting process.

> **Note: We see that the zero and one have special logical meanings for r_t. This is why the sigmoid function is used as the activation function for r_t calculation.**

Now let us consider the n_t variable:

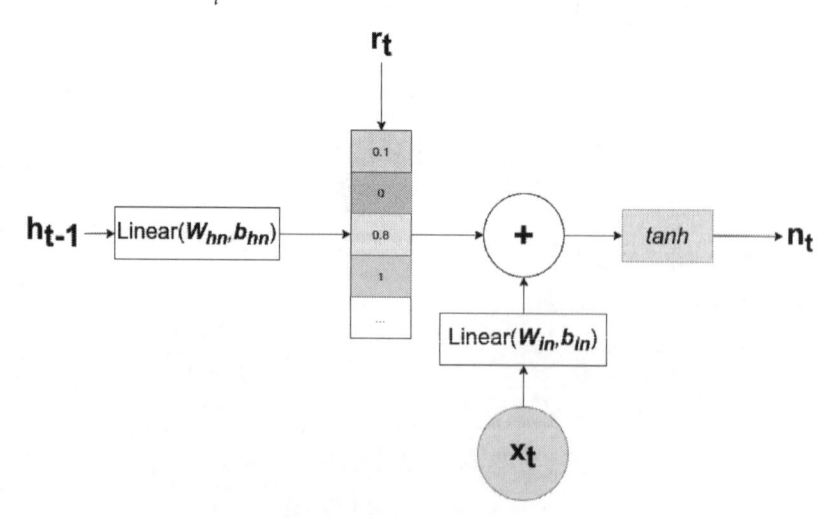

Figure 4.10: n_t variable computational graph

n_t represents the hidden state vector based on h_{t-1}, which resets some previous values. Exactly n_t variable provides long-term information storage because the r_t variable does not always allow changing something in the hidden context h_{t-1}. Thus, some values in a previously hidden state h_{t-1} can pass through the iteration without significant changes to the next hidden state h_t.

Let us finish this research with the variables z_t and h_t:

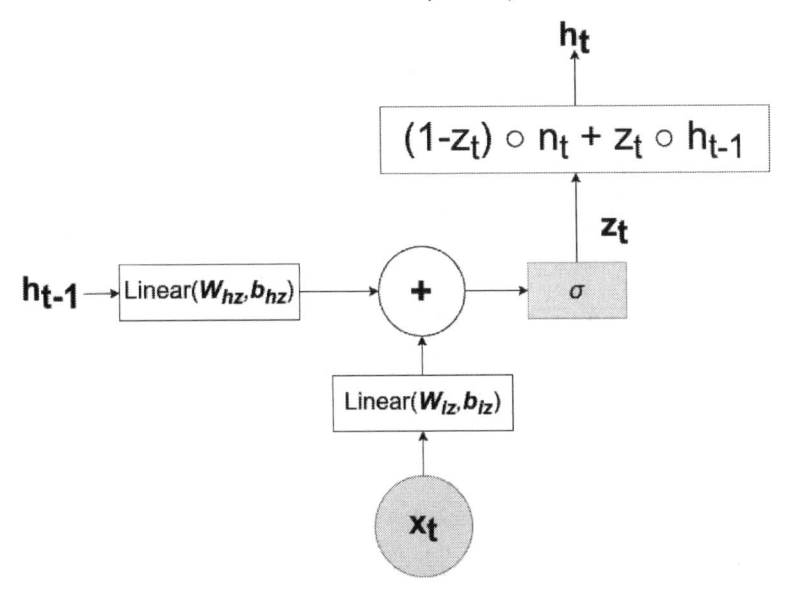

Figure 4.11: h_t variable computational graph

h_t is a simple linear combination of two hidden states: h_{t-1} - previous hidden state and n_t – candidate hidden state with long-term memory. And the variable z_t decides in what proportion to mix them.

Summarizing:

GRU selects long-term features r_t and forms a hidden state with long-term memory n_t and mixes it with the previously hidden state h_{t-1} with z_t ratio.

I really hope that these formulas do not seem so scary now:

$$r_t = \sigma(W_{ir}x_t + b_{ir} + W_{hr}h_{(t-1)} + b_{hr})$$
$$z_t = \sigma(W_{iz}x_t + b_{iz} + W_{hz}h_{(t-1)} + b_{hz})$$
$$n_t = \tanh(W_{in}x_t + b_{in} + r_t \circ (W_{hn}h_{(t-1)} + b_{hn}))$$
$$h_t = (1 - z_t) \circ n_t + z_t \circ h_{(t-1)}$$

> **Note:** Now, you might have a question in your mind: Do I need to understand the architecture principles for successful use? That is a fair question. At the moment, deep learning tools allow you to create your own complex and effective architectures. The design of new architectures is often based on borrowing ideas from the other ones. Therefore, a good understanding of time series prediction models' principles will certainly help in their correct application and the development of new ones.

Now we can show the global GRU computational graph the following way:

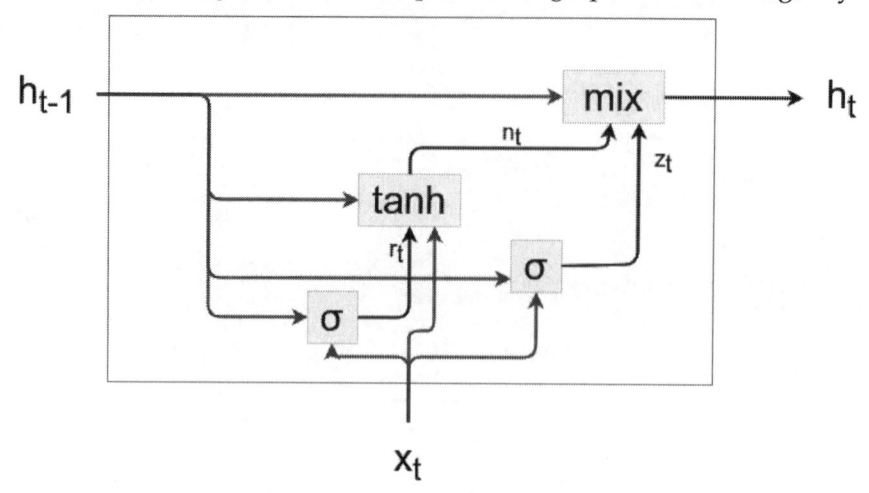

Figure 4.12: GRU computational graph

The diagram shown in *Figure 4.12* can be a good cheat sheet reminding the main principle of GRU calculation.

The GRU has the following parameters, which are adjusted during training:

- $W_{ir}, W_{hr}, W_{iz}, W_{hz}, W_{in}, W_{hn}$ – weights
- $b_{ir}, b_{hr}, b_{iz}, b_{hz}, b_{in}, b_{hn}$ – bias

GRU prediction model is very similar to RNN **ch4/model/gru.py**:

```python
import torch.nn as nn
class GRU(nn.Module):
    def __init__(self,
                 hidden_size,
                 in_size = 1,
                 out_size = 1):
        super(GRU, self).__init__()
        self.gru = nn.GRU(
            input_size = in_size,
            hidden_size = hidden_size,
            batch_first = True)
        self.fc = nn.Linear(hidden_size, out_size)
    def forward(self, x, h = None):
```

```
        out, _ = self.gru(x, h)
        last_hidden_states = out[:, -1]
        out = self.fc(last_hidden_states)
        return out, last_hidden_states
```

Let's test it on PJME dataset **ch4/pjme_hourly_timeseries.py**:

```
import matplotlib.pyplot as plt
from ch4.training_datasets import get_pjme_timeseries
plt.title('PJME Hourly')
plt.plot(get_pjme_timeseries()[:500])
plt.show()
```

Result

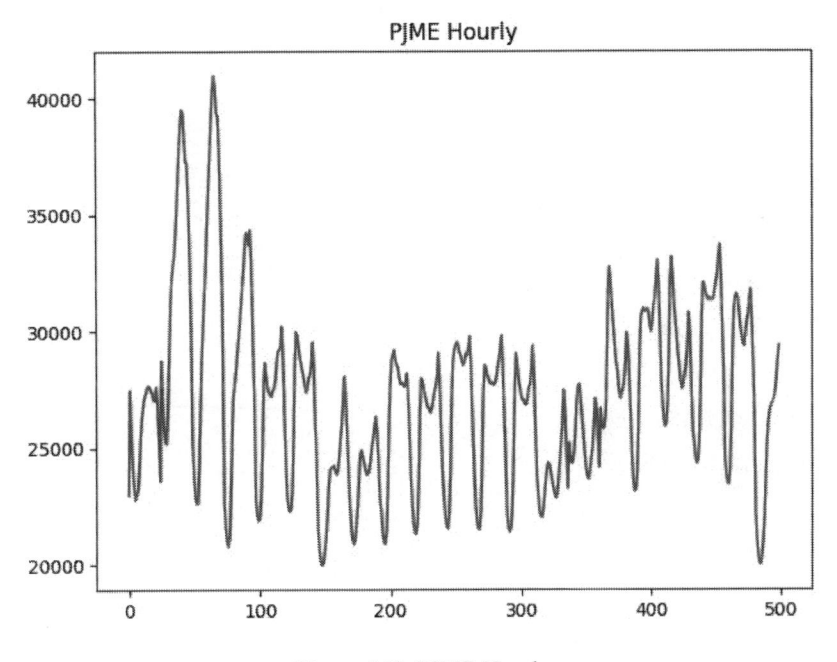

Figure 4.13: PJME Hourly

The time series shown in *figure 4.13* has complicated unobvious patterns too.

Let us examine the performance of the GRU prediction model on this time series **ch4/gru_example.py**:

Import part

```python
import copy
import random
import sys
import numpy as np
import matplotlib.pyplot as plt
import torch
from sklearn.preprocessing import MinMaxScaler
from ch4.model.gru import GRU
from ch4.training_datasets import import get_training_datasets, get_pjme_timeseries
```

Making this script reproducible

```python
random.seed(1)
torch.manual_seed(1)
```

Parameters

```python
# length of sliding window
features = 240
# length of test dataset
test_ts_len = 300
# size of GRU hidden state
gru_hidden_size = 24
# Optimizer learning rate
learning_rate = 0.02
training_epochs = 500
```

Preparing datasets for training

```python
ts = get_pjme_timeseries()
scaler = MinMaxScaler()
scaled_ts = scaler.fit_transform(ts)
x_train, x_val, x_test, y_train, y_val, y_test =\
    get_training_datasets(scaled_ts, features, test_ts_len)
```

Initializing the model

```
model = GRU(hidden_size = gru_hidden_size)
model.train()
```

Training

```
optimizer = torch.optim.Adam(params = model.parameters(), lr = learning_rate)
mse_loss = torch.nn.MSELoss()
best_model = None
min_val_loss = sys.maxsize
training_loss = []
validation_loss = []
for t in range(training_epochs):
    prediction, _ = model(x_train)
    loss = mse_loss(prediction, y_train)
    optimizer.zero_grad()
    loss.backward()
    optimizer.step()
    val_prediction, _ = model(x_val)
    val_loss = mse_loss(val_prediction, y_val)
    training_loss.append(loss.item())
    validation_loss.append(val_loss.item())
    if val_loss.item() < min_val_loss:
        best_model = copy.deepcopy(model)
        min_val_loss = val_loss.item()
    if t % 50 == 0:
        print(f'epoch {t}: train - {round(loss.item(), 4)}, '
            f'val: - {round(val_loss.item(), 4)}')
```

Evaluation

```
best_model.eval()
_, h_list = best_model(x_val)
# warm hidden state
```

```
h = (h_list[-1, :]).unsqueeze(-2)
predicted = []
for test_seq in x_test.tolist():
    x = torch.Tensor(data = [test_seq])
    # passing hidden state through each iteration
    y, h = best_model(x, h.unsqueeze(-2))
    unscaled = scaler.inverse_transform(np.array(y.item()).reshape(-1, 1))[0][0]
    predicted.append(unscaled)
```

Performance on test dataset

```
real = scaler.inverse_transform(y_test.tolist())
plt.title("Test dataset")
plt.plot(real, label = 'real')
plt.plot(predicted, label = 'predicted')
plt.legend()
plt.show()
```

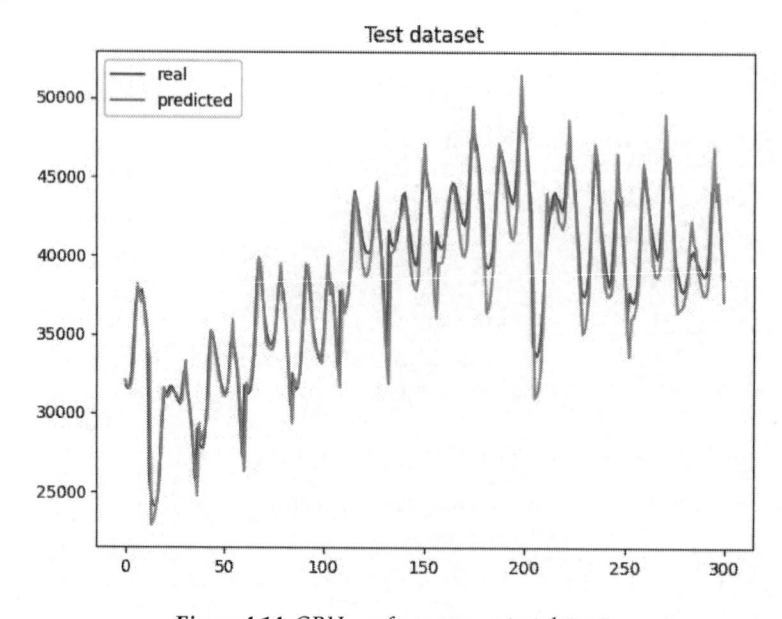

Figure 4.14: GRU performance on test dataset

We see in *figure 4.14* that the GRU model mimics original time series behavior rather accurately.

Training progress

```
plt.title('Training')
plt.yscale('log')
plt.plot(training_loss, label = 'training')
plt.plot(validation_loss, label = 'validation')
plt.ylabel('Loss')
plt.xlabel('Epoch')
plt.legend()
plt.show()
```

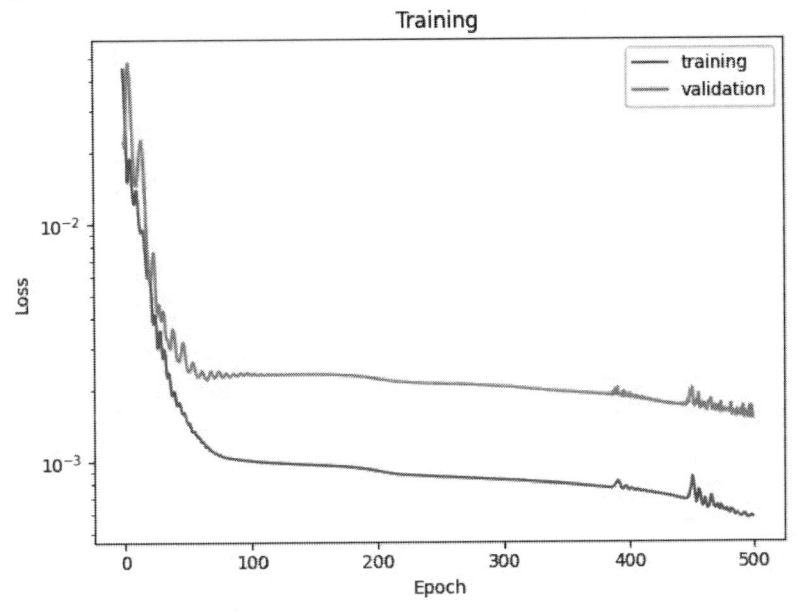

Figure 4.15: GRU training progress

Train and validation losses have asymptotical descent with a constant natural gap between them. We can conclude that the model really learns the time series behavior.

Long short-term memory

LSTM Network has been developed to overcome the vanishing gradient problem in the standard RNN by improving the network's gradient flow. It should be mentioned that the LSTM architecture appeared much earlier than the GRU. The LSTM architecture was developed in 1997, and the GRU was proposed in 2014. GRU design is simpler and more understandable than LSTM. That is why we started our study by examining GRU first.

As the name suggests, LSTM addresses the same short-term and long-term memory problems as GRU. Globally, the computational flow of the LSTM looks the following way:

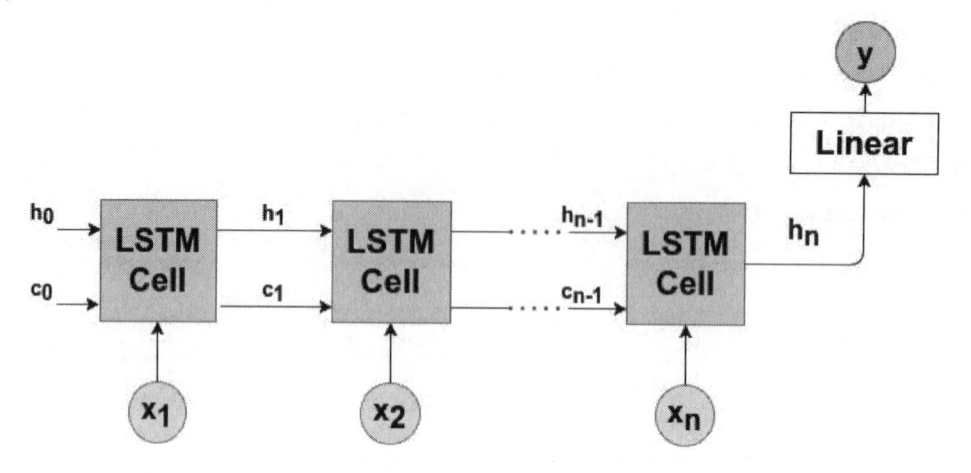

Figure 4.16: LSTM

LSTM works on the similar principles as GRU but has more variables. RNN and GRU pass only one hidden state h_t through each iteration. But LSTM passes two vectors: h_t - *hidden state* (short-term memory) and c_t - *cell state* (long-term memory).

LSTM Cell outputs are calculated via the formulas as shown follows:

$$i_t = \sigma(W_{ii}x_t + b_{ii} + W_{hi}h_{(t-1)} + b_{hi})$$

$$f_t = \sigma(W_{if}x_t + b_{if} + W_{hf}h_{(t-1)} + b_{hf})$$

$$g_t = tanh(W_{ig}x_t + b_{ig} + W_{hg}h_{(t-1)} + b_{hn})$$

$$o_t = \sigma(W_{io}x_t + b_{io} + W_{ho}h_{(t-1)} + b_{ho})$$

$$c_t = f_t \circ c_{t-1} + i_t \circ g_t$$

$$h_t = o_t \circ tanh(c_t)$$

where:

- σ is the *sigmoid* function.
- $\circ$ is the Hadamard product.

Let us go through each variable:

i_t (**input gate**) is the variable that is used to update the cell state c_t. The previously hidden state h_t and the current sequence input x_t are given as inputs to a sigmoid function. If the output is close to one, the more important the information is.

f_t (**forget gate**) is the variable that decides which information should be forgotten in the cell state c_t. The previously hidden state h_t and the current sequence input x_t are given as inputs to a sigmoid function. If the output f_t is close to zero, then the information can be forgotten, while if the output is close to one, the information must be stored.

g_t represents potentially new important information for the cell state c_t.

c_t (**cell state**) is a sum of:

- previous cell state c_{t-1} with some forgotten information f_t.
- new information from g_t selected by i_t.

o_t (**output gate**) is the variable to update hidden state h_t.

h_t (**hidden state**) is the next hidden state which is calculated by picking the important information o_t from cell state c_t.

Figure 4.17 demonstrates the computational graph of the LSTM cell:

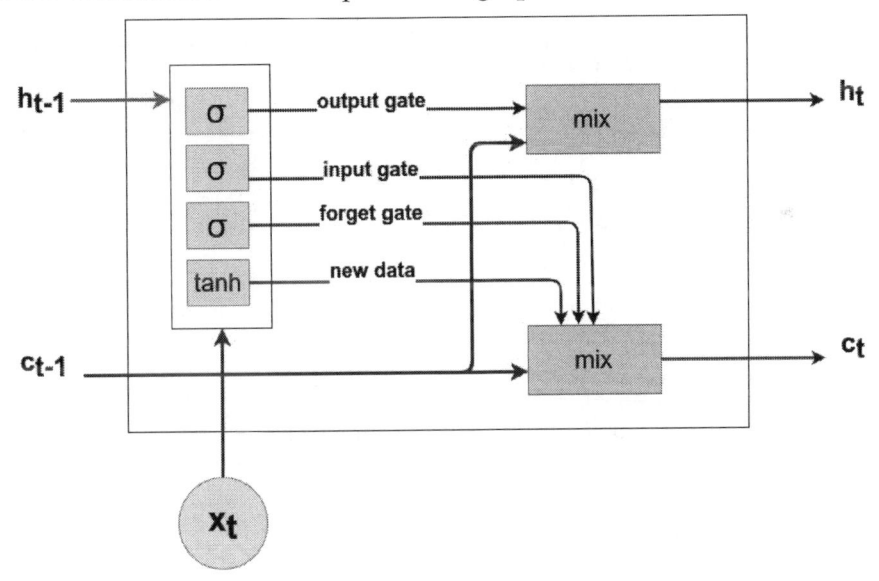

Figure 4.17: LSTM cell computational graph

The LSTM has the following parameters, which are adjusted during training:

- $W_{ii}, W_{hi}, W_{if}, W_{hf}, W_{ig}, W_{hg}, W_{io}, W_{ho}$ – weights
- $b_{ii}, b_{hi}, b_{if}, b_{hf}, b_{ig}, b_{hg}, b_{io}, b_{ho}$ – bias

Let us examine the PyTorch implementation of the LSTM prediction model **ch4/model/lstm.py**:

```python
import torch.nn as nn
class LSTM(nn.Module):
    def __init__(self,
                 hidden_size,
                 in_size = 1,
                 out_size = 1):
        super(LSTM, self).__init__()
        self.lstm = nn.LSTM(
            input_size = in_size,
            hidden_size = hidden_size,
            batch_first = True)
        self.fc = nn.Linear(hidden_size, out_size)
    def forward(self, x, h = None):
        out, h = self.lstm(x, h)
        last_hidden_states = out[:, -1]
        out = self.fc(last_hidden_states)
        return out, h
```

As we see, the implementation of the LSTM model is pretty similar to RNN and GRU implementations.

We will test the LSTM model on the following time series dataset (*NI hourly time series from Hourly Energy Consumption Data*) **ch4/ni_hourly_timeseries.py**:

```
import matplotlib.pyplot as plt
from ch4.training_datasets import get_ni_timeseries
plt.title('NI Hourly')
plt.plot(get_ni_timeseries()[:500])
plt.show()
```

Result

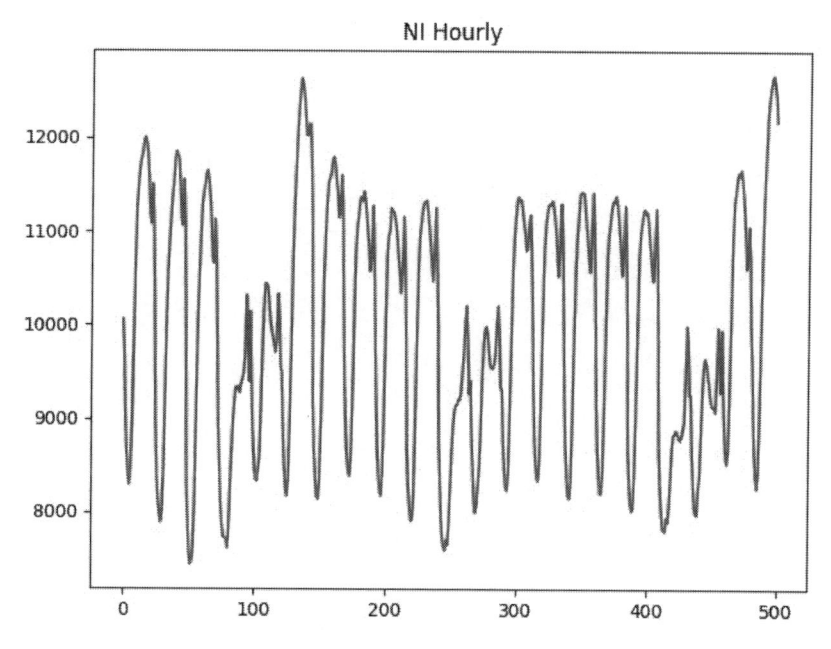

Figure 4.18: NI hourly time series

Let us go further to see the LSTM model in action **ch4/lstm_example.py**:

Import part

```
import copy
import random
import sys
import numpy as np
import matplotlib.pyplot as plt
import torch
from sklearn.preprocessing import MinMaxScaler
from ch4.model.lstm import LSTM
from ch4.training_datasets import import get_training_datasets, get_ni_timeseries
```

Making this script reproducible

```
random.seed(1)
torch.manual_seed(1)
```

Parameters

```
# length of sliding window
features = 240
# length of test dataset
test_ts_len = 300
# size of LSTM hidden state
lstm_hidden_size = 24
# Optimizer learning rate
learning_rate = 0.02
training_epochs = 100
```

Preparing datasets for training

```
ts = get_ni_timeseries()
scaler = MinMaxScaler()
scaled_ts = scaler.fit_transform(ts)
x_train, x_val, x_test, y_train, y_val, y_test =\
    get_training_datasets(scaled_ts, features, test_ts_len)
```

Initializing the model

```
model = LSTM(hidden_size = lstm_hidden_size)
model.train()
```

Training

```
optimizer = torch.optim.Adam(params = model.parameters(), lr = learning_rate)
mse_loss = torch.nn.MSELoss()
best_model = None
min_val_loss = sys.maxsize
training_loss = []
validation_loss = []
for t in range(training_epochs):
    prediction, _ = model(x_train)
    loss = mse_loss(prediction, y_train)
```

```python
        optimizer.zero_grad()
        loss.backward()
        optimizer.step()
        val_prediction, _ = model(x_val)
        val_loss = mse_loss(val_prediction, y_val)
        training_loss.append(loss.item())
        validation_loss.append(val_loss.item())
        if val_loss.item() < min_val_loss:
            best_model = copy.deepcopy(model)
            min_val_loss = val_loss.item()
        if t % 10 == 0:
            print(f'epoch {t}: train - {round(loss.item(), 4)}, '
                  f'val: - {round(val_loss.item(), 4)}')
```

Evaluation

For an evaluation of the LSTM model, we need to pass "warm" cell state and hidden state:

```python
best_model.eval()
with torch.no_grad():
    _, h_list = best_model(x_val)
    # warm hidden and cell state
    h = tuple([(h[-1, -1, :]).unsqueeze(-2).unsqueeze(-2)
               for h in h_list])
    predicted = []
    for test_seq in x_test.tolist():
        x = torch.Tensor(data = [test_seq])
        # passing hidden state and cell through each iteration
        y, h = best_model(x, h)
        unscaled = scaler.inverse_transform(
            np.array(y.item()).reshape(-1, 1))[0][0]
        predicted.append(unscaled)
```

Performance on test dataset

```
real = scaler.inverse_transform(y_test.tolist())
plt.title("Test dataset")
plt.plot(real, label = 'real')
plt.plot(predicted, label = 'predicted')
plt.legend()
plt.show()
```

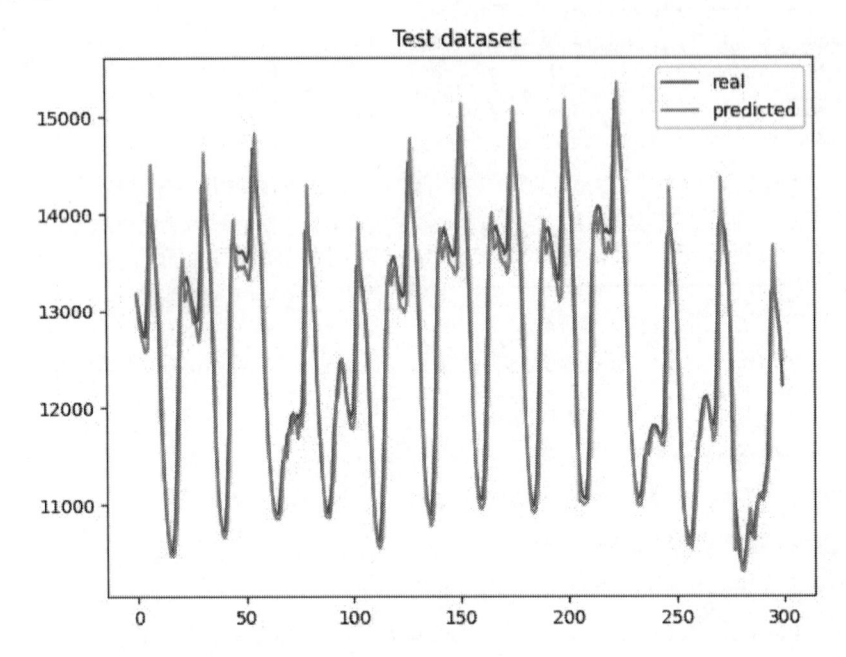

Figure 4.19: LSTM performance on the test dataset

LSTM captures time series behavior very well for making accurate predictions.

Training progress

```
plt.title('Training')
plt.yscale('log')
plt.plot(training_loss, label = 'training')
plt.plot(validation_loss, label = 'validation')
plt.ylabel('Loss')
plt.xlabel('Epoch')
```

```
plt.legend()
plt.show()
```

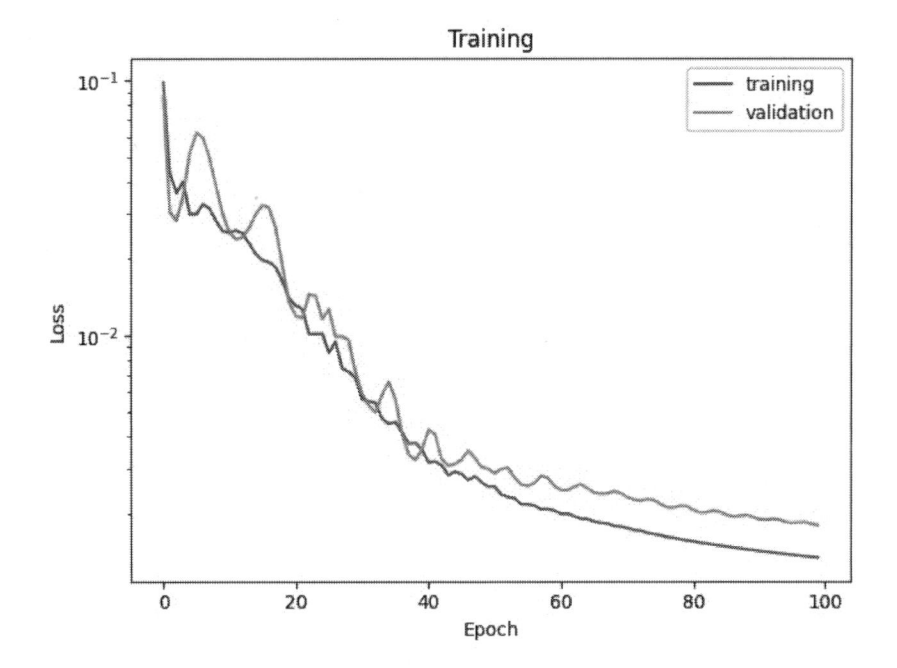

Figure 4.20: LSTM training progress

Looking at *Figure 4.20*, we conclude that we stopped the training process too early. We get more accurate models if we set more epochs for training.

We see that RNNs show excellent results and are suitable for time series forecasting problems.

Conclusion

RNNs are the very popular Deep Learning technique for Time Series Forecasting since they allow to produce reliable predictions on time series in various problems. The main problem with RNN is that it suffers from the vanishing gradient problem when applied to long sequences, and it doesn't have a long-term memory tool. LSTM and GRU were developed in order to prevent the vanishing gradient problem of RNNs with the use of gates that regulate the information flow and implement long-term memory storage. The use of LSTM and GRU gives remarkable results, but LSTM and GRU don't always perform better than RNN.

Points to remember

- RNN has a hidden state that can be treated as an internal memory of the input sequence.
- RNN recalculates the hidden state after processing each new input value recurrently.
- RNN suffers from vanishing gradient problem.
- RNN updates a hidden state on each iteration. Thus it has no long-term memory.
- GRU implements the reset gate, which declines some updates in a hidden state.
- LSTM passes two vectors through each iteration: hidden state and cell state.

Multiple choice questions

1. **GRU and LSTM use the sigmoid function as the activation for their gates. Can we change the sigmoid to ReLU to solve the gradient vanishing problem?**

   A. Yes

   B. It depends on the time series we are working with

   C. No, gate activation function should have (0, 1) return range

2. **How the length of the hidden state in RNN affects its learning ability?**

   A. Long hidden state vector can memorize more patterns and increase the performance of the model

   B. The length of the hidden state doesn't affect the model performance

Answers

1. C
2. A

Key terms

- *RNN:* recurrent neural network
- *GRU:* gated recurrent unit
- *LSTM:* long short-term memory

CHAPTER 5
Advanced Forecasting Models

Until recently, the topic of time series forecasting in deep learning has been associated mainly with recurrent neural network architectures such as LSTM and GRU. However, there is significant research breakthroughs in neural network architecture that is very efficient to predict time series. This chapter is focused on two examples of advanced deep learning architectures: Encoder–decoder model and temporal convolutional network (TCN).

Structure

In this chapter, we will discuss the following topics:

- Encoder–decoder model
- Temporal convolutional network

Objectives

After studying this chapter, the reader would have mastered the principles of building complex architectures for deep learning neural networks in time series. This chapter is a good start for diving into deep learning advances and designing your own custom deep learning architectures for particular time series problems.

Encoder–decoder model

The encoder–decoder model is a logical continuation of RNN models. These models have provided state-of-the-art results in sequence-to-sequence multistep time series forecasting, as depicted in *figure 5.1*:

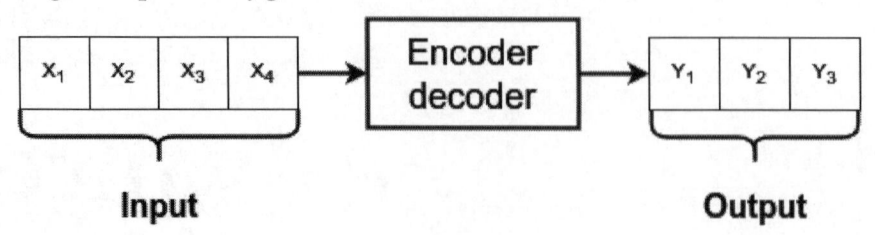

Figure 5.1: Encoder–decoder model

Encoder represents a typical recurrent neural network (RNN, GRU, LSTM) that we have studied in *Chapter 4, Recurrent Neural Networks*. The encoder is responsible for forming the internal memory (*hidden state*), which stores the time series characteristics. And the decoder is responsible for interpreting the internal memory (*hidden state*), which the encoder passed.

Encoder answers the question: *What happened?*

Decoder answers the question: *What will happen next?*

Say we have an Encoder–decoder model which predicts human activity in the evening based. Then its logic can be similar to *figure 5.2*:

Advanced Forecasting Models ▪ 143

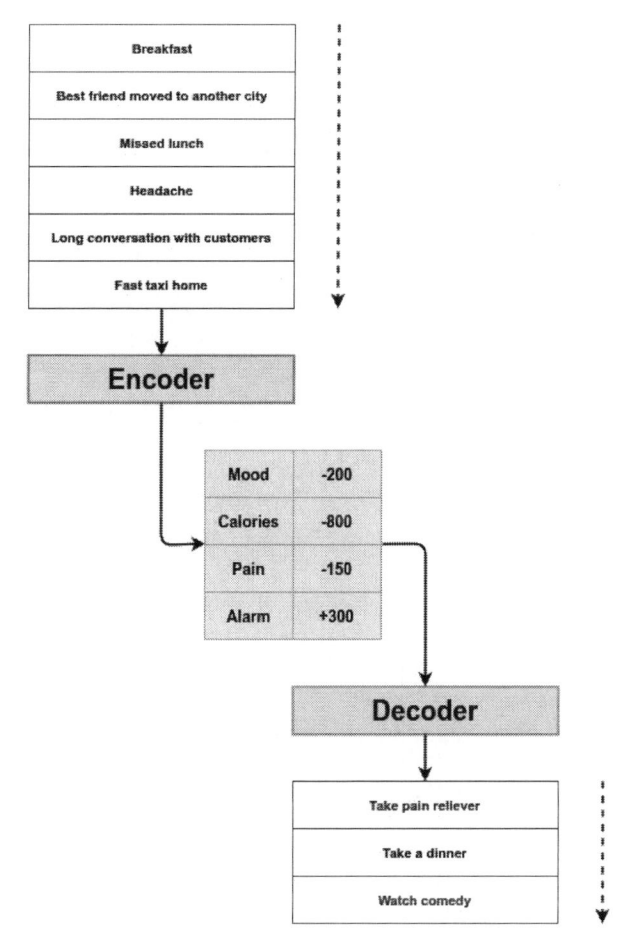

Figure 5.2: Encoder–decoder in action

Let us examine the activity presented in *figure 5.2*. At first, an encoder forms a hidden state based on events' history, the same way as classic RNN models:

Event	Effect	Hidden State
Breakfast	o Mood: +300 o Calories: +700 o Alarm: +100	o Mood: +300 o Calories: +700 o Pain: 0 o Alarm: +100
Best friend moved to another city	o Mood: -400	o Mood: -100 o Calories: +700 o Pain: 0 o Alarm: +100

Event	Effect	Hidden State
Missed lunch	o Mood: -100 o Calories: -1500	o Mood: -200 o Calories: -800 o Pain: 0 o Alarm: +100
Headache	o Mood: -100 o Pain: -100	o Mood: -300 o Calories: -800 o Pain: -100 o Alarm: 0
Long conversation with customers	o Pain: -50	o Mood: -300 o Calories: -800 o Pain: -150 o Alarm: 0
Fast taxi home	o Mood: +100	o Mood: -200 o Calories: -800 o Pain: -150 o Alarm: +300

Table 5.1: Encoding the history of events

And after a decoder analyze the hidden state and translates it to another sequence of actions, as follows:

Event	Effect	Hidden State
Take pain reliever	o Mood: +50 o Pain: +150	o Mood: -150 o Calories: -800 o Pain: 0 o Alarm: +300
Take a dinner	o Calories: +800	o Mood: -150 o Calories: 0 o Pain: 0 o Alarm: +300
Watch comedy	o Mood: +350	o Mood: +200 o Calories: 0 o Pain: 0 Alarm: +300

Table 5.2: Decoding hidden state to the sequence of actions

The encoder–decoder model mimics the human memory and decision-making mechanism. The encoder gathers experienced information, and the decoder decides what to do with it.

Let us go further and examine the architecture of the encoder–decoder model:

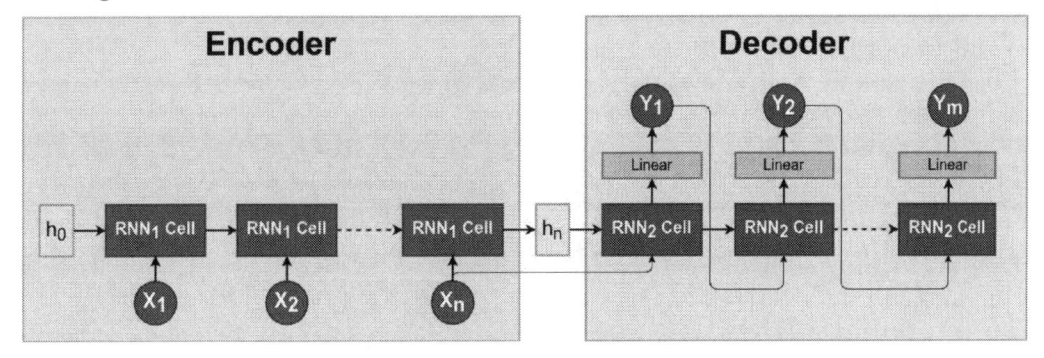

Figure 5.3: Encoder–decoder architecture

The encoder component is already familiar to us so let us examine a decoder component. The decoder component takes a hidden state formed by an encoder and returns a prediction y_1. Then the decoder model recursively takes previous prediction y_1 as the input and generates y_2. This process repeats recursively. Thus, the decoder can generate prediction sequences of unlimited length. Encoder and decoder components can have different implementations of recurrent neural networks. For example, the encoder can be based on GRU, and the decoder can be based on LSTM.

Encoder–decoder training

There are three strategies to train the decoder component: Recursive, teacher forcing, and mixed teacher forcing. Let's take a look at each of these approaches.

Recursive

Recursive training assumes that each input to the RNN cell is the result of the previous action, as shown in *figure 5.4*:

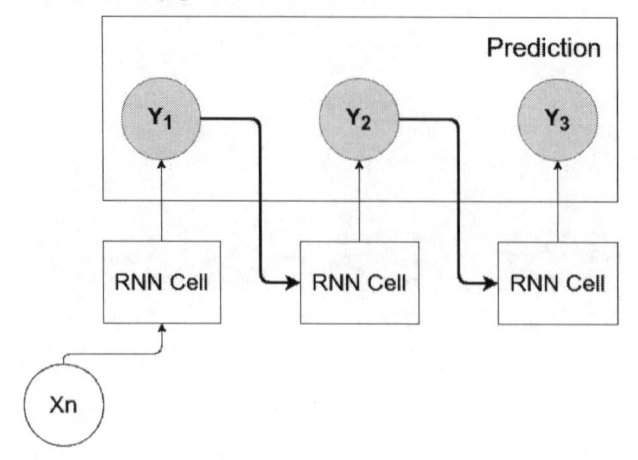

Figure 5.4: Recursive Training

Recursive training usually gives the best results for short-term predictions.

Teacher forcing

During **teacher forcing** training, the decoder RNN cell receives actual previous target values on each step, as shown in *Figure 5.5*:

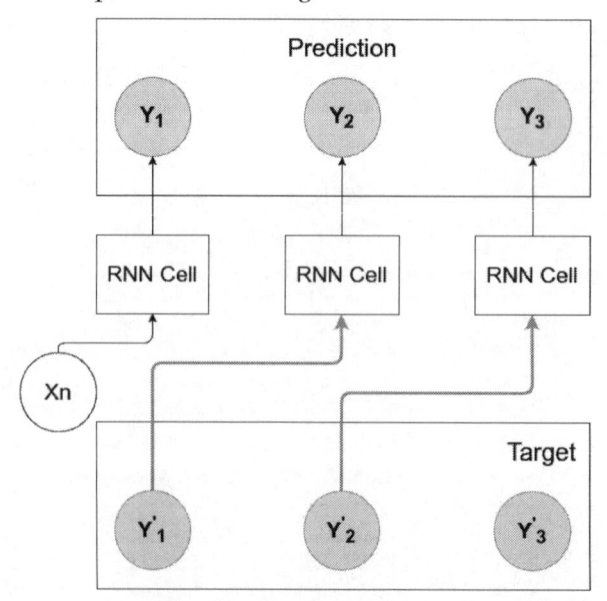

Figure 5.5: Teacher Forcing Training

Teacher forcing training adds external information to the training before loss calculation. This technique helps to learn long-term predictions.

Mixed teacher forcing

Mixed teacher forcing training combines recursive and teacher forcing methods together. It mixes decoder predictions and target sequence values. This approach usually gives the best results:

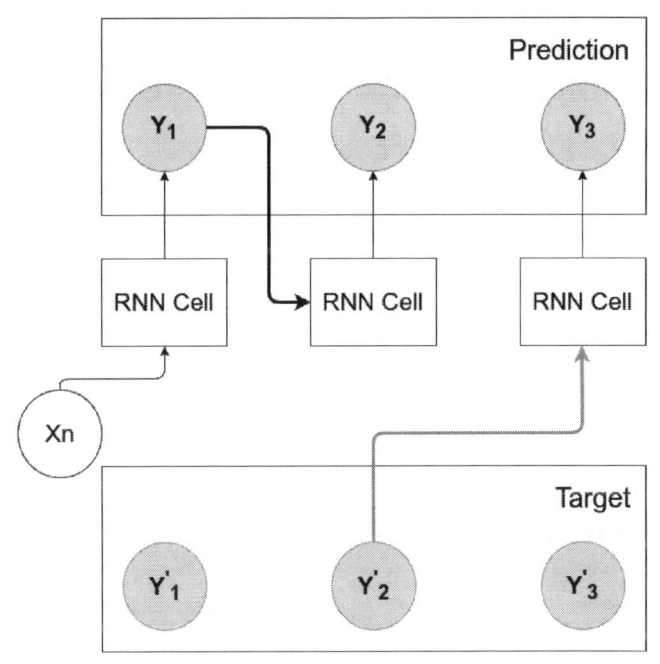

Figure 5.6: Mixed teacher forcing training

The ratio of decoder predictions and target values is usually managed by the training parameter, which takes values from 0 to 1. If the training parameter equals 0, then mixed teacher forcing training matches recursive training. If the training parameter equals 1, then mixed teacher forcing training matches pure teacher forcing training.

Implementing the encoder–decoder model

Now we are ready to examine PyTorch implementation of the encoder–decoder model `ch5/enc_dec/model.py`.

Import part

```
import numpy as np
import random
```

```
import torch
import torch.nn as nn
from torch import optim
```

Encoder layer

The **encoder layer** is a traditional recurrent neural network. We will use the LSTM model as recurrent neural network implementation:

```
class Encoder(nn.Module):
    def __init__(self, input_size, hidden_size, num_layers = 1):
        super(Encoder, self).__init__()
        self.input_size = input_size
        self.hidden_size = hidden_size
        self.num_layers = num_layers
        self.lstm = nn.LSTM(input_size = input_size, hidden_size = hidden_size, num_layers = num_layers)
    def forward(self, x):
        flat = x.view(x.shape[0], x.shape[1], self.input_size)
        out, h = self.lstm(flat)
        return out, h
```

Decoder layer

The **decoder layer** is a recurrent neural network with the linear layer. The code for this layer is as follows:

```
class Decoder(nn.Module):
    def __init__(self, input_size, hidden_size, output_size = 1, num_layers = 1):
        super(Decoder, self).__init__()
        self.input_size = input_size
        self.hidden_size = hidden_size
        self.num_layers = num_layers
        self.output_size = output_size
        self.lstm = nn.LSTM(input_size = input_size, hidden_size = hidden_size, num_layers = num_layers)
        self.linear = nn.Linear(hidden_size, output_size)
    def forward(self, x, h):
```

```
out, h = self.lstm(x.unsqueeze(0), h)
y = self.linear(out.squeeze(0))
return y, h
```

Encoder–decoder model class

Encoder–decoder model is a sequence of encoder and decoder layers. The code for this class is as follows:

```
class EncoderDecoder(nn.Module):
    def __init__(self, hidden_size, input_size = 1, output_size = 1):
        super(EncoderDecoder, self).__init__()
        self.input_size = input_size
        self.hidden_size = hidden_size
        self.encoder = Encoder(input_size = input_size, hidden_size = hidden_size)
        self.decoder = Decoder(input_size = input_size, hidden_size = hidden_size, output_size = output_size)
```

Training

The **Encoder–decoder training** contains special logic (*recursive, teacher forcing, mixed teacher forcing*). Thus the training algorithm is included in the model because this model cannot be trained with classical methods which we have used before:

```
def train_model(
        self, train, target, epochs, target_len, method = 'recursive',
        tfr = 0.5, lr = 0.01, dynamic_tf = False
):
```

Here, we define an optimizer and loss function:

```
losses = np.full(epochs, np.nan)
optimizer = optim.Adam(self.parameters(), lr = lr)
criterion = nn.MSELoss()
for e in range(epochs):
    predicted = torch.zeros(target_len, train.shape[1], train.shape[2])
    optimizer.zero_grad()
    _, enc_h = self.encoder(train)
```

```
dec_in = train[-1, :, :]
dec_h = enc_h
```

Recursive training is a passing each decoder's output to the decoder's input at another step, which is as follows:

```
if method == 'recursive':
    for t in range(target_len):
        dec_out, dec_h = self.decoder(dec_in, dec_h)
        predicted[t] = dec_out
        dec_in = dec_out
```

Teacher forcing method applies recursive training with probability *(1 − tfr)* or supplies target values to the encoder with probability *tfr*:

```
if method == 'teacher_forcing':
    # use teacher forcing
    if random.random() < tfr:
        for t in range(target_len):
            dec_out, dec_h = self.decoder(dec_in, dec_h)
            predicted[t] = dec_out
            dec_in = target[t, :, :]
    # predict recursively
    else:
        for t in range(target_len):
            dec_out, dec_h = self.decoder(dec_in, dec_h)
            predicted[t] = dec_out
            dec_in = dec_out
```

Mixed teacher forcing method mixes the decoder output with target values within the same training epoch:

```
if method == 'mixed_teacher_forcing':
    # predict using mixed teacher forcing
    for t in range(target_len):
        dec_out, dec_h = self.decoder(dec_in, dec_h)
        predicted[t] = dec_out
        # predict with teacher forcing
```

```
            if random.random() < tfr:
                dec_in = target[t, :, :]
            # predict recursively
            else:
                dec_in = dec_out
        loss = criterion(predicted, target)
        loss.backward()
        optimizer.step()
        losses[e] = loss.item()
        if e % 10 == 0:
            print(f'Epoch {e}/{epochs}: {round(loss.item(), 4)}')
```

In some cases, it is helpful to decrease the teacher forcing ratio during training:

```
        # dynamic teacher forcing
        if dynamic_tf and tfr > 0:
            tfr = tfr - 0.02
    return losses
```

Model evaluation

This model does not have a classical forward method. Model evaluation is done through the custom `predict` method.

```
    def predict(self, x, target_len):
        y = torch.zeros(target_len, x.shape[1], x.shape[2])
        _, enc_h = self.encoder(x)
        dec_in = x[-1, :, :]
        dec_h = enc_h
        for t in range(target_len):
            dec_out, dec_h = self.decoder(dec_in, dec_h)
            y[t] = dec_out
            dec_in = dec_out
        return y
```

Example

Let us go further to the practical implementation of the encoder–decoder model. We will consider following time series:

$$Y_t = sin(t) + 0.8cos(\frac{t}{2}) + R_t + \frac{5}{2}$$

This time series dataset is generated the following way **ch5/enc_dec/ts.py**:

```
import numpy as np
import matplotlib.pyplot as plt
def generate_ts(len):
    tf = 80 * np.pi
    t = np.linspace(0., tf, len)
    y = np.sin(t) + 0.8 * np.cos(.5 * t) + np.random.normal(0., 0.3, len) + 2.5
    return y.tolist()


if __name__ == '__main__':
    ts = generate_ts(2000)
    plt.plot(ts[:300])
    plt.show()
```

Result

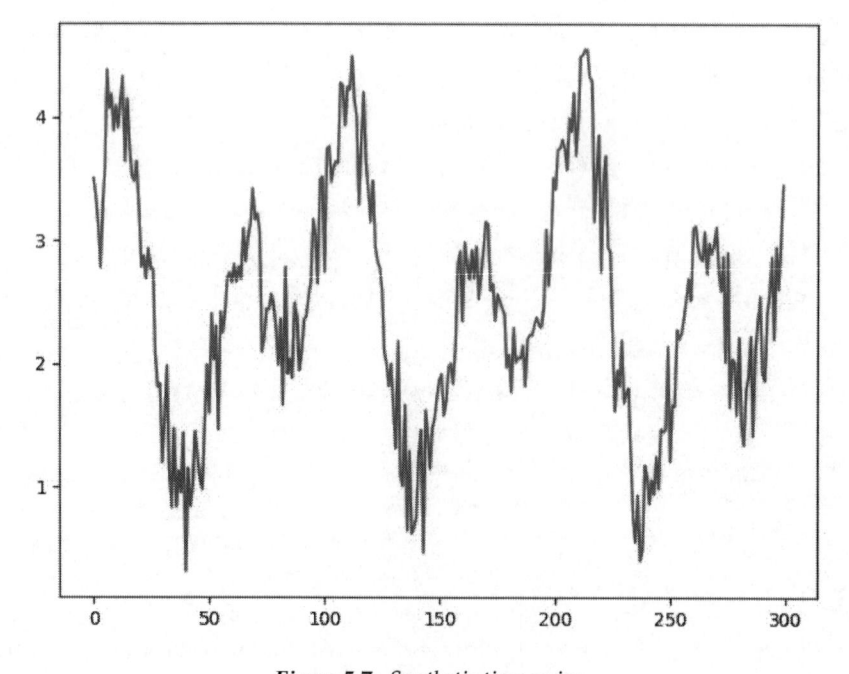

Figure 5.7: Synthetic time series

This synthetic dataset has transparent seasonality and random variable. We will create an encoder–decoder model which produces a multi-step prediction of 60 next values. It is critical to understand that multi-step prediction is much more difficult and its accuracy usually decreases with each step. Let us take a look at how the Encoder–decoder model could handle this problem **ch5/enc_dec/example.py**.

Import part

```
import random
import numpy as np
import torch
import matplotlib.pyplot as plt
from ch5.enc_dec.model import EncoderDecoder
from ch5.enc_dec.ts import generate_ts
from ch5.training_datasets import sliding_window
```

Making script reproducible

```
seed = 1
random.seed(seed)
np.random.seed(seed)
torch.manual_seed(seed)
```

Global parameters

```
# synthetic time series length
ts_len = 2000
# lstm hidden size
hidden_size = 64
# test dataset size
test_ds_len = 200
# training epochs
epochs = 500
# input history
ts_history_len = 240
# prediction length
ts_target_len = 60
```

Generating datasets

Here, we generate traditional windowed time series datasets:

```
ts = generate_ts(ts_len)
X, Y = sliding_window(ts, ts_history_len, ts_target_len)
ds_len = len(X)
def to_tensor(data):
    return torch.tensor(data = data)\
        .unsqueeze(2)\
        .transpose(0, 1).float()
x_train = to_tensor(X[:ds_len - test_ds_len])
y_train = to_tensor(Y[:ds_len - test_ds_len])
x_test = to_tensor(X[ds_len - test_ds_len:])
y_test = to_tensor(Y[ds_len - test_ds_len:])
```

Initializing Encoder–decoder model

```
model = EncoderDecoder(hidden_size = hidden_size)
```

Training

We train the model using mixed teacher forcing method:

```
model.train()
model.train_model(x_train, y_train, epochs, ts_target_len,
                  method = 'mixed_teacher_forcing',
                  tfr = .05, lr = .005)
```

Prediction

We will create the prediction for test dataset, as follows:

```
model.eval()
predicted = model.predict(x_test, ts_target_len)
```

Visualizing results

Let us analyze the model performance, with the following code:

```
fig, ax = plt.subplots(nrows = 3, ncols = 1)
fig.set_size_inches(7.5, 6)
```

```
for col in ax:
    r = random.randint(0, test_ds_len)
    in_seq = x_test[:, r, :].view(-1).tolist()
    target_seq = y_test[:, r, :].view(-1).tolist()
    pred_seq = predicted[:, r, :].view(-1).tolist()
    x_axis = range(len(in_seq) + len(target_seq))
    col.set_title(f'Test Sample: {r}')
    col.axis('off')
    col.plot(x_axis[:], in_seq + target_seq, color = 'blue')
    col.plot(x_axis[len(in_seq):],
             pred_seq,
             label = 'predicted',
             color = 'orange',
             linewidth = 3)
    col.vlines(len(in_seq), 0, 6, color = 'grey')
    col.legend(loc = "upper right")
plt.show()
```

For a multi-step prediction model, it is helpful to output several predictions from the test dataset:

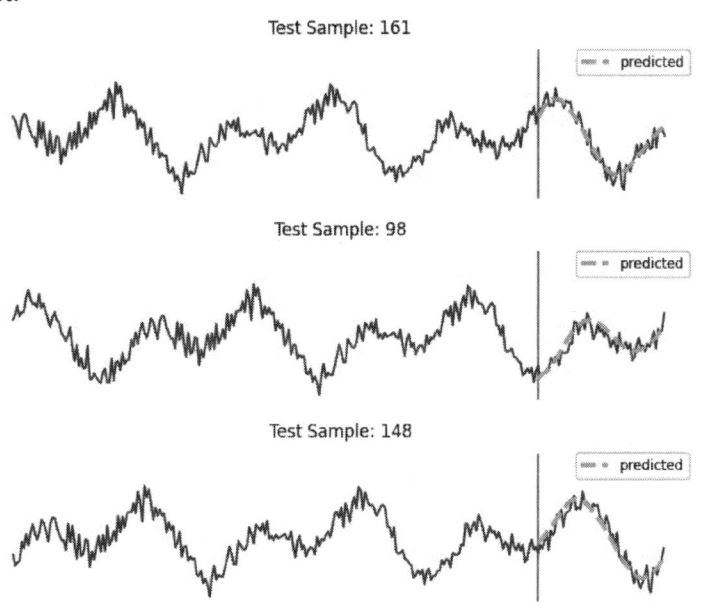

Figure 5.8: Encoder–decoder predictions

Figure 5.8 demonstrates the amazing results of the Encoder–decoder model. It gives very accurate long-term predictions. The long-term prediction (dashed line) is made on the grey vertical line. The encoder–decoder model doesn't know any future values making a long-term prediction.

One of this model's significant advantages is that the input and output sequences' lengths may differ. This opens the way for flexible multi-step forecasting applications.

Temporal convolutional network

Convolutional neural networks are generally associated with successful applications of image classification problems. Straightforward application of convolutional networks to time series analysis does not guarantee acceptable results. However, there are some advanced designs that use the full power of convolutional networks.

The idea of the TCN was proposed in 2018 in the following article: **https://arxiv.org/pdf/1803.01271.pdf**. TCN assumes a completely different approach to the problem of sequential data modeling. TCNs proved that convolutional networks could achieve better performance than RNNs in many tasks while avoiding the common drawbacks of recurrent models. Moreover, using a TCN model instead of a recurrent one can lead to performance improvements as it allows parallel computation.

Before we start exploring TCN, we will need to clarify several principles that underlie the TCN.

Casual convolution

Casual convolution means that the output sequence has the same length as the input sequence and each element in the output sequence depends on elements that come before it in the input sequence.

Casual convolution is calculated as:

$$y_i = \sum_{j=0}^{k-1} c_j x_{i-j},$$

where

- x_i – input tensor
- y_i – output tensor
- k – convolution kernel
- c_j – convolution weights

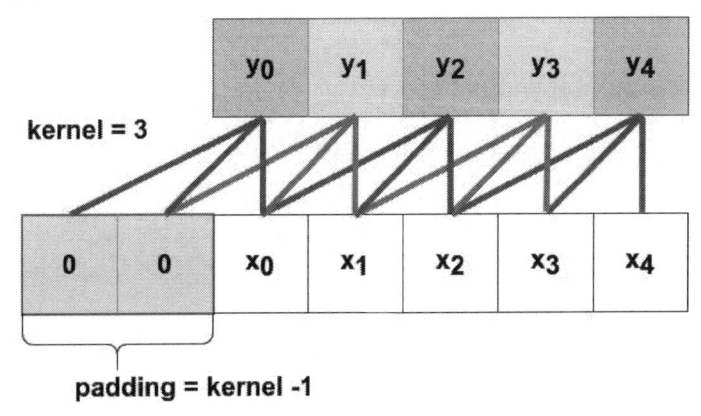

Figure 5.9 demonstrates how the casual convolution is calculated:

Figure 5.9: Casual Convolution

To calculate the casual convolution, we need to add padding (*kernel size - 1*) from the left of the input tensor.

Causal convolution has a simple logical sense: Casual convolution collects data and patterns that happened before. Deep learning models that use casual convolution layers can extract dependencies that help predict future values.

Figure 5.10 demonstrates the main principle of casual convolution layers action:

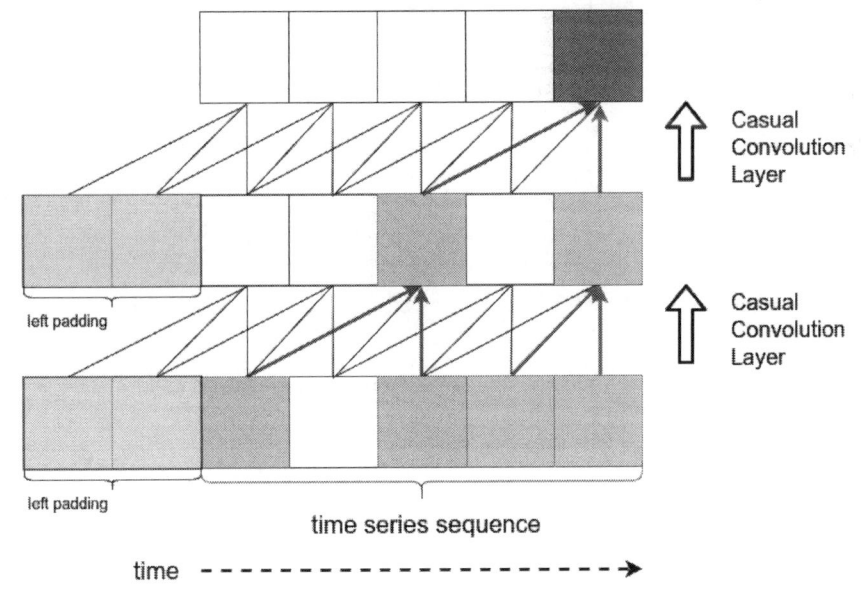

Figure 5.10: Casual convolution layers in action

PyTorch does not currently have a native casual convolution layer implementation. But it is pretty simple to implement it. To implement casual convolution, we need to apply classical 1-D convolution with padding (*kernel - 1*) and crop (*kernel - 1*) elements from the right like it is shown in the *figure 5.11*:

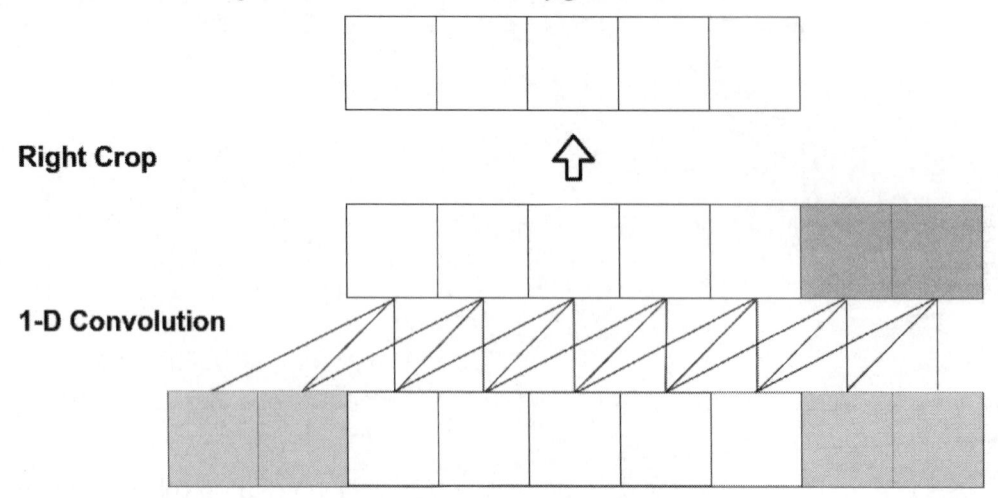

Figure 5.11: *Casual Convolution Implementation*

Let us see how the casual convolution can be implemented using PyTorch **ch5/tcn/casual_convolution.py**:

```
import torch
from torch.nn import Parameter
x = torch.tensor([[[0, 1, 2, 3, 4]]]).float()
k = 3
conv1d = torch.nn.Conv1d(1, 1, kernel_size = k, padding = k - 1, bias = False)
conv1d.weight = Parameter(torch.tensor([[[1, 0, -1]]]).float())
y1 = conv1d(x)
y2 = y1[:, :, :-(k - 1)]
print(y2.tolist())
```

The result obtained is as follows:

```
[[[0.0, -1.0, -2.0, -2.0, -2.0]]]
```

Casual convolution is a simple arithmetic operation that lies at the heart of the TCN.

Dilation

Dilation is another useful technique that is used for TCN implementation. It is the standard parameter of the convolutional layer. It sets the interval between values of the input tensor. *Figure 5.12* demonstrates the dilation principle:

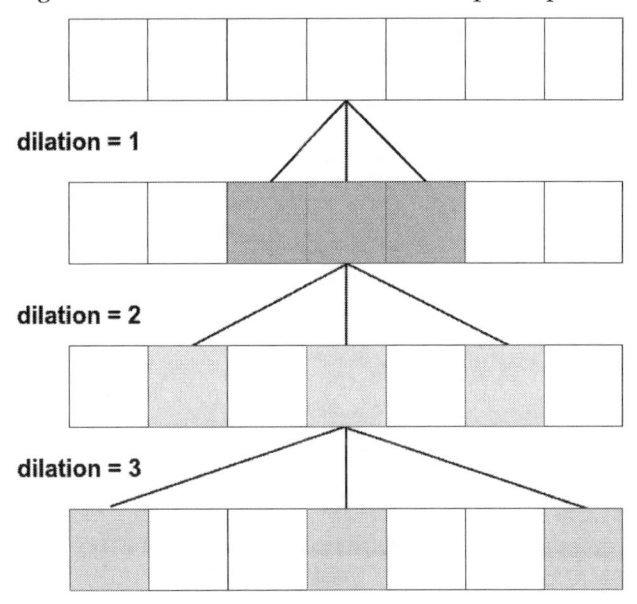

Figure 5.12: Convolution dilation

TCN assumes the sequence of casual convolutional layers with the dilation equaled to 2^{i-1}:

- 1st casual convolutional layer: dilation = $2^0 = 1$
- 2nd casual convolutional layer: dilation = $2^1 = 2$
- 3rd casual convolutional layer: dilation = $2^2 = 4$
- 4th casual convolutional layer: dilation = $2^3 = 8$

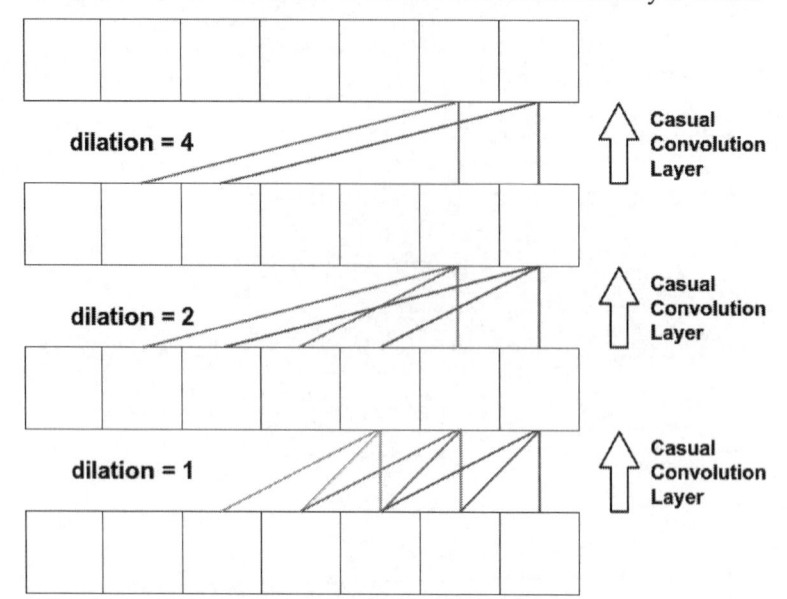

Figure 5.13 visualizes the calculation of casual convolutional layer stack:

Figure 5.13: Casual convolution with dilation

The dilation technique with a casual convolutional layer increases the input time series' coverage and reduces the computational costs significantly.

Temporal convolutional network design

Casual convolution with dilation presents an overly complex linear regression model. We need to add some deep learning techniques to make our model learn non-linear dependencies. Activation functions need to be added on top of the convolutional layers to introduce non-linearities. It is advised to use ReLU as the activation function for the TCN. To normalize the input of hidden layers (which counteracts the exploding gradient problem among other things), weight normalization is applied to every convolutional layer. The dropout regularization method is added after every convolutional layer. *Figure 5.14* shows an advanced casual convolutional layer. We will call this layer as *Temporal Casual Layer*:

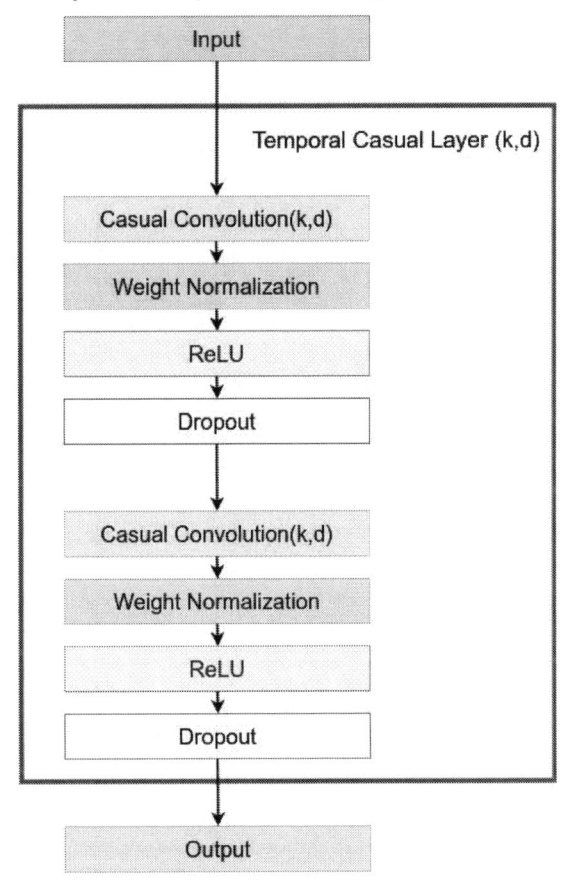

Figure 5.14: Temporal casual layer

Now we have the design of the central neural network layer of TCN. There is still one improvement left that can enhance the performance of the temporal casual layer.

That is the addition of low-kernel convolution to the input tensor is a good method that can be treated as the *"bias"* of the temporal casual layer:

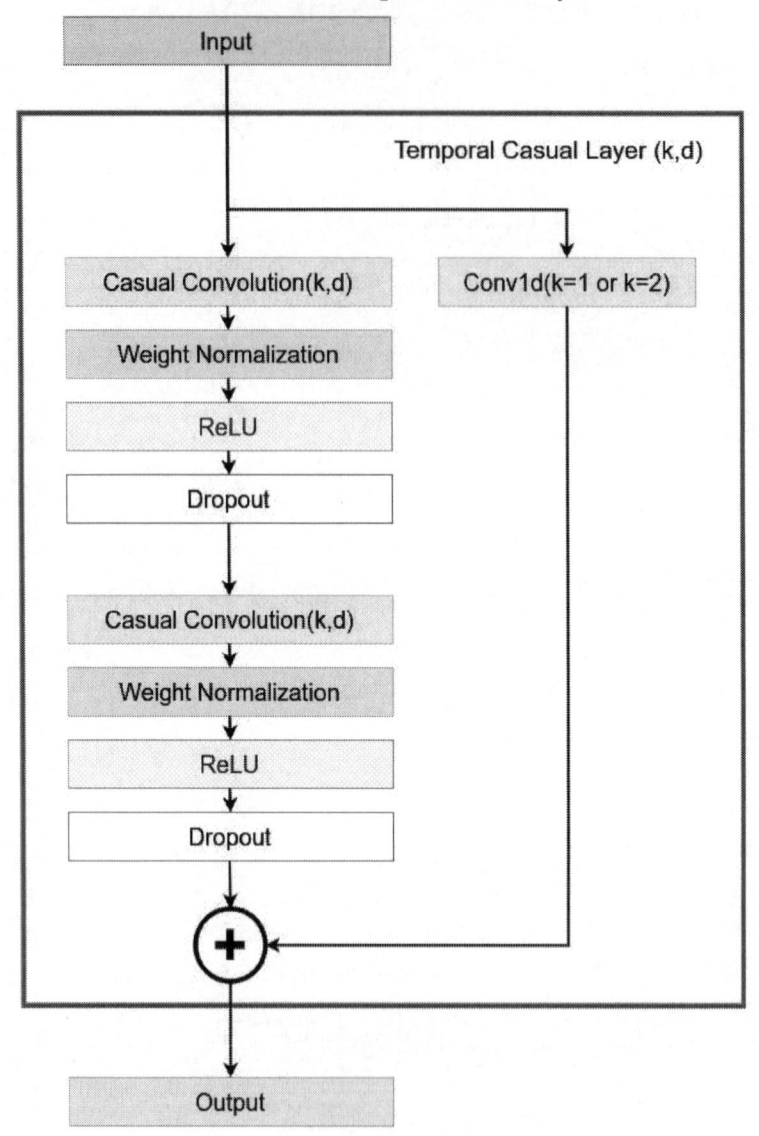

Figure 5.15: Temporal Casual Layer with bias

Well, now we are ready to put everything together and create the design of the TCN. TCN is a stack of temporal casual layers where dilation increases as the power of 2, as you can see in *figure 5.16*:

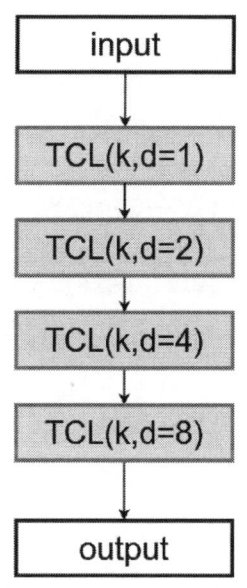

Figure 5.16: Temporal Convolutional Network

Implementing the temporal convolutional network

Now we are ready to implement the TCN **ch5/model/tcn.py**.

Import part

```
import torch.nn as nn
from torch.nn.utils import weight_norm
```

Crop layer

The **crop layer** is responsible for trimming the tensor from the right when creating a casual convolution operation:

```
class Crop(nn.Module):
    def __init__(self, crop_size):
        super(Crop, self).__init__()
        self.crop_size = crop_size
```

```python
def forward(self, x):
    return x[:, :, :-self.crop_size].contiguous()
```

Temporal casual layer

Here, we introduce the implementation of the temporal casual layer shown in *figure 5.15*:

```python
class TemporalCasualLayer(nn.Module):
    def __init__(self, n_inputs, n_outputs, kernel_size, stride,
dilation, dropout = 0.2):
        super(TemporalCasualLayer, self).__init__()
        padding = (kernel_size - 1) * dilation
        conv_params = {
            'kernel_size': kernel_size,
            'stride':      stride,
            'padding':     padding,
            'dilation':    dilation
        }
        self.conv1 = weight_norm(nn.Conv1d(n_inputs, n_outputs, **conv_params))
        self.crop1 = Crop(padding)
        self.relu1 = nn.ReLU()
        self.dropout1 = nn.Dropout(dropout)
        self.conv2 = weight_norm(nn.Conv1d(n_outputs, n_outputs, **conv_params))
        self.crop2 = Crop(padding)
        self.relu2 = nn.ReLU()
        self.dropout2 = nn.Dropout(dropout)
        self.net = nn.Sequential(self.conv1, self.crop1, self.relu1,
self.dropout1, self.conv2, self.crop2, self.relu2, self.dropout2)
        self.bias = nn.Conv1d(n_inputs, n_outputs, 1) if n_inputs !=
n_outputs else None
        self.relu = nn.ReLU()
    def forward(self, x):
        y = self.net(x)
        b = x if self.bias is None else self.bias(x)
        return self.relu(y + b)
```

Implementing temporal convolutional network

And here, we provide the TCN implementation, which is the stack of temporal casual layers:

```
class TemporalConvolutionNetwork(nn.Module):
    def __init__(self, num_inputs, num_channels, kernel_size = 2, dropout = 0.2):
        super(TemporalConvolutionNetwork, self).__init__()
        layers = []
        num_levels = len(num_channels)
        tcl_param = {
            'kernel_size': kernel_size,
            'stride':      1,
            'dropout':     dropout
        }
        for i in range(num_levels):
            dilation = 2**i
            in_ch = num_inputs if i == 0 else num_channels[i - 1]
            out_ch = num_channels[i]
            tcl_param['dilation'] = dilation
            tcl = TemporalCasualLayer(in_ch, out_ch, **tcl_param)
            layers.append(tcl)
        self.network = nn.Sequential(*layers)
    def forward(self, x):
        return self.network(x)
```

TCN prediction model

TCN does not represent a predictive model. To create a single-step prediction model based on TCN, we need to add one linear layer after applying TCN layer:

```
class TCN(nn.Module):
    def __init__(self, input_size, output_size, num_channels, kernel_size, dropout):
        super(TCN, self).__init__()
        self.tcn = TemporalConvolutionNetwork(input_size, num_channels, kernel_size = kernel_size, dropout = dropout)
```

```
        self.linear = nn.Linear(num_channels[-1], output_size)
    def forward(self, x):
        y = self.tcn(x)
        return self.linear(y[:, :, -1])
```

Example

To demonstrate the capabilities of TCN, we will consider the following multivariate input time series problem:

$$Y_t = Y_{t-1} + R_{1,t-1} + R_{1,t-2} + 4R_{2,t-3}(R_{3,t-4} + R_{3,t-6}),$$

Where:

$R_{1,t}$ – Is a random variable

$R_{2,t}$ – Is a random variable

$R_{3,t}$ – is a random variable which outputs 1 with 0.25 probability and 0 otherwise

Figure 5.17 visualizes dependencies of Y_t time series:

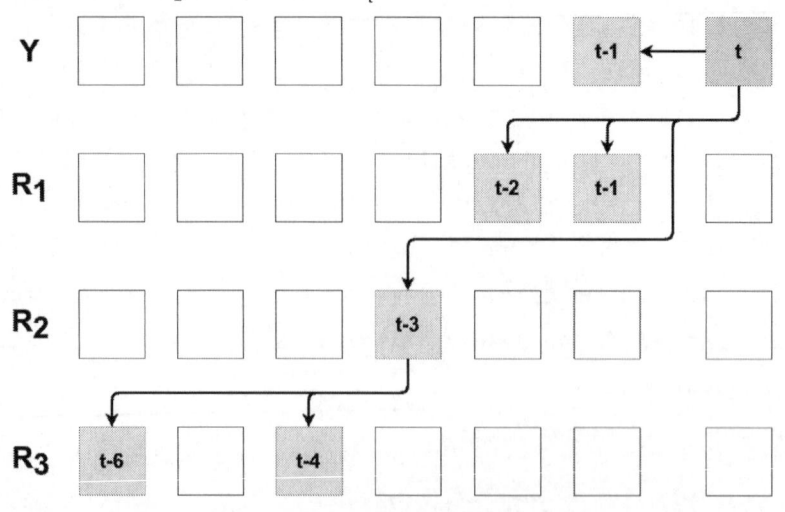

Figure 5.17: Y_t time series dependencies

These dependencies are very hard to find if you do not know about them in advance. Let us see the performance of the TCN model on this dataset **ch5/tcn/example.py**.

Import part

```
import copy
import random
```

```
import sys
import numpy as np
import matplotlib.pyplot as plt
import torch
from ch5.tcn.dummy import Dummy
from ch5.tcn.model import TCN
from ch5.tcn.ts import generate_time_series
from ch5.training_datasets import get_training_datasets, ts_diff, ts_int
```

Making script reproducible

```
seed = 12
random.seed(seed)
np.random.seed(seed)
torch.manual_seed(seed)
```

Global parameters

```
# time series input
features = 20
# training epochs
epochs = 1_000
# synthetic time series dataset
ts_len = 5_000
# test dataset size
test_len = 300
# temporal casual layer channels
channel_sizes = [10] * 4
# convolution kernel size
kernel_size = 5
dropout = .0
```

Generating time series

```
ts = generate_time_series(ts_len)
```

Preprocessing

We will use differencing preprocessing for this time series:

```
ts_diff_y = ts_diff(ts[:, 0])
ts_diff = copy.deepcopy(ts)
ts_diff[:, 0] = ts_diff_y
```

Preparing datasets

```
x_train, x_val, x_test, y_train, y_val, y_test =\
    get_training_datasets(ts_diff, features, test_len)
x_train = x_train.transpose(1, 2)
x_val = x_val.transpose(1, 2)
x_test = x_test.transpose(1, 2)
y_train = y_train[:, :, 0]
y_val = y_val[:, :, 0]
y_test = y_test[:, :, 0]
train_len = x_train.size()[0]
```

Initializing the model

```
model_params = {
    'input_size':    4,
    'output_size':   1,
    'num_channels':  channel_sizes,
    'kernel_size':   kernel_size,
    'dropout':       dropout
}
model = TCN(**model_params)
```

Defining optimizer and loss function

```
optimizer = torch.optim.Adam(params = model.parameters(), lr = .005)
mse_loss = torch.nn.MSELoss()
```

Training

```
best_params = None
min_val_loss = sys.maxsize
```

```
training_loss = []
validation_loss = []
for t in range(epochs):
    prediction = model(x_train)
    loss = mse_loss(prediction, y_train)
    optimizer.zero_grad()
    loss.backward()
    optimizer.step()
    val_prediction = model(x_val)
    val_loss = mse_loss(val_prediction, y_val)
    training_loss.append(loss.item())
    validation_loss.append(val_loss.item())
    if val_loss.item() < min_val_loss:
        best_params = copy.deepcopy(model.state_dict())
        min_val_loss = val_loss.item()
    if t % 100 == 0:
        diff = (y_train - prediction).view(-1).abs_().tolist()
        print(f'epoch {t}. train: {round(loss.item(), 4)}, '
            f'val: {round(val_loss.item(), 4)}')
```

Training progress

```
plt.title('Training Progress')
plt.yscale("log")
plt.plot(training_loss, label = 'train')
plt.plot(validation_loss, label = 'validation')
plt.ylabel("Loss")
plt.xlabel("Epoch")
```

```
plt.legend()
plt.show()
```

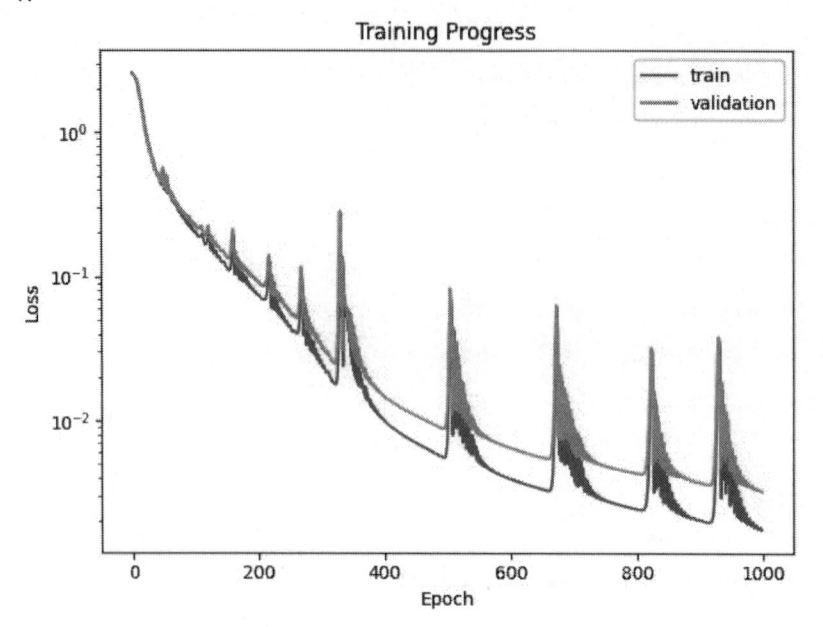

Figure 5.18: TCN training progress

TCN training and validation losses behave in a very similar way, and we can conclude that our model really learns the behavior of Y_t.

Performance on the test dataset

We will retrieve the model which has shown the best results on validation dataset:
```
best_model = TCN(**model_params)
best_model.eval()
best_model.load_state_dict(best_params)
tcn_prediction = best_model(x_test)
```

We will compare TCN prediction with dummy prediction model ($Y_t = Y_{t-1}$):
```
dummy_prediction = Dummy()(x_test)
tcn_mse_loss = round(mse_loss(tcn_prediction, y_test).item(), 4)
dummy_mse_loss = round(mse_loss(dummy_prediction, y_test).item(), 4)
```

Let us look at plotting the results:
```
plt.title(f'Test| TCN: {tcn_mse_loss}; Dummy: {dummy_mse_loss}')
plt.plot(
```

```
    ts_int(
        tcn_prediction.view(-1).tolist(),
        ts[-test_len:, 0],
        start = ts[-test_len - 1, 0]
    ),
    label = 'tcn')
plt.plot(ts[-test_len - 1:, 0], label = 'real')
plt.legend()
plt.show()
```

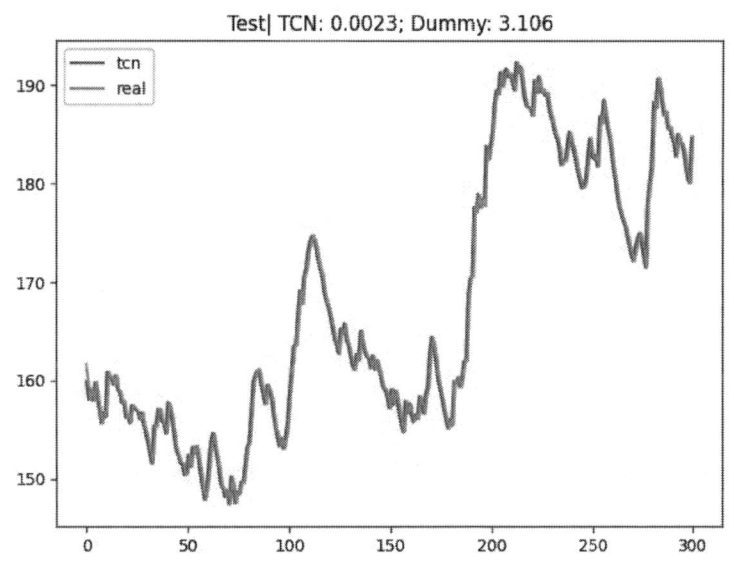

Figure 5.19: TCN performance on the test dataset

As we see, TCN model perfectly extracts hidden dependencies which drive Y_t time series.

TCN is a revolutionary approach to time series analysis. TCN basic architecture, or its variations, shows excellent results for multivariate input prediction problems.

Conclusion

This chapter has covered some of the most recent deep learning explorations in time series analysis. We have provided examples of two distinct architectures for forecasting problems. You can start experimenting with these architectures to solve your problems by adding or modifying existing deep learning blocks. There is no 'swiss knife' architecture for all types of problems. Deep learning is developing very quickly, and the ability to design, implement, and test new models will be a crucial skill for data scientists.

In the next chapter, we will look at the exciting and important topic of optimizing deep learning model architectures. We will learn to turn good models into excellent ones.

Points to remember

- Encoder–decoder model shows the best results when is applied to a multi-step forecasting problem.
- Encoder–decoder model mimics the human memory and decision-making mechanism.
- Encoder–decoder recursive training usually gives the best results for short-term predictions.
- Encoder–decoder teacher forcing training helps to learn long-term predictions.
- Casual convolution collects data and patterns that happened before.
- TCN shows the best results on multivariate input prediction problems.

Multiple choice questions

1. What implementations of recurrent neural networks (RNN, GRU, LSTM) are best suited for an Encoder–decoder model?

    A. GRU for encoder and RNN for decoder

    B. LSTM for both encoder and decoder

    C. It depends on time series. Encoder–decoder model allows using any recurrent network implementation.

2. What is the main benefit of dilation in the TCN?

    A. Dilation with increases the coverage of time series and reduces the computational costs significantly.

    B. Dilation is a regularization technique that prevents overfitting.

    C. Dilation helps to learn nonlinear dependencies.

Answer

1. C
2. A

Key terms

- *Encoder–decoder model:* **multistep forecasting model based on recurrent neural network.**
- *Temporal Convolutional Network:* **Deep learning model based on casual convolution and dilation technique.**

CHAPTER 6
PyTorch Model Tuning with Neural Network Intelligence

In the previous chapters, we studied various predictive model designs. Each of these models has many parameters and different variations. Each design we considered allows many modifications: we can change the kernel size for convolutional layers or even remove and add extra layers to the neural network architecture. But what parameters and neural network architecture are best suited for a particular time-series problem? Manual model adjustment can take too much time and effort. In this chapter, we will learn the automatic search of the optimal parameters and topologies of a deep learning model using the Neural Network Intelligence toolkit.

Structure

In this chapter, we will discuss the following topics:

- Neural Network Intelligence framework
- Hyper-parameter tuning
- Neural architecture search
- Hybrid models

Objective

After completing this chapter, the reader will be able to use the most advanced tuning, optimization, and neural architecture search (NAS) techniques. This chapter will be helpful to all data scientists who want to master the latest advances in time-series deep learning automation.

Neural Network Intelligence framework

Neural Network Intelligence (NNI) is a framework that leverages the latest advances in deep learning model tuning. NNI is a highly customizable library. It includes various open-source libraries, making it a very rich and powerful toolkit for automated machine learning tasks.

NNI's key features are as follows:

- **Native PyTorch support**: NNI supports the most popular deep learning frameworks, especially PyTorch.
- **Lightweight:** NNI has a robust and flexible architecture.
- **Scalable**: One of the key features is that NNI can execute distributed calculations on various platforms to speed up the search process.
- **Has user-friendly UI**: NNI includes a web server that allows to scroll and analyze the search process.
- **Has command line, python, and web interfaces:** The search process can be managed in different ways.
- **Highly customizable:** It is possible to integrate any custom logic and algorithms in the NNI logic core.

NNI can be installed in the following way:

```
# Requirements: python 64-bit >= 3.6
python3 -m pip install --upgrade nni
```

For additional installation information, please refer to the official site: **https://nni.readthedocs.io/en/stable/installation.html**.

Hyper-parameter tuning

Hyper-parameters are the parameters that define the model architecture and are used to control the learning process. The process of searching for the best model architecture is called **hyper-parameter tuning**.

Hyper-parameter examples are:

- Number of hidden layers in a fully connected neural network
- Activation function in deep learning model
- p parameter in dropout layer
- Number of training epochs
- Training optimization algorithm
- Optimization algorithm learning rate

Each of the parameters mentioned above can affect drastically the model performance.

To start hyper-parameter tuning, we have to consider several concepts: such as search space, trial, and tuner.

Search space

Search space is the predefined set of all hyper-parameter combinations. Usually, the search space is defined by setting all possible values of each hyper-parameter.

For example:

- Learning rate: [0.01, 0.001, 0.0001]
- Convolution kernel size: [3, 5, 7]
- LSTM hidden state size: [8, 12, 16, 32, 64]

Trial

Trial is a performance testing of a specific model constructed and trained on the passed parameters. A trial is a classical training-validating-testing script. And the testing loss function value is used as the trial metric for a given hyper-parameter combination. The trial process can be depicted in the following ways:

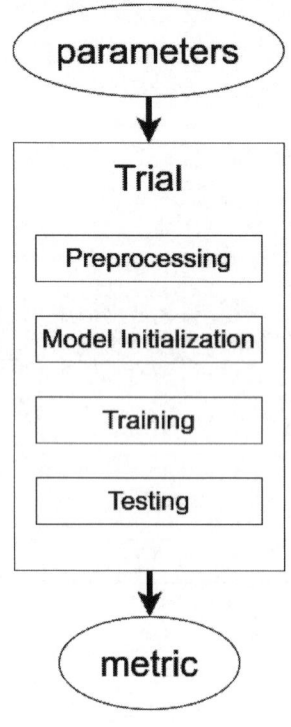

Figure 6.1: Trial

Roughly speaking, a *trial* is a simple function that takes some parameters and returns a value.

Tuner

The number of elements in search space can be extremely large. The search space can contain billions of billions of combinations, and it is physically impossible to try all of them. **Tuner** defines the strategy which aims to maximize the model performance on search space.

The most popular tuners are:

- **Random Search**: The random search picks random elements from the search space. It might be surprisingly effective despite of its simplicity. Random search is suggested as a baseline when no knowledge about the prior distribution of hyper-parameters is available.
- **Naive Evolution:** Naive evolution (or genetic algorithm) randomly initializes a population based on the search space. It selects the best ones for each

generation and does some hyper-parameter mutation on them to get the next generation. I prefer using this tuner in most cases.

- **Tree-structured Parzen Estimator (TPE)**: The TPE approach is based on conditional probabilities. It models $P(x|y)$ and $P(y)$, where x represents hyper-parameters and y the model performance.

- **Grid Search**: Grid Search executes an exhaustive search through the whole search space. Usually, it can be applied only for small search spaces.

- **Gaussian Process Tuner (GP)**: GP tuner is designed to minimize the number of steps required to find a combination of hyper-parameters close to the search space maxima.

For the complete list of NNI built-in tuners, please refer to the official documentation: https://nni.readthedocs.io/en/stable/builtin_tuner.html .

Hyper-parameter tuning in action

Now let us look at how the hyper-parameter tuning works. *Tuner* picks some elements from the *search space*. Usually, it starts with random ones. Then the *tuner* passes chosen parameters to the script, which runs the *trial*. Trial adapts given parameters, initializes the model, trains it, tests it, and returns the performance *metric*. The *metric* is stored in *result storage*. After that *tuner* analyzes completed *trials* and chooses coordinates for the next trials in the *search space*.

The process described here can be depicted in the following ways:

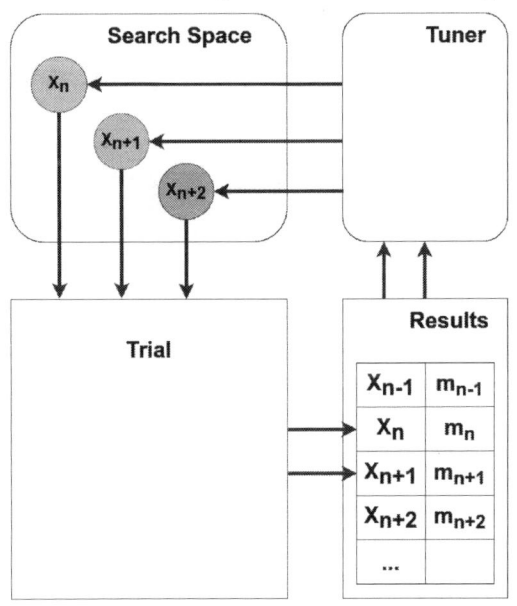

Figure 6.2: Hyper-parameter tuning in action

The tuner aims to find the best combination of hyper-parameters in a search space by minimizing the number of trials.

NNI Quick Start

Now let us go to the simple example which demonstrates NNI usage. Consider this trivial trial script **ch6/hopt/hello_world/trial.py**:

nni.get_next_parameter() returns hyper-parameters for the trial:

```
import nni
params = nni.get_next_parameter()
```

Retrieving the given parameters:

```
x = params['x']
y = params['y']
z = params['z']
```

Calculating a metric:

```
metric = x + y + z
```

nni.report_final_result() returns the trial metric to NNI:

```
nni.report_final_result(metric)
```

This is a rather trivial trial script that receives (*x, y, z*) variables and returns their sum.

Let us run hyper-parameter search **ch6/hopt/hello_world/search.py**.

Import part

```
import time
from pathlib import Path
from nni.experiment import Experiment
```

Defining search space

```
search_space = {
    "x": {"_type": "choice", "_value": [-10, -5, 0, 5, 10]},
    "y": {"_type": "choice", "_value": [-10, -5, 0, 5, 10]},
    "z": {"_type": "choice", "_value": [-10, -5, 0, 5, 10]}
}
```

Search configuration

```
search = Experiment('local')
# Search Name
search.config.experiment_name = 'Hello World Search'
search.config.trial_concurrency = 4
search.config.max_trial_number = 50
search.config.search_space = search_space
search.config.trial_command = 'python3 trial.py'
search.config.trial_code_directory = Path(__file__).parent
# Search Tuner Settings
search.config.tuner.name = 'Evolution'
search.config.tuner.class_args['optimize_mode'] = 'minimize'
search.config.tuner.class_args['population_size'] = 8
```

We start the search with the following code:

```
search.start(8080)
```

Awaiting results

```
while True:
    if search.get_status() == 'DONE':
        trials = search.export_data()
        best_trial = min(trials, key = lambda t: t.value)
        print(f'Best trial params: {best_trial.parameter}')
        input("Experiment is finished. Press any key to exit...")
        break
    time.sleep(10)
```

After running the script, NNI initializes the search process, as follows:

```
Creating experiment, Experiment ID: lh5ft9e1
Statring web server...
Setting up...
Web UI URLs: http://127.0.0.1:8080
```

NNI has a handy and straightforward web interface: **http://127.0.0.1:8080**.

After the search completes, we can view the output, which contains the best hyperparameter combinations:

```
Best trial params: {'x': -10, 'y': -10, 'z': -10}
Experiment is finished. Press any key to exit....1
```

As expected, NNI found the parameter combination (-10, -10, -10) for $x + y + z$ function minima.

NNI API

NNI toolkit has a flexible and clear API. Here, we will provide the basics of NNI. For more information, please refer to the official documentation page: https://nni.readthedocs.io/.

NNI search space

NNI defines the search spaces by setting all available values for each parameter:

- **choice**: a finite set of values
- **randint**: a finite set of integers in the given range
- **uniform**: an infinite set of values in the given range

Here is the example of search space definition:

```
{
    "dropout_rate": {"_type": "uniform", "_value": [0.1, 0.5]},
    "conv_size": {"_type": "randint", "_value": [2, 7]},
    "learning_rate": {"_type": "uniform", "_value": [0.0001, 0.1]}
}
```

Also, NNI supports nested search space definitions, which can be very useful in advanced deep learning model tuning **ch6/hopt/nested_ss.json**:

```
{
  "layer0": {
    "_type": "choice",
    "_value": [
      {
        "_name": "Empty"
      },
```

```
{
  "_name": "Conv",
  "kernel_size": {
    "_type": "choice",
    "_value": [1, 2, 3, 5]
  }
},
...
```

NNI Trial Integration

NNI has simple methods for trial implementation:

- `nni.get_next_parameter()`: Returns the parameters for the trial
- `nni.report_intermediate_result(metrics)`: Passes intermediate trial metrics
- `nni.report_final_result(metrics)`: Passes final trial metrics

Time series model hyper-parameter tuning example

Now we will study an application of hyper-parameter tuning to one of our previous models. In *Chapter 4, Recurrent Neural Networks*, we applied the GRU model for the energy prediction problem.

Deep Learning model trial

Let us start tuning the GRU model defined in *Chapter 4* **ch6/hopt/gru/trial.py**.

Import part

```
import copy
import sys
import nni
import torch
from sklearn.preprocessing import MinMaxScaler
from ch6.hopt.gru.model.gru import GRU
from ch6.hopt.gru.training_datasets import get_pjme_timeseries, get_training_datasets
```

Global parameters

```
# length of sliding window
features = 240
# length of test dataset
test_ts_len = 100
```

Here, we define hyper-parameters for tuning

```
trial_params = nni.get_next_parameter()
# optimizer name
optimizer_name = trial_params['optimizer']
# size of GRU hidden state
gru_hidden_size = trial_params['gru_hidden_size']
# Optimizer learning rate
learning_rate = trial_params['learning_rate']
```

Dataset, optimizer, and model initialization

```
training_epochs = 50
# Preparing datasets for Training
ts = get_pjme_timeseries()
scaler = MinMaxScaler()
scaled_ts = scaler.fit_transform(ts)
x_train, x_val, x_test, y_train, y_val, y_test =\
    get_training_datasets(scaled_ts, features, test_ts_len)
# Initializing the model
model = GRU(hidden_size = gru_hidden_size)
model.train()
# Training
optimizers = {
    'adam':   torch.optim.Adam,
    'sgd':    torch.optim.SGD,
    'adamax': torch.optim.Adamax
}
optimizer = optimizers[optimizer_name](params = model.parameters(), lr =
```

```
learning_rate)
mse_loss = torch.nn.MSELoss()
```

The classical training process is executed as follows:

```
best_model = None
min_val_loss = sys.maxsize
training_loss = []
validation_loss = []
for t in range(training_epochs):
    prediction, _ = model(x_train)
    loss = mse_loss(prediction, y_train)
    optimizer.zero_grad()
    loss.backward()
    optimizer.step()
    val_prediction, _ = model(x_val)
    val_loss = mse_loss(val_prediction, y_val)
    training_loss.append(loss.item())
    validation_loss.append(val_loss.item())
    if val_loss.item() < min_val_loss:
        best_model = copy.deepcopy(model)
        min_val_loss = val_loss.item()
```

The trained model is evaluated on the test dataset, and the loss value is returned to NNI:

```
best_model.eval()
_, h_list = best_model(x_val)
# warm hidden state
h = (h_list[-1, :]).unsqueeze(-2)
predicted = []
for test_seq in x_test.tolist():
    x = torch.Tensor(data = [test_seq])
    # passing hidden state through each iteration
    y, h = best_model(x, h.unsqueeze(-2))
    predicted.append(y)
```

```
test_loss = mse_loss(
    torch.tensor(predicted),
    y_test.view(-1)).item()
nni.report_final_result(test_loss)
```

As we see, a trial is a simple script with model training and evaluation.

NNI search

After defining the trial for a GRU model, we can run the search process **ch6/hopt/gru/search.py**.

Import part

```
import time
from pathlib import Path
from nni.experiment import Experiment
```

Search space

```
search_space = {
    "optimizer":
        {"_type": "choice", "_value": ['adam', 'sgd', 'adamax']},
    "gru_hidden_size":
        {"_type": "choice", "_value": [8, 12, 16, 24, 32]},
    "learning_rate":
        {"_type": "choice", "_value": [.001, .005, .01]}
}
```

Maximum number of trials

```
max_trials = 30
```

Search configuration

```
search = Experiment('local')
# Search Name
search.config.experiment_name = 'GRU Search'
search.config.trial_concurrency = 2
search.config.max_trial_number = max_trials
```

```python
search.config.search_space = search_space
search.config.trial_command = 'python3 trial.py'
search.config.trial_code_directory = Path(__file__).parent
# Search Tuner Settings
search.config.tuner.name = 'Evolution'
search.config.tuner.class_args['optimize_mode'] = 'minimize'
search.config.tuner.class_args['population_size'] = 8
```

Below code will start the search process:

```python
search.start(8080)
```

Process the output as follows:

```python
executed_trials = 0
while True:
    trials = search.export_data()
    if executed_trials != len(trials):
        executed_trials = len(trials)
        print(f'\nTrials: {executed_trials} / {max_trials}')
    if search.get_status() == 'DONE':
        best_trial = min(trials, key = lambda t: t.value)
        print(f'Best trial params: {best_trial.parameter}')
        input("Experiment is finished. Press any key to exit...")
        break
    print('.', end = ""),
    time.sleep(10)
```

After some time, NNI returns the combination of hyper-parameters that showed the best results, i.e., the minimum loss function on the test dataset:

```
Best trial params:
{'optimizer': 'adam', 'gru_hidden_size': 16, 'learning_rate': 0.01}
```

The last thing I want to mention is the hyper-parameter dependency diagram. This diagram allows you to determine which hyper-parameters are crucial for good model construction. Go to the **http://127.0.0.1:8080/detail** page, open the hyper-parameter tab and select `Top 20%` from the dropdown list:

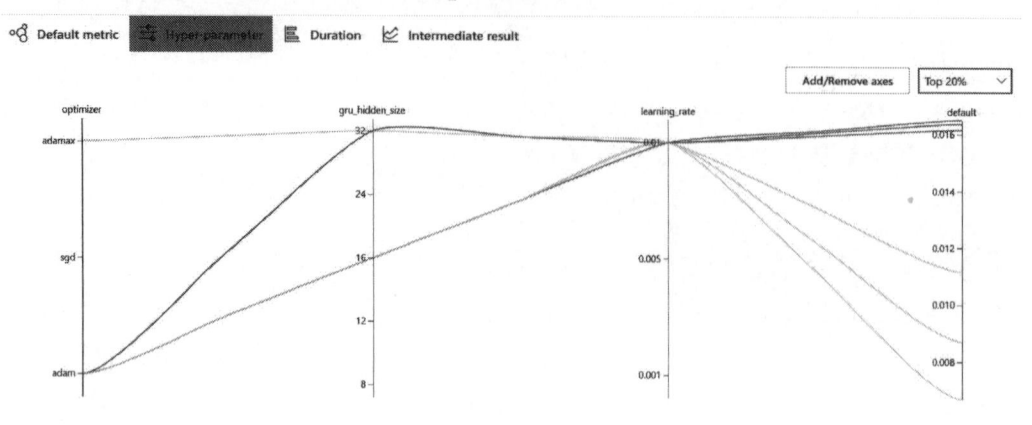

Figure 6.3: Hyper-parameter dependency diagram

We see that the *learning parameter = 0.01* is a critical hyper-parameter value because all trials in the `Top 20%` include this learning parameter value. That is predictable since the learning parameter significantly speeds up the learning process during the first training epochs.

Neural Architecture Search

NAS automates network architecture topology search. It aims to find a network topology that can produce the best performance on a particular task. Historically, the most famous and successful model architectures are created by human experts. But in any case, it is very convenient to use a well-organized and automatic way of searching robust model architectures.

NAS is a special study direction in machine learning that lies far from this book's scope. But some relatively simple techniques can help to find optimal neural network topologies in search space.

We can reduce neural network search to hyper-parameter optimization. Hyper-parameter can directly affect neural network topology.

Let us study the following example **ch6/nas/nas_to_hopt.py**. The number of hidden linear layers in this model depends on the parameter:

```
from typing import OrderedDict
import torch.nn as nn
```

```python
class FCNN(nn.Module):
    def __init__(self, hidden_layers_num):
        super(FCNN, self).__init__()
        assert hidden_layers_num >= 0, 'hidden layers number should be positive or zero'
        self.lin_first = nn.Linear(5, 10)
        hidden_layers = OrderedDict()
        for l in range(hidden_layers_num):
            hidden_layers[f'lin_hidden{l}'] = nn.Linear(10, 10)
        self.lin_hidden = nn.Sequential(hidden_layers)
        self.lin_last = nn.Linear(10, 1)
```

This concept can be visualized the following way:

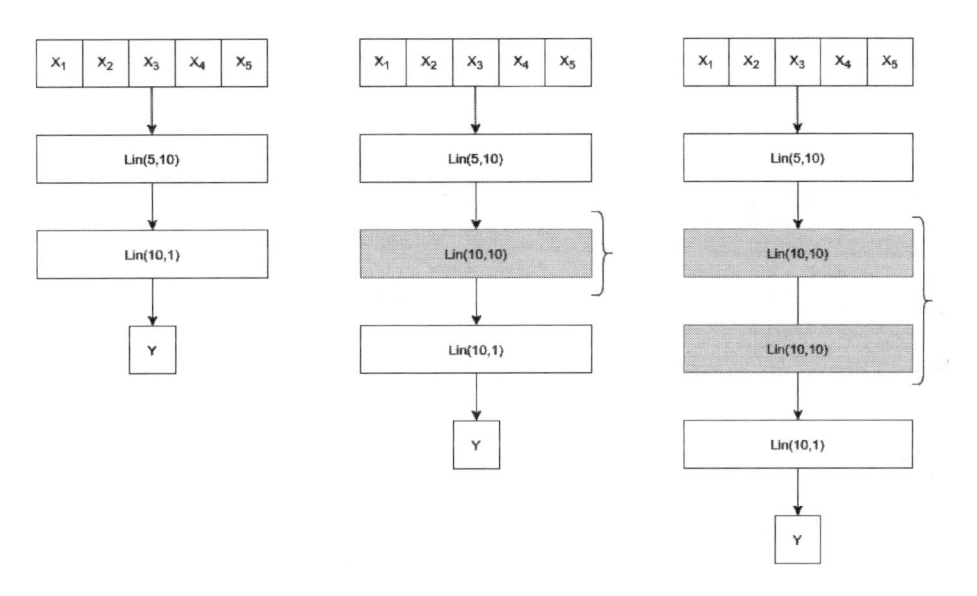

Figure 6.4: Neural Architecture Search to Hyper-parameter Optimization

We can construct very flexible models whose topology depends on input parameters. Then we can combine NAS and hyper-parameter optimization. This approach is much more effective and can create suitable models for a particular task.

Let us examine this approach in action. In *Chapter 5, Advanced Forecasting Models,* we have learned an advanced deep learning model called Temporal Convolutional Network. Let us inject some parameters into its network topology:

- activation function *parameter*
- bias usage *parameter*
- *number* of inner temporal casual layer slices
- *number* of temporal casual layers

The search space for TCN NAS can be depicted in the following way:

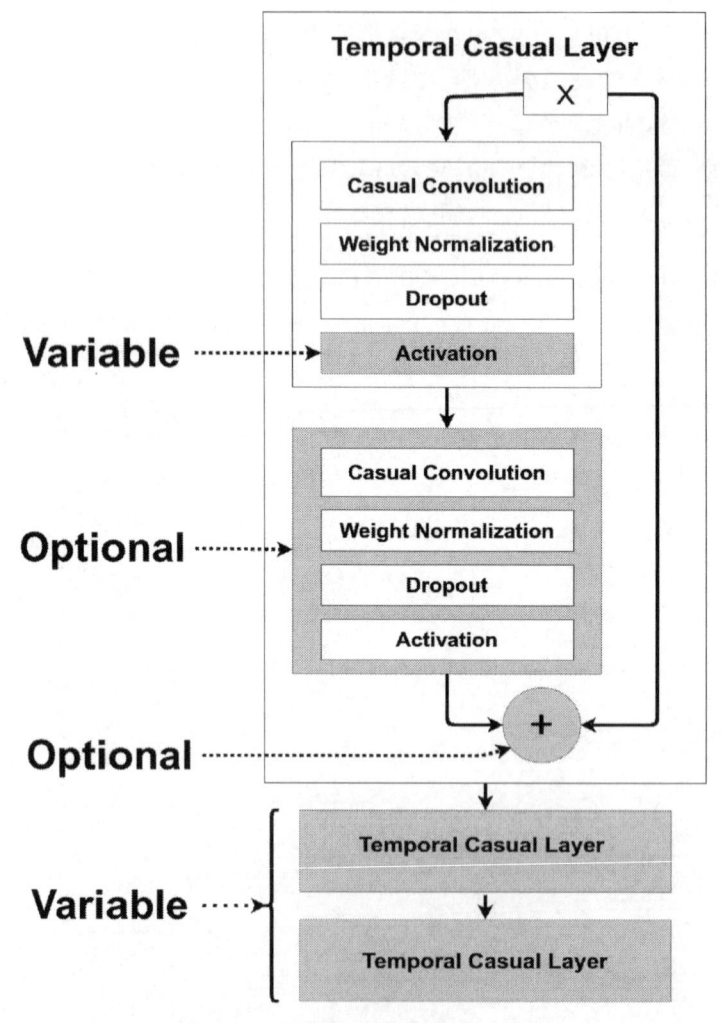

Figure 6.5: NAS search space for TCN

Let us take a look at how the TCN model with topology parameters can be implemented **ch6/nas/model.py**.

Temporal casual layer accepts: **act**, **slices** and **use_bias** parameters that defines its topology:

```python
class TemporalCasualLayer(nn.Module):
    def __init__(self,
                 n_inputs,
                 n_outputs,
                 kernel_size,
                 stride,
                 dilation,
                 dropout = 0.2,
                 act = 'relu',
                 slices = 2,
                 use_bias = True
                 ):
        super(TemporalCasualLayer, self).__init__()
        padding = (kernel_size - 1) * dilation
        conv_params = {
            'kernel_size': kernel_size,
            'stride':      stride,
            'padding':     padding,
            'dilation':    dilation
        }
        activations = {
            'relu': nn.ReLU(),
            'tanh': nn.Tanh()
        }
        self.use_bias = use_bias
        layers = OrderedDict()
        for s in range(1, slices + 1):
            if s == 1:
                layers[f'conv{s}'] = weight_norm(nn.Conv1d(n_inputs, n_outputs, **conv_params))
            else:
                layers[f'conv{s}'] = weight_norm(nn.Conv1d(n_outputs, n_outputs, **conv_params))
            layers[f'crop{s}'] = Crop(padding)
```

```python
            layers[f'act{s}'] = activations[act]
            layers[f'dropout{s}'] = nn.Dropout(dropout)
        self.net = nn.Sequential(layers)
        if n_inputs != n_outputs and use_bias:
            self.bias = nn.Conv1d(n_inputs, n_outputs, 1)
        else:
            self.bias = None
        self.relu = nn.ReLU()
    def forward(self, x):
        y = self.net(x)
        if self.use_bias:
            b = x if self.bias is None else self.bias(x)
            return self.relu(y + b)
        else:
            return self.relu(y)
```

The search space for the NAS problem we are studying looks the following way **ch6/nas/search.py**:

```
search_space = {
    "tcl_num":
        {"_type": "choice", "_value": [1, 2, 3, 4]},
    "tcl_channel_size":
        {"_type": "choice", "_value": [4, 6, 10]},
    "kernel_size":
        {"_type": "choice", "_value": [3, 5, 7]},
    "dropout":
        {"_type": "choice", "_value": [0, .1, .2]},
    "slices":
        {"_type": "choice", "_value": [1, 2]},
    "act":
        {"_type": "choice", "_value": ['relu', 'tanh']},
    "use_bias":
        {"_type": "choice", "_value": [True, False]}
}
```

Let us run the search process **ch6/nas/search.py** and analyze the results. When the search process completes, we get the best model hyper-parameters:

{'tcl_num': 2, 'tcl_channel_size': 6, 'kernel_size': 5, 'dropout': 0, 'slices': 1, 'act': 'relu', 'use_bias': True}

But we should examine some more information about the nature of successive topologies on the given dataset. As we see on the NNI overview page, the top best topologies have relatively close metrics:

Trial No.	ID	Duration	Status	Default me... ↑
170	o1Nvu	39s	SUCCEEDED	0.0002
213	FEqu2	46s	SUCCEEDED	0.0004
262	fzWCm	28s	SUCCEEDED	0.0007
242	c2UA6	40s	SUCCEEDED	0.0007
211	O8NKz	37s	SUCCEEDED	0.0008
219	FvZie	44s	SUCCEEDED	0.0008
232	ftm9F	56s	SUCCEEDED	0.0008
186	xS8Bi	34s	SUCCEEDED	0.0009
231	bsHUo	27s	SUCCEEDED	0.0009
134	DMHkL	29s	SUCCEEDED	0.0011

Figure 6.6: Top 10 best trials

If we need to know what all successful architectures have in common. NNI detail page will help us to get the answer. Open the hyper-parameter tab and display the Top 5% results on the detail page **http://127.0.0.1:8080/detail**:

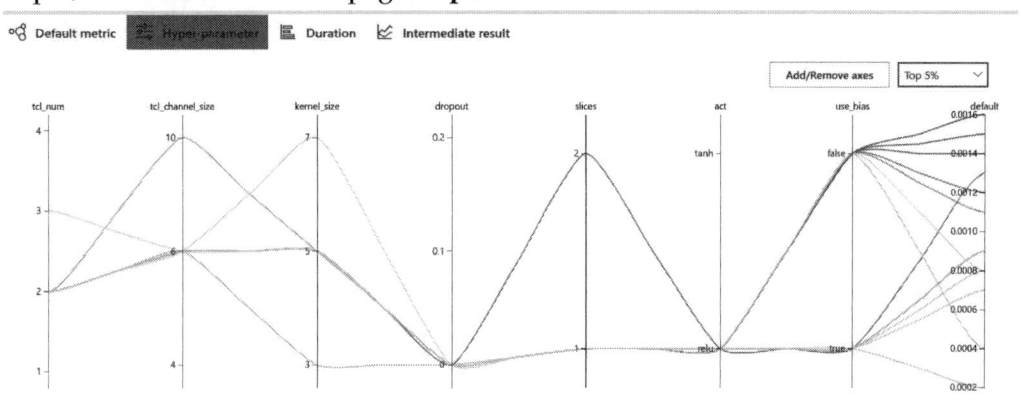

Figure 6.7: Top 5% Hyper-parameter dependencies

And we see a lot of helpful information here:

- The best number of temporal convolutional layers are 2 or 3
- 4 is not a good channel size for temporal casual layer
- Dropout technique has no effect on this model
- *tanh* is not an appropriate activation function

So the TCN topology for this particular problem can be compressed to the following one:

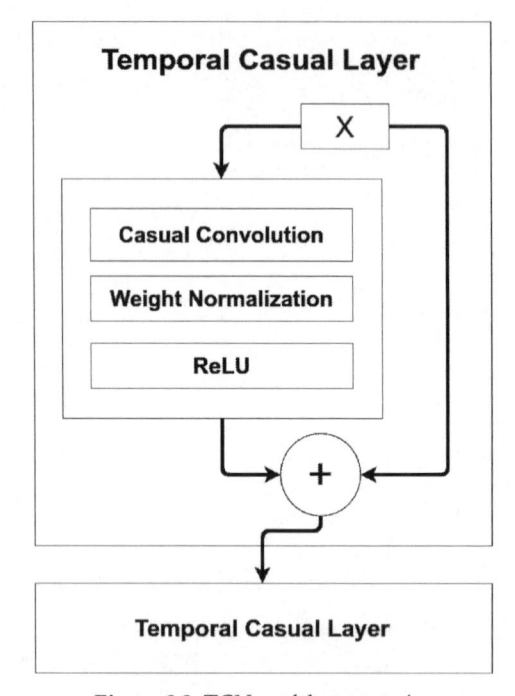

Figure 6.8: *TCN model compression*

After obtaining the best result, always analyze other trials and their hyper-parameters to understand the effectiveness of various deep learning methods for a particular task.

Hybrid models

In this section, we will study the hybrid model construction. The hybrid model contains approaches from different areas. They combine techniques from various sites of mathematics and deep learning. A hybrid model can show outstanding performance.

Mathematical statistics is a very powerful method for time-series analysis. The methods of mathematical statistics are too good to be rejected in the predictive model development. In *Chapter 3, Time Series as Deep Learning Problem*, we observed various trivial preprocessing methods: normalization, trend removal, and differencing. The main aim of preprocessing methods is to filter unnecessary information from the dataset and help the deep learning model learn hidden patterns in time series.

There are a lot of advanced statistical filters and transformers. Below are some of them:

- Kalman filter
- Hodrick–Prescott filter
- Baxter-King filter
- Christiano-Fitzgerald filter

It is totally ok if you haven't heard anything about these filters. We are not going to dive deep into their logic.

Let us demonstrate an application of two statistical filters: Hodrick–Prescott Filter and Christiano-Fitzgerald Filter. Each of these filters assumes trend filter and cycle filter **ch6/hybrid/filters.py**:

```python
import matplotlib.pyplot as plt
import statsmodels.api as sm
from ch6.hybrid.training_datasets import get_aep_timeseries
if __name__ == '__main__':
    ts = get_aep_timeseries()
    ts = ts.flatten()
    hp_cycle, hp_trend = sm.tsa.filters.hpfilter(ts)
    cf_cycle, cf_trend = sm.tsa.filters.cffilter(ts)
    fig, axs = plt.subplots(5)
    fig.set_size_inches(5, 9)
    axs[0].title.set_text('Hourly Energy Consumption')
    axs[0].plot(ts[100:200])
    axs[1].title.set_text('Hodrick-Prescott: Trend filter')
    axs[1].plot(hp_trend[100:200])
    axs[2].title.set_text('Christiano Fitzgerald: Trend filter')
    axs[2].plot(cf_trend[100:200])
    axs[3].title.set_text('Hodrick-Prescott Cycle: filter')
```

```
axs[3].plot(hp_cycle[100:200])
axs[4].title.set_text('Christiano Fitzgerald: Cycle filter')
axs[4].plot(cf_cycle[100:200])
plt.show()
```

Result

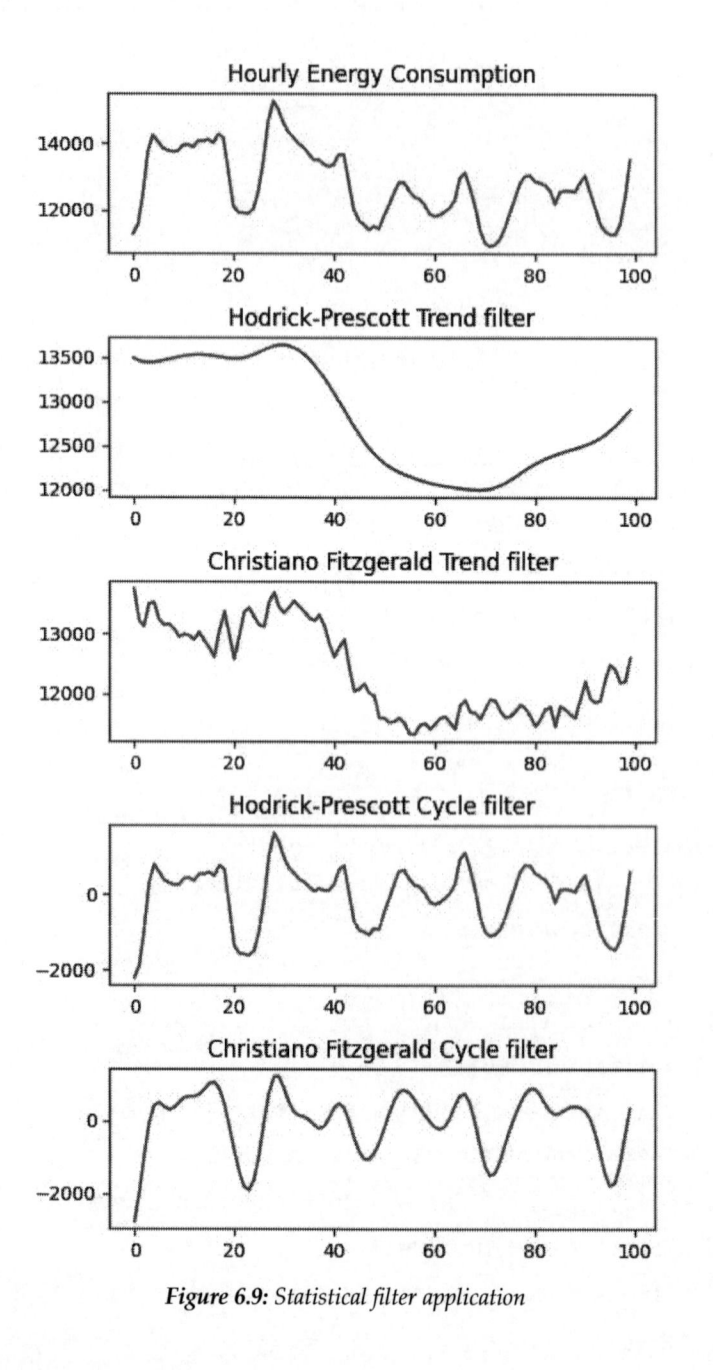

Figure 6.9: Statistical filter application

Statistical filters can be applied to create additional time-series sequences for the deep learning model, as shown here:

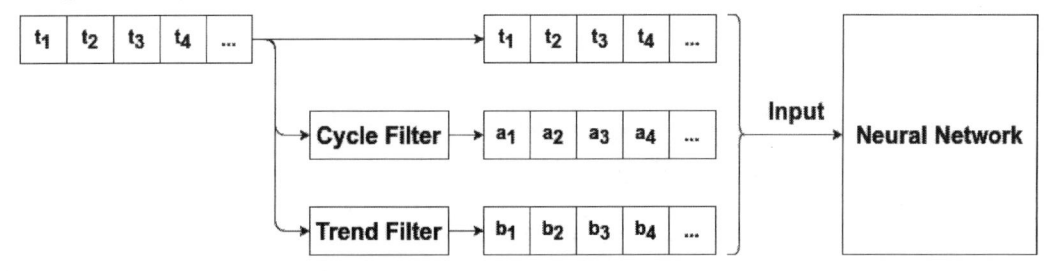

Figure 6.10: Statistical filters as neural network input

We can use hyper-parameter tuning to find filters that show the best performance with the deep learning model collaboration.

Another way to create a robust deep learning model is to combine ideas from different designs. You can try to integrate various approaches in the same model and study how they perform together. For example, you can combine fully connected neural networks, recurrent neural networks, convolutional layers, etc. Of course, you can use hyper-parameter tuning to find an optimal design.

Let us consider the RNN model, which we have examined in *Chapter 4, Recurrent Neural Networks*, for energy consumption prediction, and build a hybrid model on top of it.

- **Optional Statistical Preprocessing**: We will add optional statistical preprocessing with Hodrick–Prescott and Christiano–Fitzgerald filters for input.

- **Optional Casual Convolution**: Casual convolution can extract many hidden dependencies. We will add casual convolution as an optional layer for our hybrid model.

- **RNN hyper-parameter tuning**: We'll try to find the optimal hidden state size for RNN layer.

- **Optional Fully Connected Neural Network**: We can assume that a flat linear layer is not enough for interpreting an RNN output. We will add an optional FCNN layer to our hybrid model.

The search space for the hybrid model can be depicted in the following way:

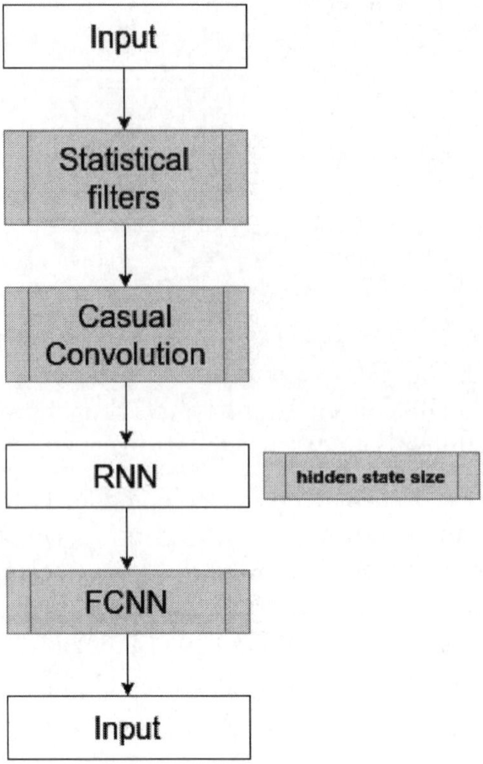

Figure 6.11: Hybrid model search space

Implementing hybrid model

Let us examine the implementation of the hybrid model **ch6/hybrid/model.py**.

Import part

```
import torch
from typing import OrderedDict
import torch.nn as nn
from torch.nn.utils import weight_norm
```

Casual convolution layer

Here, we define the casual convolution layer, which we studied in *Chapter 5, Advanced Forecasting Models*:

```python
class CasualConvolution(nn.Module):
    def __init__(self, n_inputs, n_outputs, kernel_size = 5):
        super(CasualConvolution, self).__init__()
        self.kernel_size = kernel_size
        self.conv = weight_norm(
            nn.Conv1d(n_inputs, n_outputs,
                      kernel_size = kernel_size,
                      padding = kernel_size - 1))
    def forward(self, x):
        x1 = torch.swapaxes(x, 1, 2)
        x1 = self.conv(x1)
        x1 = x1[:, :, :-(self.kernel_size - 1)].contiguous()
        x = torch.swapaxes(x1, 2, 1)
        return x
```

Hybrid model

```python
class Hybrid(nn.Module):
    def __init__(self,
                 hidden_size,
                 in_size = 1,
                 out_size = 1,
                 use_casual_convolution = False,
                 casual_convolution_kernel = 5,
                 fcnn_layer_num = 0,
                 fcnn_layer_size = 8
                 ):
        super(Hybrid, self).__init__()
```

Optional casual convolution layer

```python
        if use_casual_convolution:
            self.cc = CasualConvolution(in_size, in_size, casual_convolution_kernel)
        else:
            self.cc = None
```

Obligatory RNN layer

```
self.rnn = nn.RNN(
    input_size = in_size,
    hidden_size = hidden_size,
    batch_first = True)
```

Optional fully connected layer

```
lin_layers = OrderedDict()
for l in range(fcnn_layer_num):
    if l == 0:
        lin_layers[f'lin_hidden_{l}'] = nn.Linear(hidden_size, fcnn_layer_size)
    else:
        lin_layers[f'lin_hidden_{l}'] = nn.Linear(fcnn_layer_size, fcnn_layer_size)
if fcnn_layer_num == 0:
    lin_layers['lin_final'] = nn.Linear(hidden_size, out_size)
else:
    lin_layers['lin_final'] = nn.Linear(fcnn_layer_size, out_size)
self.fc = nn.Sequential(lin_layers)
```

Hybrid model

```
def forward(self, x, h = None):
    if self.cc:
        x = self.cc(x)
    out, _ = self.rnn(x, h)
    last_hidden_states = out[:, -1]
    out = self.fc(last_hidden_states)
    return out, last_hidden_states
```

Hybrid model trial

Statistical filtering is performed during trial execution in the dataset preparation stage **ch6/hybrid/trial.py**:

```
# Preparing datasets for Training
ts = get_aep_timeseries()
scaler = MinMaxScaler()
scaled_ts = scaler.fit_transform(ts)
hp_cycle, hp_trend = sm.tsa.filters.hpfilter(scaled_ts)
cf_cycle, cf_trend = sm.tsa.filters.cffilter(scaled_ts)
cycle_filters = {'hp': hp_cycle, 'cf': cf_cycle}
trend_filters = {'hp': hp_trend, 'cf': cf_trend}
```

Hybrid model search space

Let us examine the search space **ch6/hybrid/search.py**:

```
search_space = {
```

We add one of the statistical trend filters or none of them:

```
    "trend_filter":        {
        "_type":   "choice",
        "_value": [{"_name": "None"}, {"_name": "hp"}, {"_name": "cf"}]
    },
```

We add one of the statistical cycle filters or none of them:

```
    "cycle_filter":        {
        "_type":   "choice",
        "_value": [{"_name": "None"}, {"_name": "hp"}, {"_name": "cf"}]
    },
```

Optional addition of casual convolution layer. This hyper-parameter has nested options:

```
    "casual_convolution": {
        "_type":   "choice",
        "_value": [
            {
                "_name": False
            },
            {
                "_name": True,
```

```
                "kernel": {"_type": "choice", "_value": [3, 5, 7, 9]},
            },
        ]
    },
}
```

RNN hidden state size tuning:

```
    "rnn_hidden_size":    {"_type": "choice", "_value": [8, 16, 24]},
```

`Addition of FCNN layer. If fcnn_layer_num is 0, then no FCNN layer is added`:

```
    "fcnn_layer_num":     {"_type": "choice", "_value": [0, 1, 2]},
    "fcnn_layer_size":    {"_type": "choice", "_value": [4, 8, 12]},
}
```

Hybrid model architecture search

Let us run the search **ch6/hybrid/search.py**. After the search completes, we can analyze its results **http://127.0.0.1:8080/oview**:

Trial No.	ID	Duration	Status	Default me... ↑
139	afeyr	43s	SUCCEEDED	0.000984
232	IfHD4	1m 17s	SUCCEEDED	0.001015
289	Qyrm1	1m 14s	SUCCEEDED	0.001017
211	XGWqM	1m 20s	SUCCEEDED	0.001026
285	rJogC	1m 23s	SUCCEEDED	0.00103
147	gAawn	1m 1s	SUCCEEDED	0.001052
138	dcLGc	1m 2s	SUCCEEDED	0.00107
183	SSM9B	1m 18s	SUCCEEDED	0.001077
149	Al2rF	1m 11s	SUCCEEDED	0.001077
126	hV3Jo	52s	SUCCEEDED	0.001079

Figure 6.12: Hybrid model architecture search top 10 trials

The top 10 results are very close to each other, and it would be reasonable to analyze what the best trials have in common. Let us look at the hyper-parameter tab for Top 5% trials **http://127.0.0.1:8080/detail**:

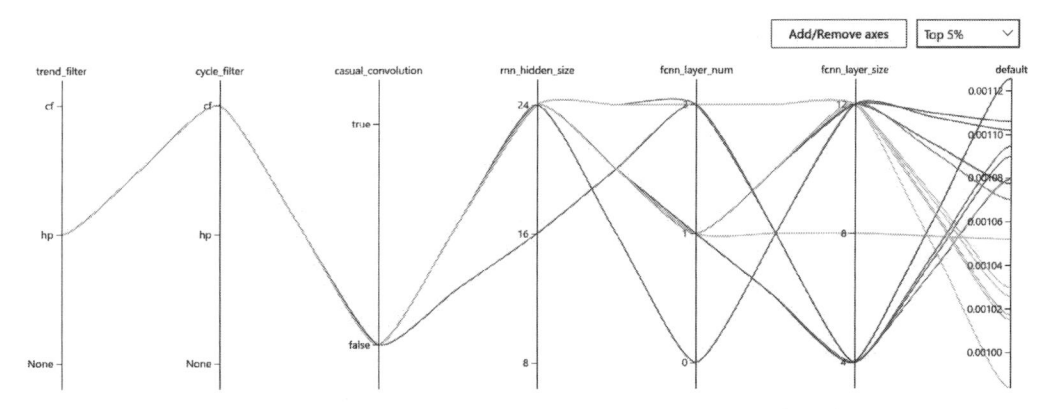

Figure 6.13: Hybrid model architecture search hyper-parameter dependencies

And here, we have very interesting results:

- All successful models use statistical filtering, which proves the benefit of this approach.
- Hodrick–Prescott Trend Filter and Christiano–Fitzgerald Cycle Filter are the best preprocessors for this model.
- Casual convolution is useless for this model.
- FCNN layer is optional.

After our research, we can conclude that this hybrid model is optimal for the energy consumption prediction problem, as shown in the following figure:

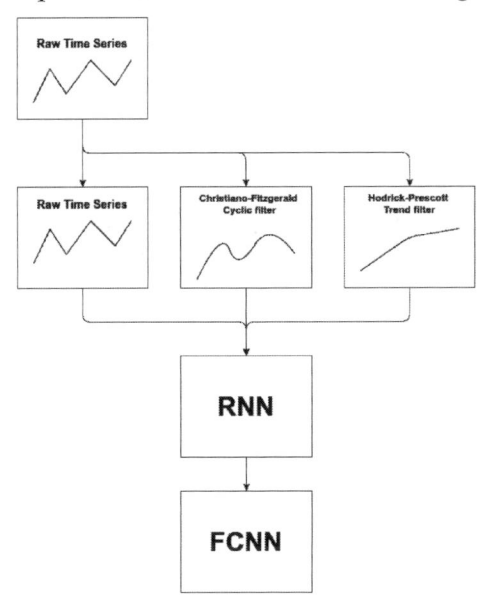

Figure 6.14: Hybrid model for energy consumption prediction problem

Well, that is it! We have constructed a unique deep learning model for particular time-series prediction problem after injecting different mathematical and machine learning methods.

In this section, we analyzed some of the promising possibilities for hybrid model construction. The application of hyper-parameter tuning and statistical methods inclusion can significantly increase the variability and likelihood of finding robust architectures.

Conclusion

In this chapter, we have learned the basics of hyper-parameter tuning applications. We have shown how simple concepts of finding optimal parameters can lead to radically new architectures. The selection of the optimal parameters is a simple task, which significantly increases the efficiency of the developed model. The next chapter will be wholly dedicated to real-world forecasting problems. We will study how to apply our theoretical knowledge in practice.

Points to remember

- Hyper-parameter trial is a simple script that receives input parameters and returns output metric.
- After hyper-parameter tuning, analyze top trial results together through hyper-parameter dependency diagram.
- In some cases, NAS can be reduced to hyper-parameter tuning.
- Hybrid models combine techniques from various sites of mathematics and deep learning.

Multiple choice questions

1. Say we a fully connected neural network with the following variables: number_of_hidden_layers, hidden_layer_size. What kind of search space is better to use for hyper-parameter tuning?

    A. number_of_hidden_layers: [1]

    hidden_layer_size: [8, 10, 12, 14, 16]

    B. number_of_hidden_layers: [1, 2, 3]

    hidden_layer_size: [8, 12, 16]

    C. number_of_hidden_layers: [1, 2, 3, 4, 5, 6]

    hidden_layer_size: [10]

2. Can we exclude the validation stage (evaluation on validation dataset) from hyper-parameter tuning trials?

   A. No

   B. Yes, if we are not worried about the overfitting problem.

Answers

1. B
2. B

Key terms

- *Hyper-parameters:* are the parameters that define the model architecture and are used to control the learning process.

- *Hyper-parameter tuning:* an optimal model hyper-parameter search.

- *Search space:* is the predefined set of all hyper-parameter combinations.

- *Tuner:* defines the strategy which aims to maximize the model performance on search space.

- *Neural architecture search (NAS):* automates network architecture topology search.

CHAPTER 7
Applying Deep Learning to Real-world Forecasting Problems

In the previous chapters, we explored the theoretical aspects of applying deep learning to forecasting problems. Now, we are ready to start developing deep learning models for real-world tasks. This chapter is entirely dedicated to solving real-world forecasting problems. Here, we will apply all the knowledge that we have gained in the previous chapters to construct robust time series prediction models.

Structure

In this chapter, we will discuss the following topics:

- Rain prediction
- COVID-19 confirmed cases forecast
- Algorithmic trading

Objectives

After studying this chapter, you will be able to apply complex deep learning models to different types of forecasting data problems. This chapter provides a bridge from theory to practice and shows various deep learning implementations to real-world tasks.

Rain prediction

Since ancient times, humanity has tried to learn how to predict the weather. People quickly realized that a year consists of 365 days, that there are different seasons throughout the year: dry seasons, rainy or snowy seasons. But predicting the weather in the near future has been and remains a highly complex task.

How often have you asked yourself a simple question: *Will it rain tomorrow?* And how often did the forecast match with reality? No forecast with 100% probability can guarantee the answer to this question. Nevertheless, let us try to apply deep learning methods to solve this problem and study the results of this model.

Okay, let us pretend we are in Australia at the end of 2015. We live in Sydney, the capital of Australia. And we want to build a predictive model that answers the question, "*Will it rain tomorrow?*":

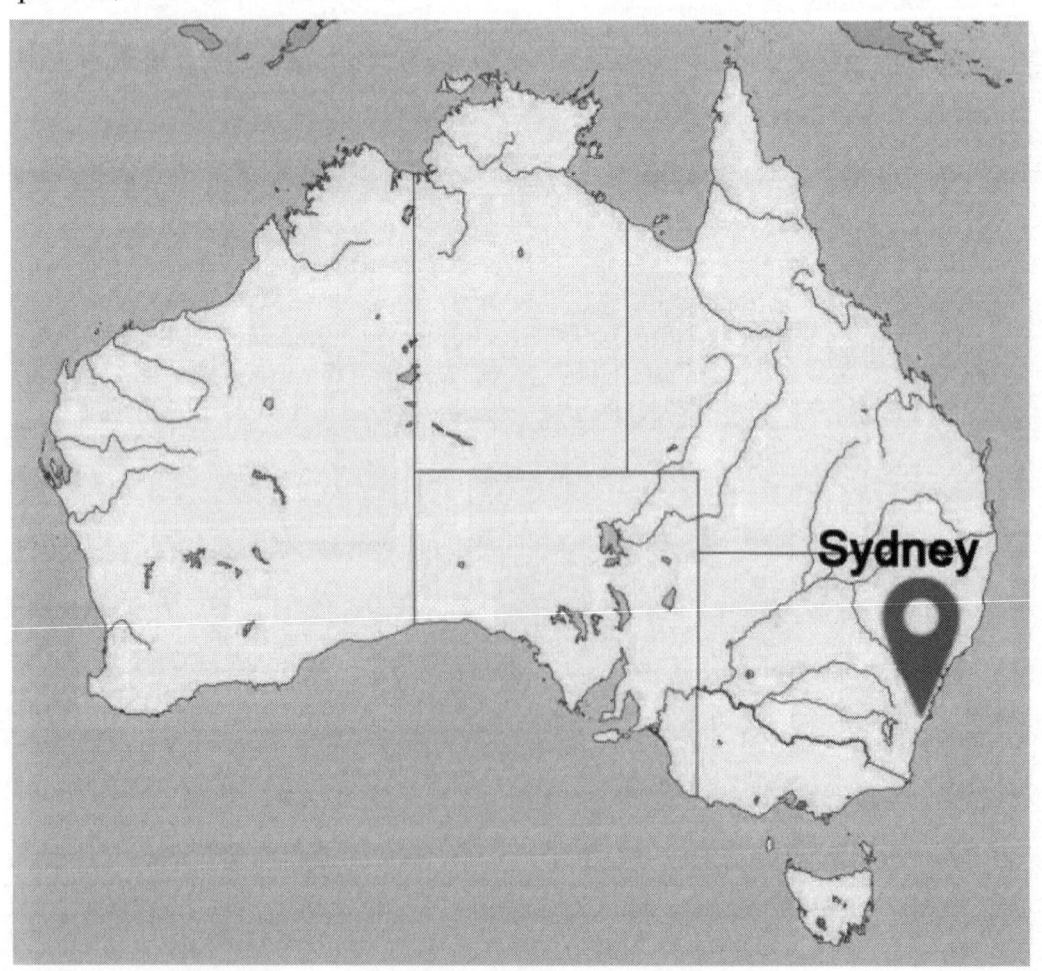

Figure 7.1: Sydney, Australia

Before diving into the depths of this problem, let us give a meteorological definition: *Rain is considered to be an excess of precipitation by 1 mm*. This definition is necessary to handle a precise analysis of the problem. It should be understood that not every drop of water means that it was raining today.

We have a dataset of historical observations dating back to 2008: `ch7/weather/data/weatherAUS_until_2016_01_01.csv`. This dataset contains the following columns:

Date	The date of observation
Location	The common name of the location of the weather station
MinTemp	The minimum temperature in degrees Celsius
MaxTemp	The maximum temperature in degrees Celsius
Rainfall	The amount of rainfall recorded for the day in mm
Sunshine	The number of hours of bright sunshine in the day
WindGustDir	The direction of the strongest wind gust in the 24 h to midnight
WindGustSpeed	The speed (km/h) of the strongest wind gust in the 24 h to midnight
WindDir9am	Direction of the wind at 9 am
WindDir3pm	Direction of the wind at 3 pm
WindSpeed9am	Wind speed (km/hr) averaged over 10 min prior to 9 am
WindSpeed3pm	Wind speed (km/hr) averaged over 10 min prior to 3 pm
Humidity9am	Humidity (percent) at 9 am
Humidity3pm	Humidity (percent) at 3 pm
Pressure9am	Atmospheric pressure (hpa) reduced to mean sea level at 9 am
Pressure3pm	Atmospheric pressure (hpa) reduced to mean sea level at 3 pm
Cloud9am	Fraction of sky obscured by cloud at 9 am. This is measured in "oktas", which are a unit of eigths. It records how many eigths of the sky are obscured by clouds. A 0 measure indicates a completely clear sky whilst an 8 indicates that it is completely overcast.
Cloud3pm	Fraction of sky obscured by cloud (in "oktas": eighths) at 3 pm. See Cload9am for a description of the values

Temp9am	Temperature (degrees C) at 9 am
Temp3pm	Temperature (degrees C) at 3 pm
RainToday	Boolean: 1 if precipitation (mm) in the 24 h exceeds 1mm, otherwise 0

Table 7.1: Weather dataset columns

As you can see, we have a fairly rich historical dataset with a large amount of various weather data.

Note: For the sincerity of the experiment, we will explicitly separate the datasets. ch7/weather/data/weatherAUS_until_2016_01_01.csv - dataset contains data until 2015-12-31, and we use this dataset for training only. To evaluate the prediction model and test its effectiveness, we will use another dataset ch7/weather/data/weatherAUS_complete.csv that contains data for 2016. Of course, you could use one dataset and do all the restrictions in the code, but I prefer and strongly recommend explicitly separate data files.

So, we have historical data. Let's visualize the precipitation data in Sydney **ch7/weather/visualize.py**:

```python
import matplotlib.pyplot as plt
from ch7.weather.dataset import get_df_until_2016_01_01
df = get_df_until_2016_01_01()
df_syd = df[(df['Location'] == 'Sydney') &
            (df.index > '2015-01-01')]
rainfall = df_syd['Rainfall'].values
raintoday = df_syd['RainToday']\
    .map({'Yes': 1, 'No': 0}).values
fig, axs = plt.subplots(2)
axs[0].set_title('Rainfall')
axs[0].plot(rainfall)
axs[1].set_title('Rain Classification')
axs[1].bar(range(len(raintoday)), raintoday, color = 'red')
plt.show()
```

Result

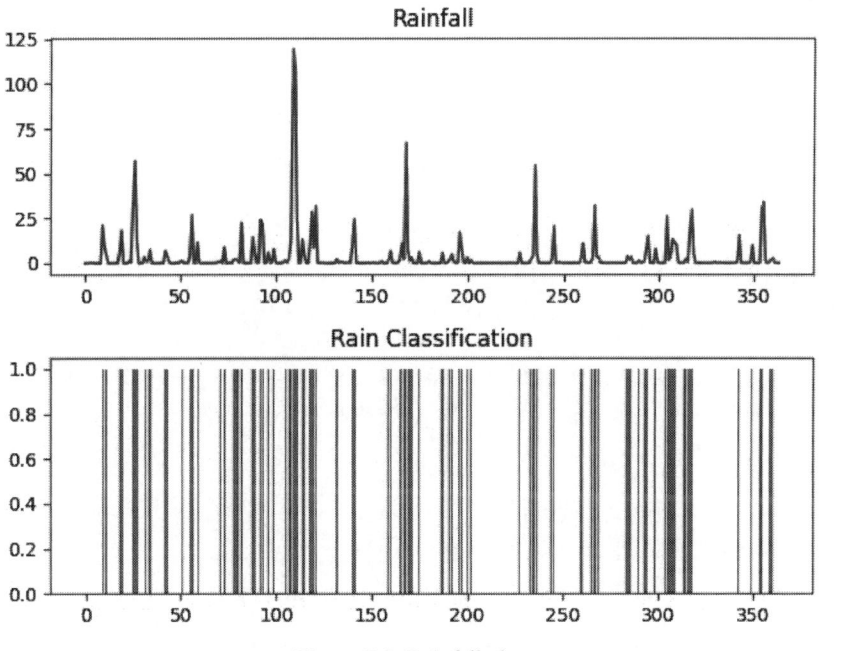

Figure 7.2: Rainfall plot

Based on the data in *figure 7.2*, the rainfall distribution does not have remarkable straightforward patterns. Therefore, developing a predictive deep learning model makes sense because we need a tool to extract the hidden dependencies in the time series dataset.

Let us formulate the problem: *we need to create a multivariate input single-step classification model*:

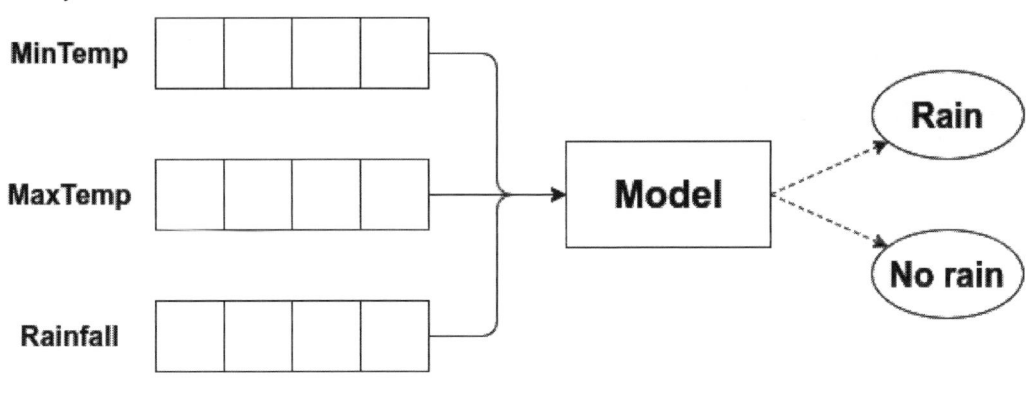

Figure 7.3: Multivariate single-step classification model

We will use the following features from the historical dataset for model training: MinTemp, MaxTemp, Rainfall, WindGustSpeed, WindSpeed9am, WindSpeed3pm, Humidity9am, Humidity3pm, Pressure9am, Pressure3pm, Cloud9am, Cloud3pm, Temp9am, Temp3pm, and RainToday.

To expand the dataset, we will use observations made in *Sydney* and four more locations in Australia: *Albury, Newcastle, Richmond,* and *Canberra*.

In *Chapter 5, Advanced forecasting models*, we examined the Temporal Convolutional Network, which shows promising results for multivariate input single-step forecasting problems. And in *Chapter 6, PyTorch Model Tuning with Neural Network Intelligence*, we have constructed the flexible TCN architecture, which allows different designs depending on the given parameters. Let's use the same model for a rain forecasting prediction problem. The only difference now is that the TCN model will be used as a classifier **ch7/weather/model/model.py**:

```python
class TcnClassifier(nn.Module):
    def __init__(self, **params):
        super(TcnClassifier, self).__init__()
        self.num_channels = params['num_channels']
        self.num_classes = params.pop('num_classes')
        self.tcn = TemporalConvolutionNetwork(**params)
        self.linear = nn.Linear(self.num_channels[-1], self.num_classes)
    def forward(self, x):
        x = self.tcn(x)
        x = self.linear(x[:, :, -1])
        y = torch.log_softmax(x, dim = 1)
        return y
```

Now, let us explicitly define the algorithm according to which we will be building a predictive model. We will create a sliding window time series dataset for different locations in Australia. After that, we will randomly pick a sample for the validation dataset with $p = 0.2$ probability.

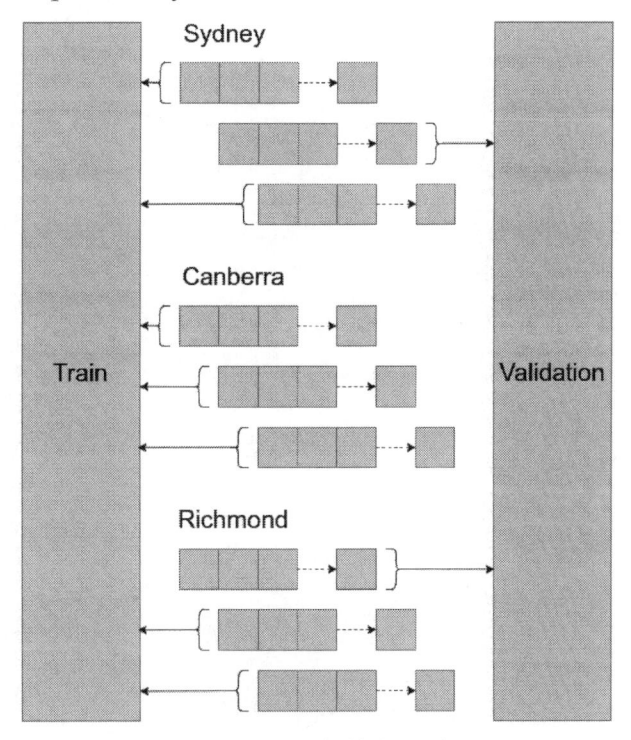

Figure 7.4: Train and validation datasets

We will launch the process of hyper-parameter tuning using NNI to pick the optimal model hyper-parameters for this task. The model's performance on the validation dataset will be used as a model quality metric. We record the best hyper-parameters obtained by the NNI, train the model on dataset from 2008-12-01 to 2015-12-31, and save it.

Let us examine the training process **ch7/weather/train.py**.

Import part

```
import copy
import os
import random
import torch
from ch7.weather.dataset import get_df_until_2016_01_01
from ch7.weather.model.model import TcnClassifier
from ch7.weather.utils import sliding_window
```

Model preparation function

This function receives model and training parameters and saves the best model parameters to disk if necessary:

```
def prepare_model(params, save_model = False, model_name = 'tcn_rain'):
```

Global parameters

Here, we initialize the historical dataset and set the length of the sliding window and the number of epochs to train:

```
    dir_path = os.path.dirname(os.path.realpath(__file__))
    # Explicitly define the end date
    end_date = '2016-01-01'
    # Historical data
    df = get_df_until_2016_01_01()
    df = df[df.index < end_date]
    # 14 days as sliding window
    w = 14
    # Number of epochs for training
    epochs = 5_00
```

Model hyper-parameters

We have used the same set of hyper-parameters for TCN that were used in *Chapter 6, PyTorch Model Tuning with Neural Network Intelligence*:

```
    # Hyper-parameters:
    tcl_num = params['tcl_num']
    tcl_channel_size = params['tcl_channel_size']
    # temporal casual layer channels
    channel_sizes = [tcl_channel_size] * tcl_num
    # convolution kernel size
    kernel_size = params['kernel_size']
    dropout = params['dropout']
    slices = params['slices']
    use_bias = params['use_bias']
    lr = params['lr']
```

Locations and features to train on

We have choosed only five cities from the historical dataset:

```
# Australia Location for training
    locations = ['Albury', 'Newcastle', 'Richmond', 'Sydney', 'Canberra']
    # features
    features_cont = ['MinTemp', 'MaxTemp', 'Rainfall', 'WindGustSpeed', 'WindSpeed9am',
                     'WindSpeed3pm', 'Humidity9am', 'Humidity3pm', 'Pressure9am',
                     'Pressure3pm', 'Cloud9am', 'Cloud3pm', 'Temp9am', 'Temp3pm']
    features_cat = ['RainToday']
```

Sliding window dataset

Preparing the sliding window dataset:

```
X, Y = [], []
    for l in locations:
        df_l = df[df['Location'] == l]
        D = []
        for f in features_cont:
            D.append(df_l[f].interpolate('linear').fillna(0).values)
        for f in features_cat:
            D.append(df_l[f].map({'Yes': 1, 'No': 0}).fillna(0).values)
        # transpose to time series
        TS = []
        for i in range(df_l.shape[0]):
            row = []
            for c in D:
                row.append(c[i])
            TS.append(row)
        in_seq, out_seq = sliding_window(TS, w, 1)
        rain_seq = [r[0][-1] for r in out_seq]
```

```
        X.extend(in_seq)
        Y.extend(rain_seq)
```

Train-validation split

We randomly split the dataset for train and validation datasets:

```
    X_train, Y_train = [], []
    X_val, Y_val = [], []
    for i in range(len(X)):
        if random.random() > .8:
            X_val.append(X[i])
            Y_val.append(Y[i])
        else:
            X_train.append(X[i])
            Y_train.append(Y[i])
```

Converting all datasets to tensors:

```
    x_train = torch.tensor(X_train).float().transpose(1, 2)
    y_train = torch.tensor(Y_train).long()
    x_val = torch.tensor(X_val).float().transpose(1, 2)
    y_val = torch.tensor(Y_val).long()
```

Initializing the model

The model initializes based on the hyper-parameters passed to the function:

```
    model_params = {
        'num_inputs':   len(features_cont) + len(features_cat),
        'num_classes':  2,
        'num_channels': channel_sizes,
        'kernel_size':  kernel_size,
        'dropout':      dropout,
        'slices':       slices,
        'act':          'relu',
        'use_bias':     use_bias
    }
    model = TcnClassifier(**model_params)
```

Optimizer

```
optimizer = torch.optim.Adam(params = model.parameters(), lr = lr)
```

Loss function

We will use Cross Entropy Loss function for this classification problem:

```
cl_loss = torch.nn.CrossEntropyLoss()
```

Training

Classical training with validation dataset:

```
best_params = None
min_val_loss = 1000_000
training_loss = []
validation_loss = []
for t in range(epochs):
    prediction = model(x_train)
    loss = cl_loss(prediction, y_train)
    optimizer.zero_grad()
    loss.backward()
    optimizer.step()
    val_prediction = model(x_val)
    val_loss = cl_loss(val_prediction, y_val)
    training_loss.append(loss.item())
    validation_loss.append(val_loss.item())
    if val_loss.item() < min_val_loss:
        best_params = copy.deepcopy(model.state_dict())
        min_val_loss = val_loss.item()
    if t % 10 == 0:
        print(f'Epoch {t}| test: {round(loss.item(),4)}, '
            f'val: {round(val_loss.item(),4)}')
```

Saving the model if necessary:

```
if save_model:
    torch.save(best_params, f'{dir_path}/data/{model_name}.pth')
```

Model's best performance and validation dataset:

```
return min_val_loss
```

So far, so good. Now we need to define the search space for hyper-parameter tuning **ch7/weather/search.py**:

```
search_space = {
    "tcl_num":
        {"_type": "choice", "_value": [1, 2, 3]},
    "tcl_channel_size":
        {"_type": "choice", "_value": [8, 16, 24, 32]},
    "kernel_size":
        {"_type": "choice", "_value": [3, 5, 7]},
    "dropout":
        {"_type": "choice", "_value": [0, .1, .2, .4]},
    "slices":
        {"_type": "choice", "_value": [1, 2]},
    "use_bias":
        {"_type": "choice", "_value": [True, False]},
    "lr":
        {"_type": "choice", "_value": [.01, .005, .0001]}
}
```

Now let us launch the optimization process **ch7/weather/search.py**. This process can take several hours. Therefore you can use the results obtained by the author:

```
Best trial params:
{
    "tcl_num":          2,
    "tcl_channel_size": 32,
    "kernel_size":      7,
    "dropout":          0.1,
    "slices":           1,
    "use_bias":         true,
    "lr":               0.005
}
```

Let us take a look at the Top 10 trials:

	Trial No.	ID	Duration	Status	Default me... ↑
>	104	sW4UL	14m 51s	SUCCEEDED	0.344522
>	8	S7KgX	2m 30s	SUCCEEDED	0.355779
>	103	Uv3Rd	9m 56s	SUCCEEDED	0.358348
>	90	gfCz3	1m 41s	SUCCEEDED	0.362978
>	49	kLzHv	5m 3s	SUCCEEDED	0.363063
>	22	xyfXM	6m 47s	SUCCEEDED	0.36347
>	71	Y5vPY	6m 44s	SUCCEEDED	0.365744
>	42	eTCe9	5m 59s	SUCCEEDED	0.365832
>	58	RR3n4	2m 16s	SUCCEEDED	0.366578
>	53	O4Obx	4m 38s	SUCCEEDED	0.36709

Figure 7.5: Rain prediction Top 10 hyper-parameter tuning trials

Figure 7.5 shows that the performance on the validation set is pretty close between all top trials. Now let us take a look at the hyper-parameter dependency graph:

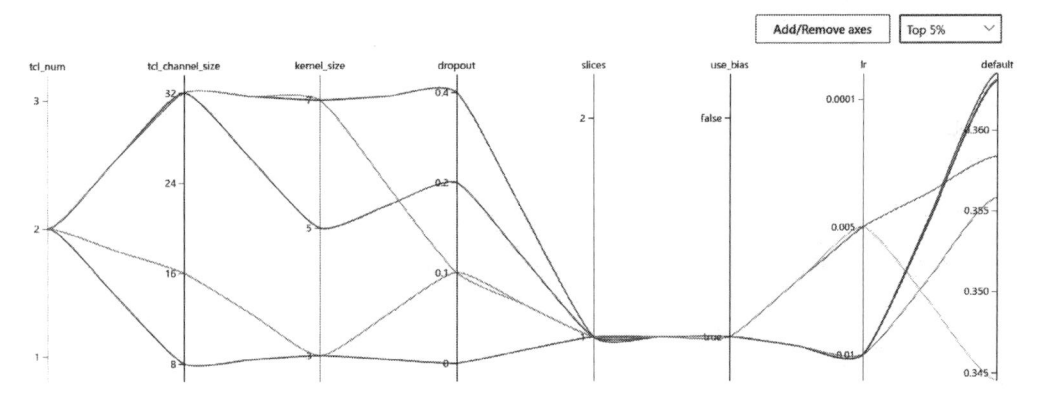

Figure 7.6: Rain prediction Top 5% hyper-parameter dependencies

Here, we see that all successful architectures have the following features:
- Have 2 temporal convolutional layers
- Have 1 slice of casual layers
- Use bias

The best model design for rain prediction problem can be depicted the following ways:

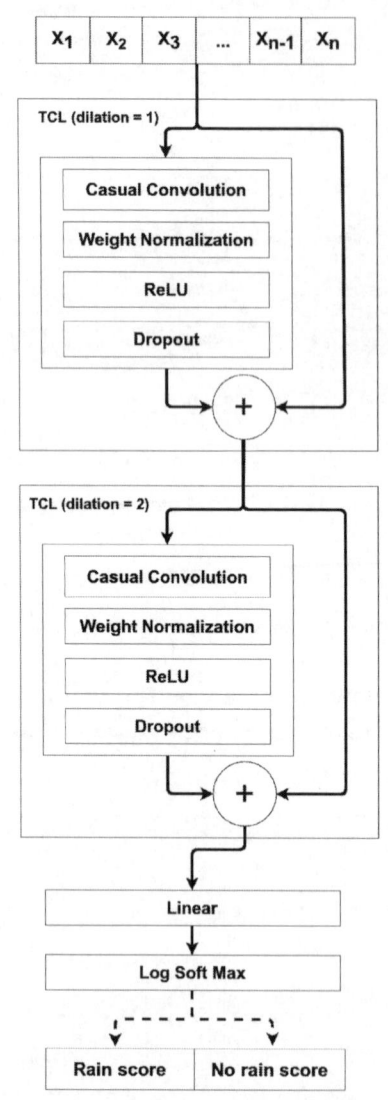

Figure 7.7: Rain prediction best deep learning model design

I hope that the design depicted in *Figure 7.7* no longer confuses you. Let us train and save the model based on the result of the hyper-parameter tuning **ch7/weather/train_and_save.py**:

```
from ch7.weather.train import prepare_model
import random
import numpy as np
```

```
import torch
seed = 1
random.seed(seed)
np.random.seed(seed)
torch.manual_seed(seed)
# NNI result:
# Best trial params:
params = {
    "tcl_num":          2,
    "tcl_channel_size": 32,
    "kernel_size":      7,
    "dropout":          0.1,
    "slices":           1,
    "use_bias":         True,
    "lr":               0.005
}
prepare_model(params, save_model = True, model_name = 'best_model')
```

The result of this script is the model saved in **ch7/weather/data/best_model.pth**.

And now, we come to the most exciting part. Let us try to evaluate the predictive ability of our model. But first, we need to define a criterion for evaluation. There are many different metrics for estimating the quality of a binary classification. For this task, we will use *balanced accuracy* as a common classification metric.

But before moving on to the model evaluation, we need to have several alternative models to compare the quality. We will define several simple forecasts:

- *No rain forecast*. Always assumes that there will be no rain tomorrow.
- *Rain forecast*. It always assumes there will be rain tomorrow.
- *Coin flip forecast*. The forecast is based on a random number.
- *Tomorrow like today forecast*. We know that sunny and rainy days usually follow each other, that's why this forecast can give a lot of *true* predictions.

Let us go to the model evaluation on 2016 **ch7/weather/evaluate.py**.

Import part

```
import os
import random
import torch
from sklearn.metrics import balanced_accuracy_score
from ch7.weather.dataset import get_df_complete
from ch7.weather.model.model import TcnClassifier
from ch7.weather.utils import sliding_window
```

Global parameters

```
dir_path = os.path.dirname(os.path.realpath(__file__))
location = 'Sydney'
w = 14
# We pick 14 before the 2016-01-01 for the sliding window
from_date = '2015-12-17'
to_date = '2017-01-01'
date_fmt = '%Y-%m-%d'
df = get_df_complete()
```

Preparing datasets

```
# features
features_cont = ['MinTemp', 'MaxTemp', 'Rainfall', 'WindGustSpeed', 'WindSpeed9am',
                 'WindSpeed3pm', 'Humidity9am', 'Humidity3pm', 'Pressure9am',
                 'Pressure3pm', 'Cloud9am', 'Cloud3pm', 'Temp9am', 'Temp3pm']
features_cat = ['RainToday']
X, Y = [], []
df_l = df[(df['Location'] == location) & (df.index < to_date) & (df.index > from_date)]
D = []
for f in features_cont:
    D.append(df_l[f].interpolate('linear').fillna(0).values)
```

```python
for f in features_cat:
    D.append(df_1[f].map({'Yes': 1, 'No': 0}).fillna(0).values)
    # transpose to time series
TS = []
for i in range(df_1.shape[0]):
    row = []
    for c in D:
        row.append(c[i])
    TS.append(row)
in_seq, out_seq = sliding_window(TS, w, 1)
rain_seq = [r[0][-1] for r in out_seq]
X.extend(in_seq)
Y.extend(rain_seq)
x_test = torch.tensor(X).float().transpose(1, 2)
```

Initializing the model

```python
model_name = 'best_model'
model_params = {
    'num_inputs':    len(features_cont) + len(features_cat),
    'num_classes':   2,
    'num_channels':  [32] * 2,
    'act':           'relu',
    "kernel_size":   7,
    "dropout":       0.1,
    "slices":        1,
    "use_bias":      True
}
model = TcnClassifier(**model_params)
```

Loading the trained model

```python
model.load_state_dict(torch.load(f'{dir_path}/data/{model_name}.pth'))
model.eval()
```

Making the predictions

```
predicted_prob = model(x_test)
model_prediction = predicted_prob.data.max(1, keepdim = True)[1].view(-1).tolist()
```

Alternative predictions

```
no_rain_prediction = [0] * len(Y)
no_sun_prediction = [1] * len(Y)
coin_flip_prediction = [random.randint(0, 1) for _ in range(len(Y))]
tomorrow_like_today_prediction = x_test[:, -1, -1].view(-1).tolist()
```

Computing scores

```
ba_sc = balanced_accuracy_score
model_score = round(ba_sc(Y, model_prediction), 4)
no_rain_score = round(ba_sc(Y, no_rain_prediction), 4)
no_sun_score = round(ba_sc(Y, no_sun_prediction), 4)
coin_flip_score = round(ba_sc(Y, coin_flip_prediction), 4)
tlt_score = round(ba_sc(Y, tomorrow_like_today_prediction), 4)
```

Printing the results

```
print(f'Model Prediction Score: {model_score}')
print(f'No Rain Prediction Score: {no_rain_score}')
print(f'Rain Prediction Score: {no_sun_score}')
print(f'Coin Flip Prediction Score: {coin_flip_score}')
print(f'Tomorrow like Today Prediction Score: {tlt_score}')
```

Result

Model Prediction Score	0.7644
No Rain Prediction Score	0.5
Rain Prediction Score	0.5
Coin Flip Prediction Score	0.4934
Tomorrow like Today Prediction Score	0.623

Table 7.2: Rain Prediction Models Results

If you are familiar with the methodology of calculating balanced accuracy, you could immediately assume that *No Rain Forecast*, *Rain Forecast*, and *Coin Flip Forecast* will have a score of about 0.5. The model we have developed shows a fairly high result for this type of problem. We can certainly accept this model as a successful one.

COVID-19 confirmed cases forecast

In 2020, humanity was attacked by a deadly virus for which we were not ready. The nature of the COVID-19 virus was completely obscure. Initially, it was not obvious how exactly it spreads and the experts do not know how to properly heal people. Many intellectual resources of mankind have been directed to cope with this disaster.

One of the apparent problems was the attempt to predict the increase of confirmed cases of COVID-19 diseases. The problem was complicated by the fact that the nature of the virus was totally unknown. Different countries have taken diverse measures to combat with the virus, and there was not any historical data. But despite all these facts, let's try to make a long-term forecast for the number of confirmed cases.

Let's assume we are in Austria in 2021-01-31. We want to make a forecast for the number of cases for the next 60 days - a pretty ambitious and challenging task.

We have the following historical data `ch7/covid/data/COVID_19_until_2021_02_01.csv`:

Date	Date of observation
Country	Country of observation
Province	Province of observation
Confirmed	Confirmed disease cases
Recovered	Successful recoveries
Deaths	Lethal cases

Table 7.3: Covid-19 dataset columns

Let us analyze this dataset `ch7/covid/analyze.py`.

We load the dataset and set global parameters:

```
df = get_df_until_2021_02_01()
date_fmt = '%Y-%m-%d'
start_date = datetime.datetime.strptime('2020-01-22', date_fmt)
end_date = datetime.datetime.strptime('2021-02-01', date_fmt)
date_list = mdates.drange(start_date, end_date, dt.timedelta(days = 1))
```

Let us plot total number of cases in Austria:

```
aus_df = df[df['Country'] == 'Austria']
aus_confirmed = aus_df['Confirmed'].values
plt.title('Total number of Confirmed cases')
plt.gca().xaxis.set_major_formatter(mdates.DateFormatter(date_fmt))
plt.gca().xaxis.set_major_locator(mdates.DayLocator(interval = 90))
plt.plot(date_list[:], aus_confirmed, color = 'blue')
plt.show()
```

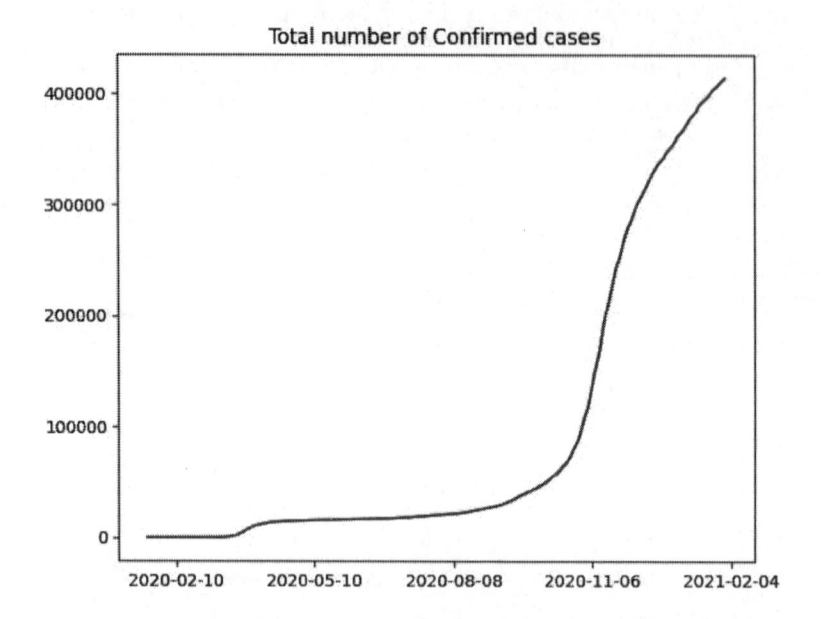

Figure 7.8: Total number of confirmed cases in Austria

This time series has an apparent upward nonlinear trend, which is evident since it is the sum of non-negative numbers (a cumulative sum). Let us use time series differencing:

```
aus_confirmed_diff = df[df['Country'] == 'Austria']['Confirmed'].diff().fillna(0)
plt.title('Daily Increase of Confirmed cases')
plt.gca().xaxis.set_major_formatter(mdates.DateFormatter(date_fmt))
plt.gca().xaxis.set_major_locator(mdates.DayLocator(interval = 90))
plt.plot(date_list[:], aus_confirmed_diff, color = 'blue')
plt.show()
```

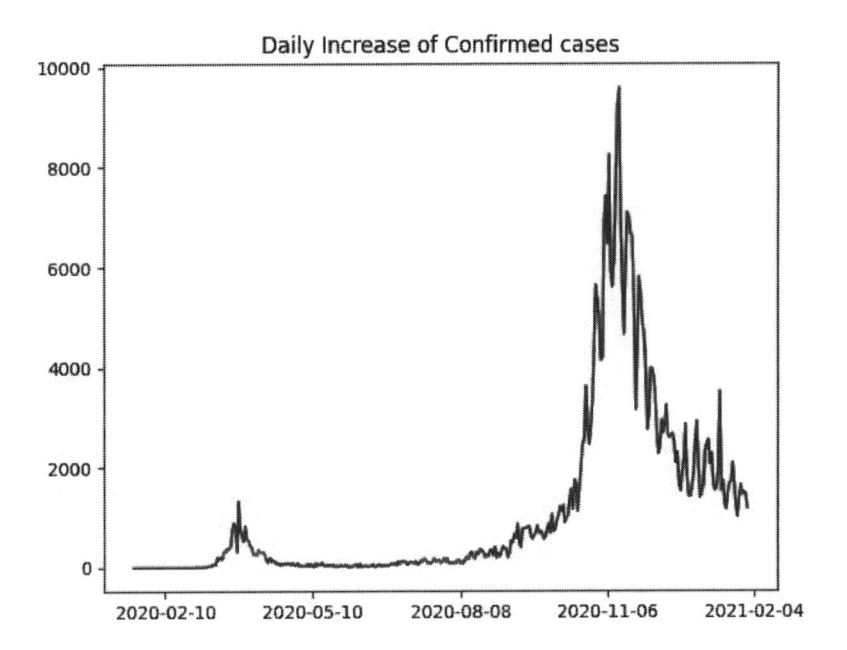

Figure 7.9: Daily increase of confirmed cases in Austria

Time series shown in *figure 7.9* has no obvious patterns. The main problem here is the lack of historical data. We have no choice but to start analyzing data from neighboring countries: Italy, Russia, Hungary, Israel, and Poland. Since all these countries differ in the number of citizens, it would be reasonable to normalize the time series for each country:

```
countries = ['Austria', 'Italy', 'Russia', 'Hungary', 'Israel',
'Poland']
plt.title('Daily Increase of Confirmed cases by Countries')
plt.gca().xaxis.set_major_formatter(mdates.DateFormatter(date_fmt))
plt.gca().xaxis.set_major_locator(mdates.DayLocator(interval = 90))
for c in countries:
    plt.title(f'Confirmed')
    ts = df[df['Country'] == c]['Confirmed'].diff().fillna(0).values
    ts = ts / max(ts)
    plt.plot(ts, label = c)
```

```
plt.legend()
plt.show()
```

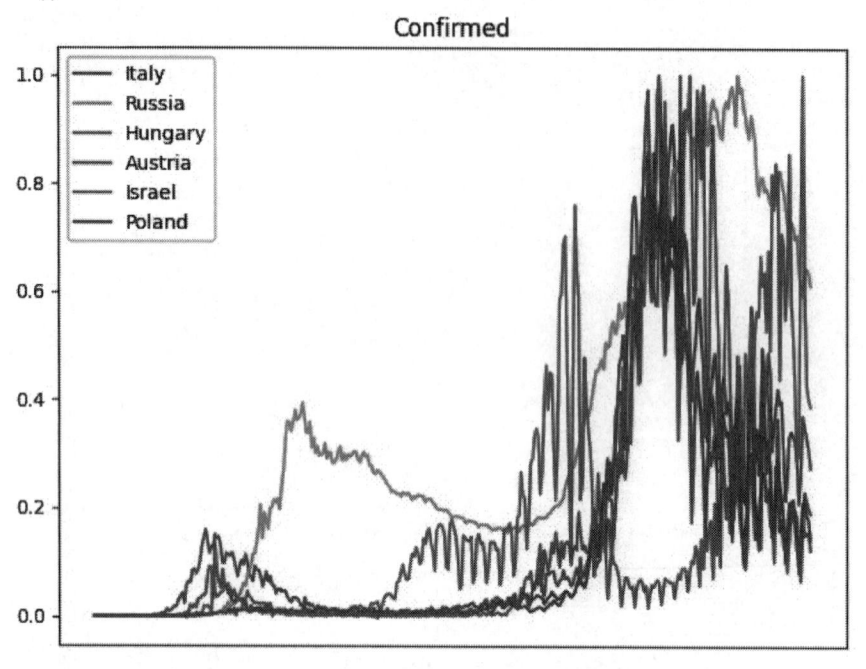

Figure 7.10: Daily increase of Confirmed cases in different countries

We can see that time series have a lot of spikes. That happens due to the specifics of observations in each country. It makes sense to apply statistical filters: Hodrick–Prescott Trend filter and Christiano Fitzgerald Cycle filter:

```
aus_confirmed_diff_norm = aus_confirmed_diff / max(aus_confirmed_diff)
_, train_hp_trend = sm.tsa.filters.hpfilter(aus_confirmed_diff_norm)
train_cf_cycle, _ = sm.tsa.filters.cffilter(aus_confirmed_diff_norm)
plt.title('Trend and Cycle filters')
plt.gca().xaxis.set_major_formatter(mdates.DateFormatter(date_fmt))
plt.gca().xaxis.set_major_locator(mdates.DayLocator(interval = 90))
plt.plot(date_list[:], aus_confirmed_diff_norm, color = 'blue', label = 'original')
plt.plot(date_list[:], train_hp_trend, color = 'orange', label = 'trend filter', linewidth = 3)
plt.plot(date_list[:], train_cf_cycle, color = 'green', label = 'cycle filter')
plt.show()
```

Trend and Cycle filters

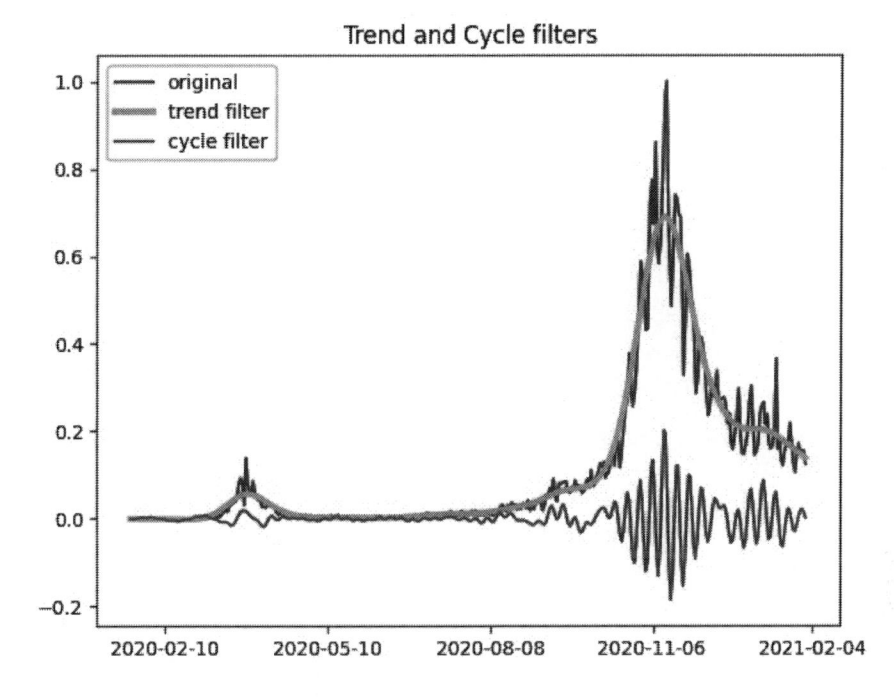

Figure 7.11: Daily increase of confirmed cases with statistical filters

We can see that statistical filters make a good separation of the time series into trend and cyclical fluctuations.

So, our training dataset will contain 18 features. Three time series types: *original, trend filter, cycle filter* for six countries: *Austria, Italy, Russia, Israel, Poland,* and *Hungary*.

```
countries_count = len(countries)
fig = plt.figure()
fig.set_size_inches(5, 8)
for i in range(countries_count):
    c = countries[i]
    ax = fig.add_subplot(countries_count * 100 + 10 + i + 1)
    ts = df[df['Country'] == c]['Confirmed'].diff().fillna(0).values
    ts = ts / max(ts)
    _, train_hp_trend = sm.tsa.filters.hpfilter(ts)
    train_cf_cycle, _ = sm.tsa.filters.cffilter(ts)
    ax.set_title(c)
    ax.axis('off')
```

```
    ax.plot(ts)
    ax.plot(train_hp_trend, color = 'orange')
    ax.plot(train_cf_cycle, color = 'green')
plt.show()
```

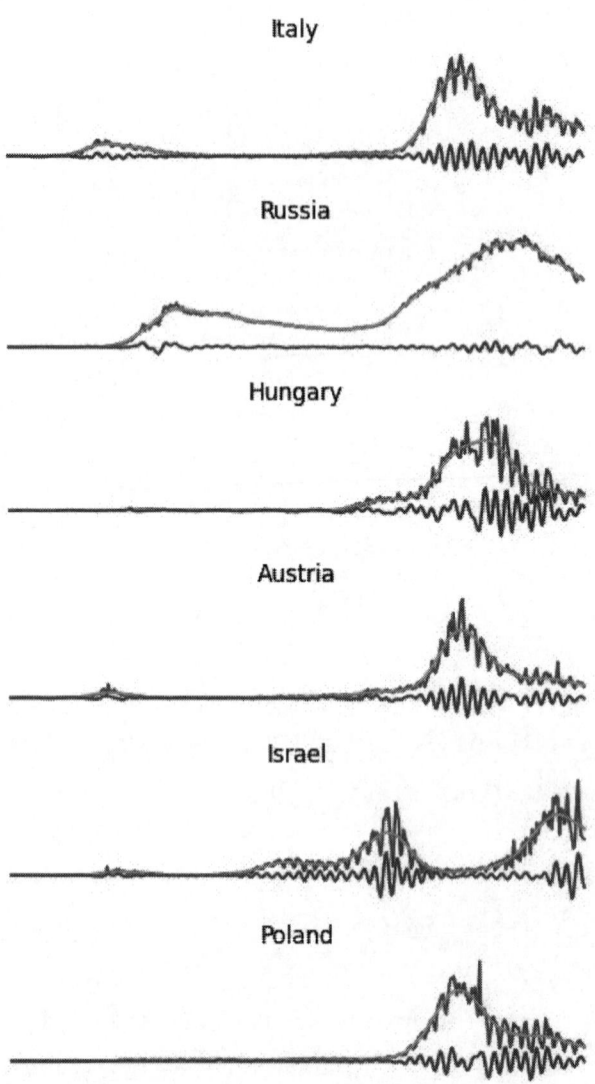

Figure 7.12: All 18 input time series

Here, we have a multivariate input multi-step prediction problem. In *Chapter 5, Advanced Forecasting Models*, we have studied the encoder–decoder model, which is well suited for multi-step prediction problems. Let us use it for this task as well **ch7/covid/model/model.py**.

For this task, we will use a similar approach as we used for the rain prediction task. From the sliding window dataset, we randomly select samples for the validation set. We start the process of finding the optimal hyper-parameters for the encoder–decoder model. The best model is the one that will perform best on the validation set. We initialize the model with the best hyper-parameters, train, and save it.

Let's consider the training process `ch7/covid/train.py`:

Import part

```
import os
import random
import torch
import statsmodels.api as sm
from ch7.covid.dataset import get_df_until_2021_02_01
from ch7.covid.model.model import EncoderDecoder
from ch7.covid.utils import sliding_window
```

Model preparation function

The function receives model and training parameters and saves the best model parameters to disk if necessary:

```
def prepare_model(params, save_model = False, model_name = 'enc_dec'):
```

Global parameters

```
    dir_path = os.path.dirname(os.path.realpath(__file__))
    df = get_df_until_2021_02_01()
    start_date = '2020-01-01'
    end_date = '2021-02-01'
    countries = ['Italy', 'Russia', 'Hungary', 'Austria', 'Israel', 'Poland']
    # size of the sliding window
    w = 120
    # length of prediction
    out = 60
    # number of training epochs
    epochs = 2_00
```

Model hyper-parameters

```
hidden_size = params['hidden_size']
hidden_dl_size = params['hidden_dl_size']
lr = params['lr']
tfr = params['tfr']
```

Preparing sliding window datasets

As we discussed before, this dataset contains 18 features. Normalized original time series, trend filter, and cycle filter for each of six countries:

```
X, Y = [], []
for c in countries:
    # diff
    ts_df = df[df['Country'] == c]['Confirmed'].diff().dropna()
    train = ts_df[start_date:end_date].values
    # Normalized time series
    train = train / max(train)
    # Statistical pre-processing
    _, train_hp_trend = sm.tsa.filters.hpfilter(train)
    train_cf_cycle, _ = sm.tsa.filters.cffilter(train)
    D = []
    for i in range(len(train)):
        D.append([train[i], train_hp_trend[i], train_cf_cycle[i]])
    # input - output for country
    X_c, Y_c = sliding_window(D, w, out)
    X.extend(X_c)
    Y.extend(Y_c)
```

Creating train/validation datasets

```
X_train, Y_train = [], []
X_val, Y_val = [], []
for i in range(len(X)):
    if random.random() > .8:
        X_val.append(X[i])
```

```
            Y_val.append(Y[i])
    else:
        X_train.append(X[i])
        Y_train.append(Y[i])
```

Converting datasets to tensors

```
x_train = torch.tensor(X_train).float().transpose(0, 1)
y_train = torch.tensor(Y_train).float().transpose(0, 1)[:, :, 0]
x_val = torch.tensor(X_val).float().transpose(0, 1)
y_val = torch.tensor(Y_val).float().transpose(0, 1)[:, :, 0]
```

Initializing the model

```
model_params = {
    'hidden_size':    hidden_size,
    'hidden_dl_size': hidden_dl_size,
    'input_size':     3,
    'output_size':    1
}
model = EncoderDecoder(**model_params)
model.train()
```

Training and getting the results

```
model_params, val = model.train_model(
    x_train, y_train, x_val, y_val, epochs, out,
    method = 'mixed_teacher_forcing', tfr = tfr, lr = lr)
# Saving the model if necessary
if save_model:
    torch.save(model_params, f'{dir_path}/data/{model_name}.pth')
return val
```

The encoder–decoder model, like all recurrent models, takes a lot of training time. Therefore, we will not use a vast search space for hyper-parameter tuning **ch7/covid/search.py**:

```
search_space = {
    "hidden_size":    {"_type": "choice", "_value": [8, 12, 16, 24, 32, 64]},
```

```
    "hidden_dl_size": {"_type": "choice", "_value": [4, 6, 8, 12]},
    "lr":             {"_type": "choice", "_value": [.001, .005, .01]},
    "tfr":            {"_type": "choice", "_value": [.1, .2, .3, .4, .5]}
}
```

Now let us launch the optimization process `ch7/covid/search.py`. This process can take several hours. Therefore you can use the results obtained by the author:

Best trial params:

```
{
    'hidden_size':    32,
    'hidden_dl_size': 12,
    'lr':             .01,
    'tfr':            .1,
}
```

Let's analyze the results:

Trial No.	ID	Duration	Status	Default me... ↑
7	YRSxx	5m 1s	SUCCEEDED	0.013064
148	NyWAs	4m 6s	SUCCEEDED	0.013331
263	MewXP	6m 27s	SUCCEEDED	0.013673
222	D6pmo	3m 54s	SUCCEEDED	0.013696
53	JlWmv	5m 47s	SUCCEEDED	0.01418
160	ELUSJ	4m 15s	SUCCEEDED	0.014606
238	LST4d	4m 0s	SUCCEEDED	0.014641
298	tg3XG	5m 45s	SUCCEEDED	0.014908
13	XOBu8	12m 41s	SUCCEEDED	0.014922
205	ztO1a	5m 47s	SUCCEEDED	0.01536

Figure 7.13: Top 10 trials for the COVID-19 prediction problem

All the results are pretty close to each other. Let's look at the hyper-parameter dependency matrix:

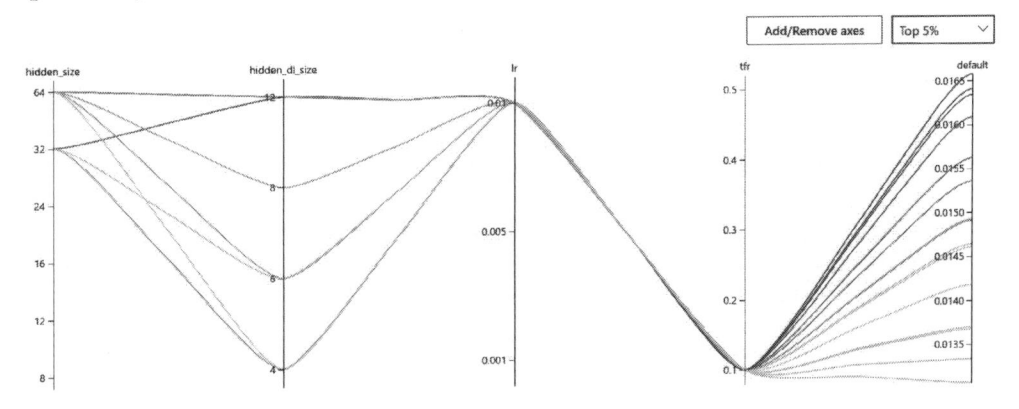

Figure 7.14: Top 10 trials for the COVID-19 prediction problem

Figure 7.14 shows that all successive trials have common features:

- 32 or 64 hidden size
- The size of the hidden decision layer is not so important
- High *learning rate* = 0.01
- Very low *teacher forcing rate* = 0.1

Let us train and save the model with the best hyper-parameters **ch7/covid/train_and_save.py**:

```
from ch7.covid.train import prepare_model
import random
import numpy as np
import torch
seed = 1
random.seed(seed)
np.random.seed(seed)
torch.manual_seed(seed)
# NNI result:
# Best trial params:
# {'hidden_size': 32, 'hidden_dl_size': 12, 'lr': 0.01, 'tfr': 0.1}
params = {
```

```
    'hidden_size':      32,
    'hidden_dl_size': 12,
    'lr':               .01,
    'tfr':              .1,
}
prepare_model(params, save_model = True, model_name = 'best_model')
```

Our model is trained and saved in **ch7/covid/data/best_model.pth**. So, now we are ready to make the long-term prediction we have been looking for **ch7/covid/prediction.py**.

Import part

```
import datetime
import os
import datetime as dt
import torch
import statsmodels.api as sm
import matplotlib.pyplot as plt
import matplotlib.dates as mdates
from ch7.covid.dataset import get_df_until_2021_02_01
from ch7.covid.model.model import EncoderDecoder
```

Global parameters

```
dir_path = os.path.dirname(os.path.realpath(__file__))
# we need only one time sequence with 120 length
from_date = '2020-10-04'
to_date = '2021-02-01'
date_fmt = '%Y-%m-%d'
country = 'Austria'
```

Creating the input

Our model makes only one long-term prediction and needs only one input for that:

```
df = get_df_until_2021_02_01()
au_ts_df = df[df['Country'] == country]['Confirmed'].diff().dropna()
```

```
test = au_ts_df[from_date:to_date].values
max_test = max(test)
test = test / max_test
test_hp_cycle, test_hp_trend = sm.tsa.filters.hpfilter(test)
test_cf_cycle, test_cf_trend = sm.tsa.filters.cffilter(test)
X = []
for i in range(len(test)):
    X.append([test[i], test_hp_trend[i], test_cf_cycle[i]])
x = torch.tensor([X]).float().transpose(0, 1)
```

Initializing the model

```
model_name = 'best_model'
model_params = {
    'hidden_size':    32,
    'hidden_dl_size': 12,
    'input_size':     3,
    'output_size':    1
}
model = EncoderDecoder(**model_params)
model.load_state_dict(torch.load(f'{dir_path}/data/{model_name}.pth'))
model.eval()
```

Making the prediction

```
predicted = model.predict(x, 60)
```

Plotting the prediction

```
in_seq = [e * max_test for e in x[:, -1, 0].view(-1).tolist()]
pred_seq = [e * max_test for e in predicted[:, -1, 0].view(-1).tolist()]
x_axis = range(len(in_seq) + len(pred_seq))
start_date = datetime.datetime.strptime(from_date, date_fmt)
end_date = start_date + datetime.timedelta(days = len(in_seq))
prediction_date = start_date + datetime.timedelta(days = len(in_seq) + len(pred_seq))
date_list = mdates.drange(start_date, prediction_date, dt.timedelta(days = 1))
```

```
plt.title(f'Prediction for next 60 days')
plt.gca().xaxis.set_major_formatter(mdates.DateFormatter(date_fmt))
plt.gca().xaxis.set_major_locator(mdates.DayLocator(interval = 35))
plt.plot(date_list[:], in_seq + pred_seq, color = 'blue')
plt.plot(date_list[len(in_seq):],
         pred_seq,
         label = 'Model prediction',
         color = 'orange',
         linewidth = 3)
plt.vlines(end_date, 0, max_test, color = 'grey')
plt.legend(loc = "upper right")
plt.gcf().autofmt_xdate()
plt.show()
```

Result

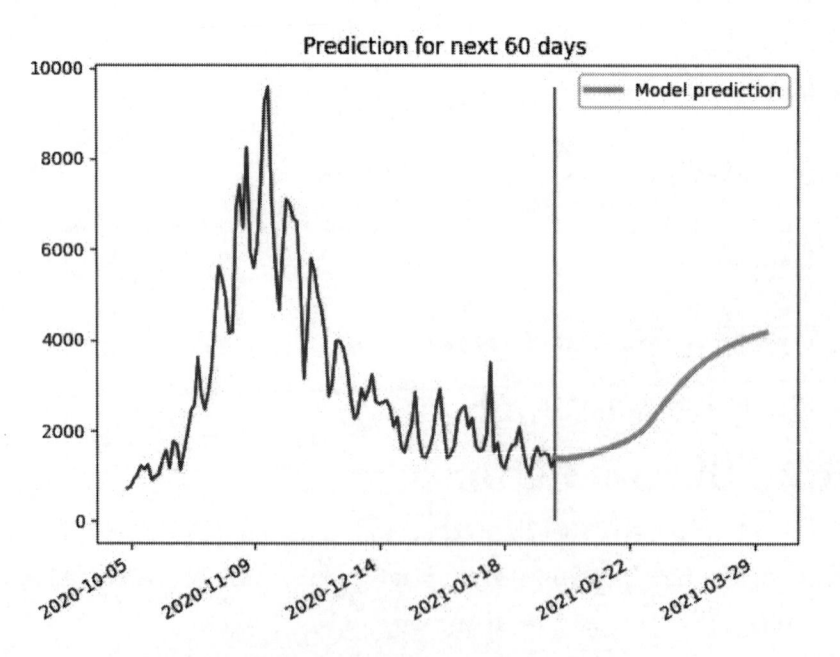

Figure 7.15: COVID-19 confirmed cases prediction for Austria

The forecast is not very optimistic. The model shows that there will be no recession, and after a while, the growth will resume. Let us compare our prediction with the actual data we know so far **ch7/covid/evaluate.py**:

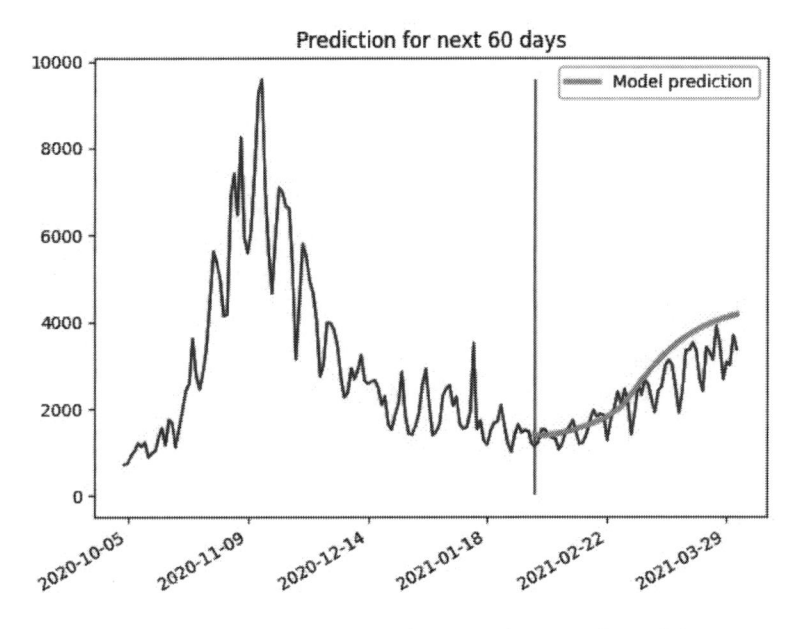

Figure 7.16: COVID-19 confirmed cases prediction and actual data

And that is a fantastic result! We can visually confirm that our model made a pretty accurate prediction. Long-term forecasts are very complicated and have a high error degree. But the prediction made by the encoder–decoder model is pretty accurate. The significance of this forecast is that it has predicted the start of growth in a downtrend. Such forecasts are especially difficult because most predictive models tend to support the current trend rather than make predictions against its movement.

Algorithmic trading

Yes, I know you have been waiting for it! Now, we are starting to consider one of the most common applications of time series analysis. We must admit that many people are trying to apply their knowledge in statistics, game theory, and deep learning to predict changes in financial markets because successful forecasts yield good profits. Even though quote prices are often difficult to distinguish from a random walk, many scientists try to find a robust predictive model for the trading. We will try to do the same in this section.

Algorithmic trading uses a predefined set of rules (an algorithm) to place a trade. Here, we will use a simplified trading model.

Now let us define the trading mechanics. Say we bought today 1 share of stock for 100$. Tomorrow its prices rise to 110$. We sell our share for 110$, and we earn 110$ - 100$ = 10$. This section will consider daily trading, which means that the trade is made once per day.

Let us analyze the trader's diary:

	Shares	Stock Daily Close Price	Returns
Day #1	No Shares	100$	0
Day #2	2 Shares	110$	(110 – 100) ×2 + 0 = 20$
Day #3	2 Shares	105$	(105 – 110)×2 + 20 = 10$
Day #4	-1 Share	100$	(100 - 105)×(-1) + 10 = 15$
Day #5	-1 Share	95$	(95 - 100) ×(-1) + 15 = 20$

So the trading returns can be defined in the following way:

$$\sum (C_{i+1} - C_i) S_i$$

where

- C_i - Stock Close Price
- S_i – Number of Shares

Algorithmic trading is similar to the following prediction model:

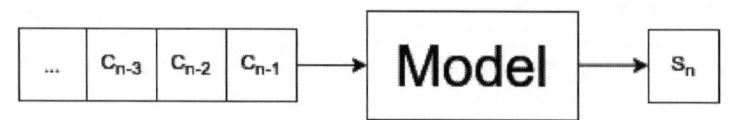

Figure 7.17: Algorithmic Trading as a prediction model

Knowing the previous values of a price sequence or events, we must define the number of shares to buy to maximize our profit. Naturally, you should attempt to buy shares before the price goes up and sell shares before the price goes down.

Please install these additional packages to continue further:

pip install yfinance

pip install pandas_ta

Suppose, we are at the end of 2019 and want to build a predictive model for trading in the stock market. We will choose Microsoft stock as a trading tool. Let us visualize quotes for Microsoft from 2009 to the end of 2019 **ch7/stock/visualize.py**:

```
import matplotlib.pyplot as plt
from ch7.stock.dataset import get_df_until_2020
q = get_df_until_2020()
q['Close'].plot()
plt.show()
```

Result

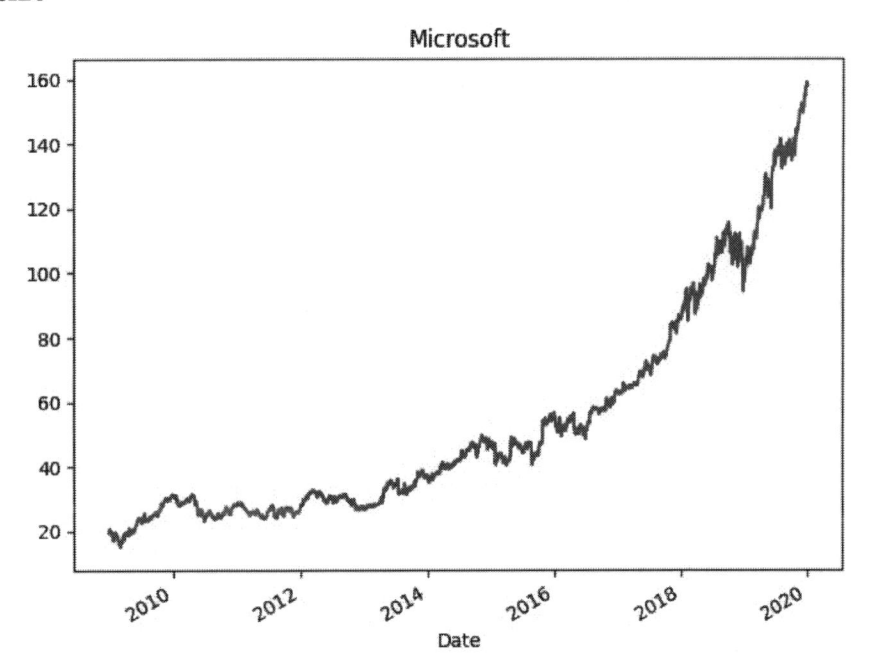

Figure 7.18: Microsoft quotes history from 2009 to the end of 2019

This time series has a clear upward trend. *Buy-and-Hold* may seem like the best strategy for this stock. This strategy implies a one-time purchase of shares and holding them for a long time. We will definitely compare the results of our model with the *Buy-and-Hold* strategy.

Trading has become an isolated research area with its own tools and approaches. Technical indicators are essential tools in helping a trader identify to get insights from the market **ch7/stock/indicators.py**:

```
import pandas_ta as ta
import matplotlib.pyplot as plt
from ch7.stock.dataset import get_df_until_2020
q = get_df_until_2020()
fig, axes = plt.subplots(nrows = 3)
fig.set_size_inches(5, 7)
axes[0].set_title('Microsoft Quotes')
q['Close'].plot(ax = axes[0])
axes[1].set_title('Momentum Indicator')
```

```
q.ta.ao(9, 14).plot(ax = axes[1])
axes[2].set_title('RSI Indicator')
q.ta.rsi(20).plot(ax = axes[2])
axes[0].xaxis.set_visible(False)
axes[1].xaxis.set_visible(False)
axes[2].xaxis.set_visible(False)
plt.show()
```

Result

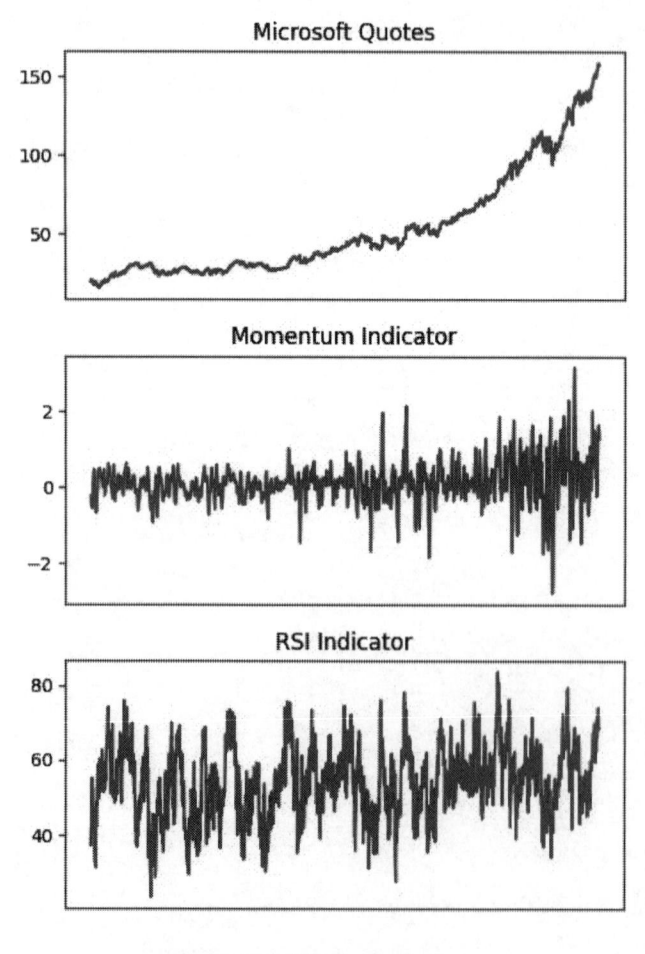

Figure 7.19: Trading Indicators

The description of technical indicators and their interpretation rules lies far beyond the scope of this book. We will not be doing this here. But let us leave our deep learning model to choose the best indicators for its prediction ability. In our prediction model, we will use the following indicators:

- Awesome Oscillator (ao)
- Absolute Price Oscillator (apo)
- Commodity Channel Index (cci)
- Chande Momentum Oscillator (cmo)
- Momentum (mom)
- Relative Strength Index (rsi)
- True strength index (tsi)

We will use **pandas_ta** library for the implementation of indicators mentioned above **ch7/stock/utils.py**:

```
import pandas_ta as ta
def get_indicator(q, ind_name, params):
    ts = None
    if ind_name == 'ao':
        ts = q.ta.ao(params['fast'], params['slow'])
    elif ind_name == 'apo':
        ts = q.ta.apo(params['fast'], params['slow'])
    elif ind_name == 'cci':
        ts = q.ta.cci(params['length']) / 100
    elif ind_name == 'cmo':
        ts = q.ta.cmo(params['length']) / 100
    elif ind_name == 'mom':
        ts = q.ta.mom(params['length'])
    elif ind_name == 'rsi':
        ts = q.ta.rsi(params['length']) / 100
    elif ind_name == 'tsi':
        ts = q.ta.tsi(params['fast'], params['slow']) / 100
    return ts
```

Trading income does not depend on the absolute close price value but only on the difference between the close prices. Therefore, it will be natural to use time series differencing for the close prices **ch7/stock/ts_diff.py**:

242 ■ Time Series Forecasting using Deep Learning

```
import matplotlib.pyplot as plt
from ch7.stock.dataset import get_df_until_2020
q = get_df_until_2020()
(q['Close'] - q['Close'].shift(1)).plot()
plt.title('Microsoft Quotes Absolute Change')
plt.show()
```

Result

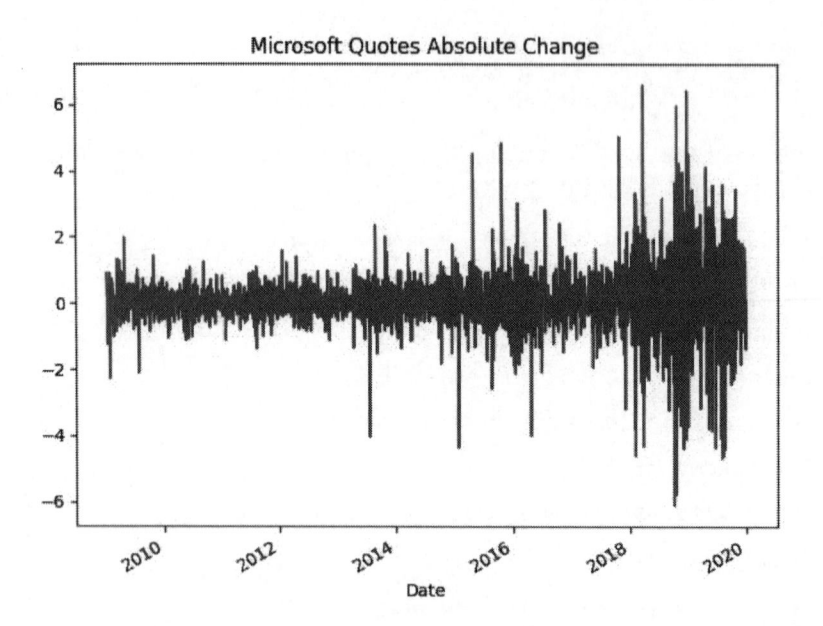

Figure 7.20: Quotes absolute change

Figure 7.20 demonstrates that the absolute price changes increase over time. It is easy to explain that the more expensive a stock is, the higher the absolute deviation in its price. Therefore, we can also use relative price changes C_i / C_{i-1}:

```
(q['Close'] / q['Close'].shift(1)).plot()
plt.title('Microsoft Quotes Relative Change')
plt.show()
```

Result

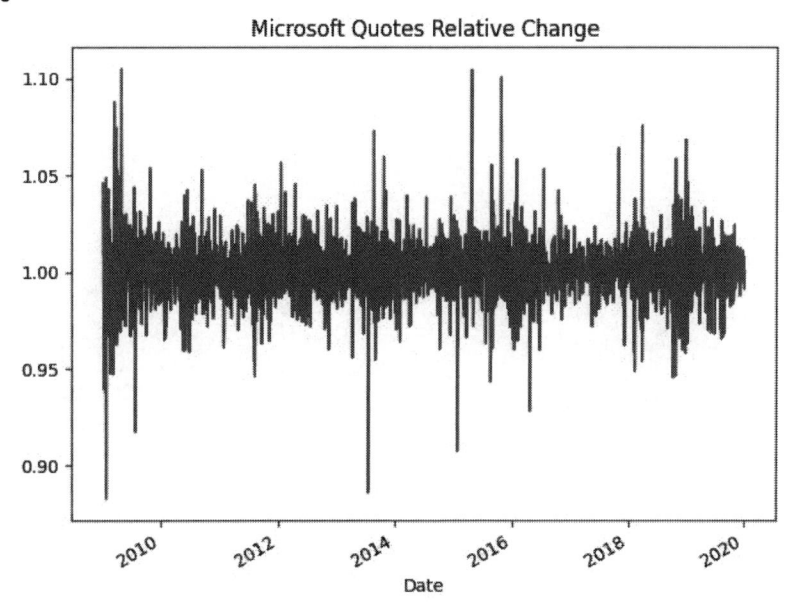

Figure 7.21: *Quotes Relative Change*

We see in *Figure 7.21* that the relative changes have a much more regular structure.

So far we have done the following:

- We defined the *trading rules*.
- We determined how *trading returns* are calculated.
- We decided that we will use *absolute* and *relative* quote changes as input for the deep learning model.
- We decided which trading *indicators* we will use for our trading model.

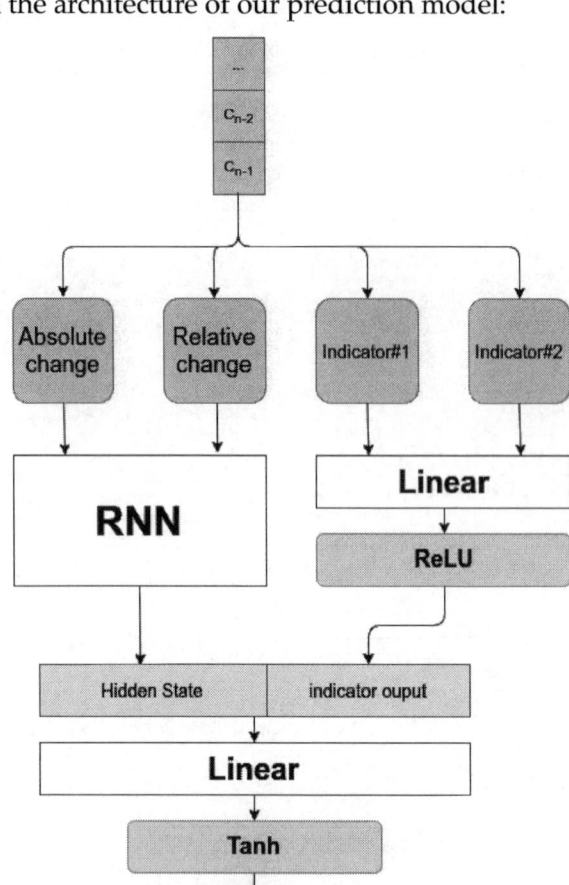

Now let us design the architecture of our prediction model:

Figure 7.22: Algorithmic Trading Prediction Model

The model depicted in *figure 7.22* assumes two input types:

- *Absolute* and *relative* time series change for a Recurrent Neural Network Layer.
- Two indicator values for a Linear Layer.

Trading indicators are calculated on a historical time series sequence, so its output is slightly similar to RNN's hidden state output. Let us consider Chande Momentum Oscillator formula:

$$CMO(n) = \frac{\sum_{i=1}^{n} pos(i) - \sum_{i=1}^{n} neg(i)}{n} \times 100$$

where

- $pos(i) = 1$ if $C_{i-1} < C_i$ and 0 otherwise
- $neg(i) = 1$ if $C_{i-1} > C_i$ and 0 otherwise

Simply speaking, Chande Momentum Oscillator calculates the ratio of positive price changes to negative ones for n days ago. For example, if we have the following time series: 100, 101, 105, 100, 102, then CMO (4) will be equal to 75 because we have three positive moves and one negative. This example shows that trading indicators analyze the history of price changes and return a number characterizing the dynamics of price changes in the past, which can be interpreted as a hidden memory of price movements. That is why we do not apply RNN to the indicator value sequence. RNN's hidden state is concatenated with the result of the indicator's linear layer. After that, the decision linear layer with *tanh* activation function is applied. The result of this neural network is the number of shares to buy in the next step. The number of shares should be normalized and be in [-1, 1] range. Therefore, we cannot replace *tanh* with another activation function.

Tanh is a continuous function and can take any value in the range [-1, 1]. In the real world, we cannot buy stocks in any proportion. So, we need to use rounding anyway. But any rounding function has a derivative equal to zero almost everywhere:

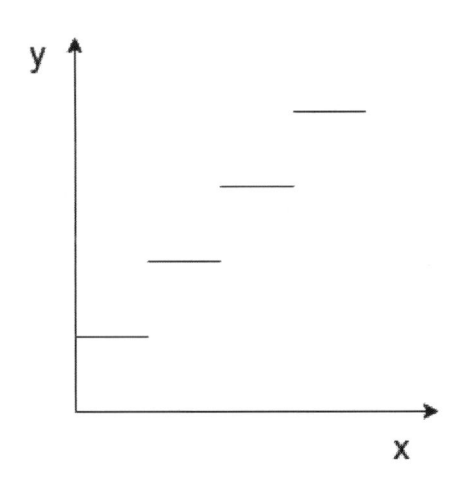

Figure 7.23: Rounding function graph

And hence, it cannot be applied in the gradient descent algorithm. We will not use any rounding during model training and will assume that it is allowed to buy shares in any pieces. But we will use shares rounding in evaluation mode.

Let us take a look at implementation of this model **ch7/stock/model/model.py**:

```
import torch
import torch.nn as nn
```

```python
class AlgoTrader(nn.Module):
    def __init__(self,
                 rnn_input_size,
                 ind_input_size,
                 rnn_type = 'gru',
                 rnn_hidden_size = 16,
                 ind_hidden_size = 4,
                 des_size = 4,
                 ind_dropout = 0,
                 des_dropout = 0
                 ):
        super(AlgoTrader, self).__init__()
        rnn_params = {
            'input_size':  rnn_input_size,
            'hidden_size': rnn_hidden_size,
            'batch_first': True
        }
        if rnn_type == 'gru':
            self.rnn = nn.GRU(**rnn_params)
        elif rnn_type == 'rnn':
            self.rnn = nn.RNN(**rnn_params)
        else:
            raise Exception(f'This type is not supported: {rnn_type}')
        self.rnn_input_size = rnn_input_size
        self.ind_input_size = ind_input_size
        self.lin_ind = nn.Linear(ind_input_size, ind_hidden_size)
        self.lin_des = nn.Linear(rnn_hidden_size + ind_hidden_size, des_size)
        self.lin_pos = nn.Linear(des_size, 1)
        self.ind_drop = nn.Dropout(p = ind_dropout)
        self.des_drop = nn.Dropout(p = des_dropout)
    def forward(self, raw, indicators, rnn_h = None):
        _, h = self.rnn(raw, rnn_h)
        z = torch.relu(self.lin_ind(indicators))
```

```
x = torch.cat((z, h[0]), dim = 1)
x = torch.relu(self.lin_des(x))
p = torch.tanh(self.lin_pos(x))
return p.view(-1)
```

The model we defined has the following hyper-parameters:

- *rnn_type*. The type of RNN network: *rnn* or *gru* allowed.
- *rnn_hidden_size*. The hidden state size of RNN network.
- *ind_hidden_size*. The size of the indicator linear layer.
- *des_size*. The size of decision linear layer.

So, we are almost ready to start the training process. But what will be the training loss function? We use the mean income as a quality score of our model:

$$\frac{\sum_i (C_{i+1} - C_i) S_i}{n}$$

PyTorch does not have a built-in function to calculate this formula. But we can implement this custom loss function by ourselves **ch7/stock/utils.py**:

```
class NegativeMeanReturnLoss(nn.Module):
    def __init__(self):
        super(NegativeMeanReturnLoss, self).__init__()
    def forward(self, lots, price_diff):
        abs_return = torch.mul(lots.view(-1), price_diff)
        ar = torch.mean(abs_return)
        return torch.neg(ar)
```

PyTorch model training aims to minimize the loss function. But in our case, on the contrary, we want to maximize the income that the model produces. Therefore, we will use a negative value for our loss function. That is the typical pattern when we want to maximize a loss function.

As in the previous examples, we started the hyper-parameter tuning process. We pick the parameters which makes the best performance on the validation dataset:

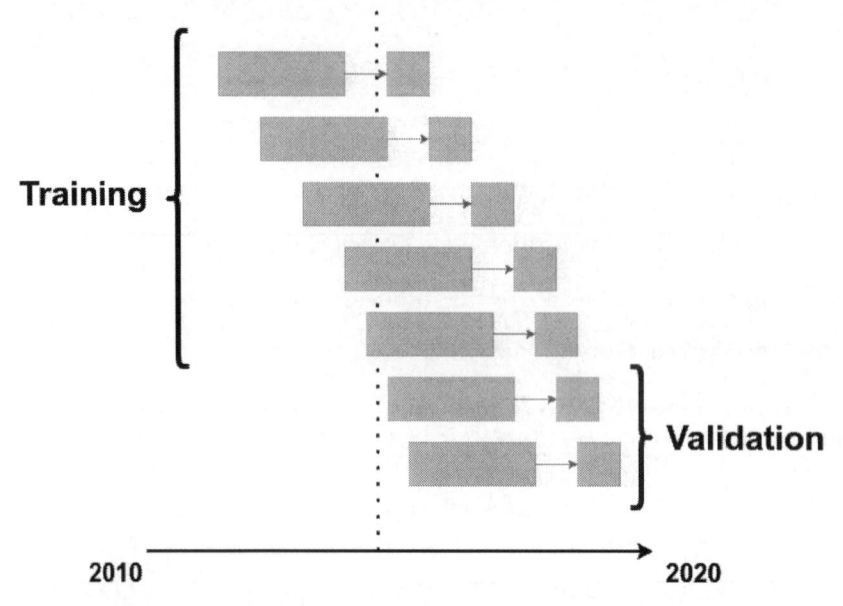

Figure 7.24: Algorithmic trading Training and Validation datasets

After that, we train the model with the best parameters and save it. Let us examine the training process **ch7/stock/train.py**.

Import part

```
import copy
import os
import torch
from typing import OrderedDict
from torch import optim
from ch7.stock.dataset import get_df_until_2020
from ch7.stock.model.model import AlgoTrader
from ch7.stock.utils import sliding_window, NegativeMeanReturnLoss, get_indicator
```

Model preparation function

The function receives model and training parameters and saves the best model parameters to disk if necessary:

```
def prepare_model(params, save_model = False, model_name = 'algo_
trader'):
```

Global parameters

```
    dir_path = os.path.dirname(os.path.realpath(__file__))
    start_date = '2010-01-01'
    end_date = '2020-01-01'
    w = 40
    epochs = 5_00
    train_val_ratio = .8
```

Model hyper-parameters

We are using a hybrid model here. Therefore, hyper-parameter tuning will try to find the best combination of indicators that will be used for model training and evaluation:

```
    lr = params['lr']
    rnn_type = params['rnn_type']
    rnn_hidden_size = params['rnn_hidden_size']
    ind_hidden_size = params['ind_hidden_size']
    des_size = params['des_size']
    ind1_name = params['ind1']['_name']
    ind2_name = params['ind2']['_name']
```

Preparing sliding window dataset

```
    q = get_df_until_2020()
    q = q[q.index < end_date]
    ts_len = q[q.index > start_date].shape[0]
    train_len = int(ts_len * train_val_ratio)
    data_source = OrderedDict()
    data_source['close_diff'] = (q['Close'] - q['Close'].shift(1))
    data_source['close_roc'] = (q['Close'] / q['Close'].shift(1))
    data_source['ind1'] = get_indicator(q, ind1_name, params['ind1'])
    data_source['ind2'] = get_indicator(q, ind2_name, params['ind2'])
    # Cut to 'start date'
```

```
for k, v in data_source.items():
    data_source[k] = v[v.index > start_date].dropna().values
D = []
for i in range(ts_len):
    row = []
    for k, v in data_source.items():
        row.append(v[i])
    D.append(row)
X, Y = sliding_window(D, w)
```

Creating train and validation datasets

```
X_test, Y_test = X[:train_len], Y[:train_len]
X_val, Y_val = X[train_len:], Y[train_len:]
```

Preparing tensors

```
x_test = torch.tensor(X_test).float()
y_test = torch.tensor(Y_test).float()
x_val = torch.tensor(X_val).float()
y_val = torch.tensor(Y_val).float()
c_test, c_val = x_test[:, :, :2], x_val[:, :, :2]
ind_test, ind_val = x_test[:, -1, 2:], x_val[:, -1, 2:]
p_test, p_val = y_test[:, :, 0].view(-1), y_val[:, :, 0].view(-1)
```

Model initializing

```
model_params = {
    'rnn_input_size':   2,
    'ind_input_size':   2,
    'rnn_type':         rnn_type,
    'rnn_hidden_size':  rnn_hidden_size,
    'ind_hidden_size':  ind_hidden_size,
    'des_size':         des_size
}
model = AlgoTrader(**model_params)
```

Training

```
    optimizer = optim.Adam(model.parameters(), lr = lr)
    criterion = NegativeMeanReturnLoss()
    min_val_loss = 1000_000
    best_params = None
    for e in range(epochs):
        predicted = model(c_test, ind_test)
        loss = criterion(predicted, p_test)
        optimizer.zero_grad()
        optimizer.zero_grad()
        loss.backward()
        optimizer.step()
        val_predicted = model(c_val, ind_val)
        val_loss = criterion(val_predicted, p_val)
        if val_loss.item() < min_val_loss:
            min_val_loss = val_loss.item()
            best_params = copy.deepcopy(model.state_dict())
        if e % 10 == 0:
            print(f'Epoch {e}| test:{round(loss.item(), 4)},'
                  f'val: {round(val_loss.item(), 4)}')
    # Saving the best model if necessary
    if save_model:
        torch.save(best_params, f'{dir_path}/data/{model_name}.pth')
    return min_val_loss
```

Now let us go to the tuning. The search space for hyper-parameter tuning can be depicted the following way:

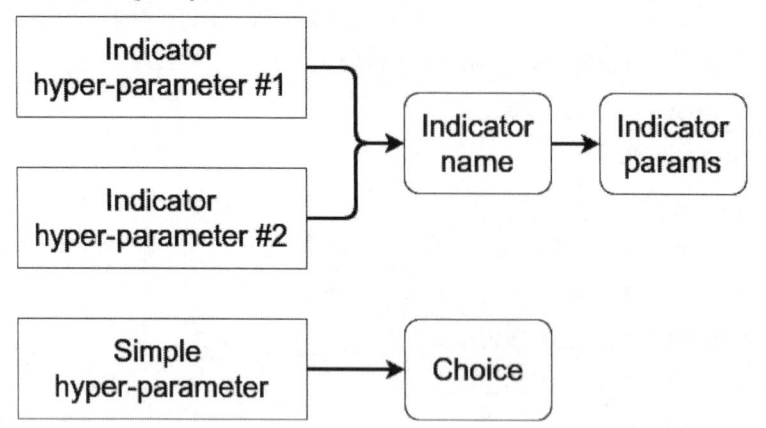

Figure 7.25: Algorithmic trading hyper-parameter tuning search space structure

Let us examine the implementation of hyper-parameter search space **ch7/stock/search.py**:

```
fast_choices = {"_type": "choice", "_value": [3, 5, 7, 9]}
slow_choices = {"_type": "choice", "_value": [14, 20, 40]}
length_choices = {"_type": "choice", "_value": [5, 10, 20]}
ind_choices = [
    {"_name": "ao", "fast": fast_choices, "slow": slow_choices},
    {"_name": "apo", "fast": fast_choices, "slow": slow_choices},
    {"_name": "cci", "length": length_choices},
    {"_name": "cmo", "length": length_choices},
    {"_name": "mom", "length": length_choices},
    {"_name": "rsi", "length": length_choices},
    {"_name": "tsi", "fast": fast_choices, "slow": slow_choices},
]
search_space = {
    "lr":              {"_type": "choice", "_value": [.01, .005, .001, .0005]},
    "rnn_type":        {"_type": "choice", "_value": ['rnn', 'gru']},
    "rnn_hidden_size": {"_type": "choice", "_value": [8, 16, 24]},
    "ind_hidden_size": {"_type": "choice", "_value": [1, 2, 4]},
    "des_size":        {"_type": "choice", "_value": [2, 4, 8, 16]},
```

```
    "ind1":              {"_type": "choice", "_value": ind_choices},
    "ind2":              {"_type": "choice", "_value": ind_choices},
}
```

Now let us launch the optimization process **ch7/stock/search.py**. This process can take several hours. Therefore you can use the results obtained by the author:

Best trial params:

```
{
    "lr":                0.01,
    "rnn_type":          "rnn",
    "rnn_hidden_size":   24,
    "ind_hidden_size":   1,
    "des_size":          2,
    "ind1":              {
        "_name":   "rsi",
        "length":  20
    },
    "ind2":              {
        "_name":   "cmo",
        "length":  20
    }
}
```

Now let us train and save the model with the best hyper-parameter combination **ch7/stock/train_and_save.py**.

And this brings us to the most intriguing part of our research. Let us evaluate our model for 2020 **ch7/stock/evaluate.py**.

Import part

```python
import os
import matplotlib.pyplot as plt
import torch
from typing import import OrderedDict
from ch7.stock.dataset import import get_df_until_2021
```

```
from ch7.stock.model.model import AlgoTrader
from ch7.stock.utils import get_indicator, sliding_window
```

Best hyper-parameters

Best model parameters found by hyper-parameter tuning process:

```
params = {
    "lr":               0.01,
    "rnn_type":         "rnn",
    "rnn_hidden_size":  24,
    "ind_hidden_size":  1,
    "des_size":         2,
    "ind1":             {
        "_name":  "rsi",
        "length": 20
    },
    "ind2":             {
        "_name":  "cmo",
        "length": 20
    }
}
```

Global parameters

```
dir_path = os.path.dirname(os.path.realpath(__file__))
start_date = '2020-01-01'
end_date = '2021-01-01'
w = 40
q = get_df_until_2021()
q = q[q.index < end_date]
ts_len = q[q.index > start_date].shape[0]
```

Sliding window dataset

```
data_source = OrderedDict()
data_source['close_diff'] = (q['Close'] - q['Close'].shift(1))
```

```python
data_source['close_roc'] = (q['Close'] / q['Close'].shift(1))
data_source['ind1'] = get_indicator(q, params['ind1']['_name'],
params['ind1'])
data_source['ind2'] = get_indicator(q, params['ind2']['_name'],
params['ind2'])
# Cut to 'start date'
for k, v in data_source.items():
    data_source[k] = v[v.index > start_date].dropna().values
data_source['close_diff'][0] = 0
data_source['close_roc'][0] = 1
D = []
for i in range(ts_len):
    row = []
    for k, v in data_source.items():
        row.append(v[i])
    D.append(row)
X, Y = sliding_window(D, w)
```

Creating tensors

```python
x = torch.tensor(X).float()
y = torch.tensor(Y).float()
c = x[:, :, :2]
ind = x[:, -1, 2:]
tomorrow_price_diff = y[:, :, 0].view(-1)
```

Initializing and loading the model

```python
model_name = 'best_model'
model_params = {
    'rnn_input_size':   2,
    'ind_input_size':   2,
    'rnn_type':         params['rnn_type'],
    'rnn_hidden_size':  params['rnn_hidden_size'],
    'ind_hidden_size':  params['ind_hidden_size'],
    'des_size':         params['des_size']
```

```
}
model = AlgoTrader(**model_params)
model.load_state_dict(torch.load(f'{dir_path}/data/{model_name}.pth'))
model.eval()
```

Evaluating

And here we are evaluating the trading on **2020-01-01 - 2021-01-01** time range:

```
with torch.no_grad():
    trades = model(c, ind)
    # Rounded Trades
    trades = torch.round(trades * 100) / 100
    # Calculating Absolute Returns
    abs_return = torch.mul(trades, tomorrow_price_diff)
    cumsum_return = [0] + torch.cumsum(abs_return, dim = 0)\
        .view(-1).tolist()
    # Buy and Hold Strategy Returns
    cumsum_price = [0] + torch.cumsum(tomorrow_price_diff, dim = 0)\
        .view(-1).tolist()
    plt.title('Trading evaluation on 2020')
    plt.plot(cumsum_return, label = 'Model Returns')
    plt.plot(cumsum_price, label = 'Buy and Hold Returns')
    plt.axhline(y = 0, color = 'black', linestyle = '--')
    plt.legend()
    plt.show()
    print(f'Model Returns: {round(cumsum_return[-1], 4)}')
    print(f'Buy and Hold Returns: {round(cumsum_price[-1], 4)}')
```

Result

```
Model Returns: 191.4051
Buy and Hold Returns: 60.41
```

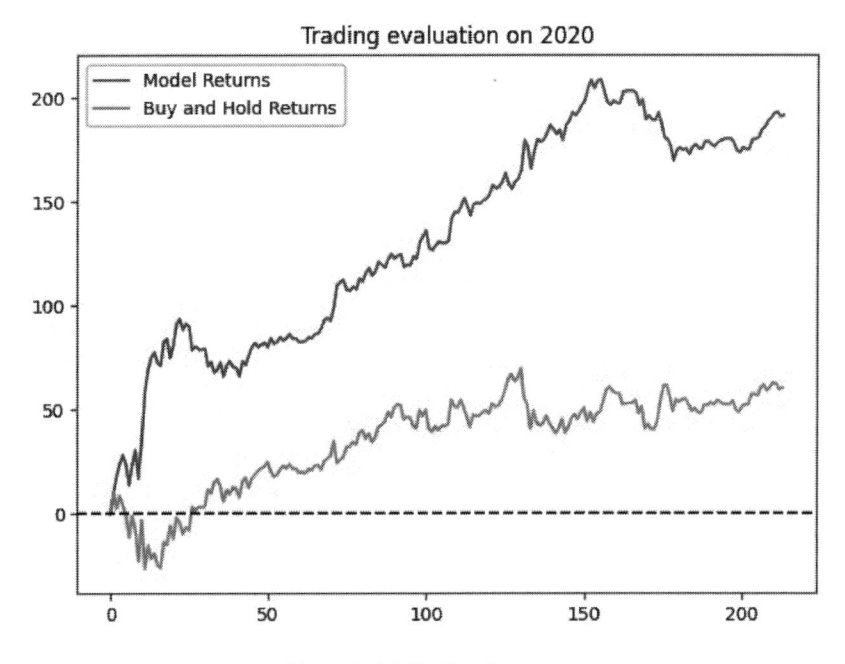

Figure 7.26: Trading Returns

Figure 7.26 shows the returns of the trading model we made. It shows a good positive result. The Buy and Hold strategy also shows a positive result, but the income of this strategy is significantly lower than the income of our deep learning model. This example shows the promise of deep learning applications for time series analysis. This problem was analyzed exclusively within the theoretical research. Trading in the financial market is associated with significant risks and can differ from paper trading, which we modeled in our study. Nevertheless, the accurate application of neural networks can show encouraging results in helping to develop trading strategies.

Conclusion

In this chapter, we have studied the application of deep learning models to real-world forecasting problems. We saw the potential of neural networks for time series analysis. Each of our examples had its own specifics and required an individual solution. I sincerely hope that these examples will help you in applying theoretical knowledge in practice.

In the next chapter, we will look at popular time series frameworks.

Points to remember

- You can use the custom loss function to train the model if needed.
- If there is a lack of historical data for a specific location, you can use the historical information of neighboring areas if they have similar characteristics.

Multiple choice questions

1. Is it mandatory to use hyper-parameter tuning to create a predictive model?

   A. Yes

   B. No, but hyper-parameter tuning increases the likelihood of developing an efficient model.

2. What should we do if we want to maximize the loss function F?

   A. Use -F function.

   B. This is impossible because the backward method always minimizes the loss function.

Answers

1. B
2. A

CHAPTER 8
PyTorch Forecasting Package

In this book, we studied developing time series-specific deep learning models. We have used the various features of PyTorch to create architectures of varying complexity. This approach is called the low-level design. The significance of this approach is that we have maximum flexibility to solve a specific problem. However, sometimes it is useful to use high-level libraries for particular tasks. This chapter will introduce the PyTorch Forecasting package, which aims to ease state-of-the-art time series forecasting with neural networks.

Structure

In this chapter, we will discuss the following topics:

- Introduction PyTorch Forecasting package
- Working with TimeSeriesDataset
- Initializing built-in PyTorch Forecasting model
- Creating custom PyTorch Forecasting model
- A complete example
- **Objectives**

After studying this chapter, you will be able to use additional forecasting tools to develop PyTorch deep learning models. This chapter is a good start for exploring deep learning libraries related to time series analysis.

Introduction to PyTorch Forecasting package

PyTorch Forecasting package is built on PyTorch that makes it possible to implement any PyTorch features in the forecasting model. The package provides a high-level API for dealing with the real-world problems.

The main features of the PyTorch Forecasting package are as follows:

- Methods that allow operating with time series datasets.
- Base forecasting model class which has specific forecasting methods and logic.
- Ready-to-use deep learning architectures.
- Range optimizer, early stop conditions, and so on.

The package can be installed in the following way:

```
$ pip install pytorch-forecasting
```

> Note: For more information, please refer to the official documentation: https://pytorch-forecasting.readthedocs.io/en/latest/index.html.

One of the most significant advantages of using the PyTorch Forecasting package is having fewer limitations. Though, sometimes it is rather tricky to inject custom features into an existing library. But here, you can use any idea and implemented it in PyTorch. PyTorch Forecasting only aims to make it easier to solve everyday time series tasks.

Also, one of the main advantages of this package is the availability of ready-made models for time series forecasting: Autoregressive model, Deep Autoregressive model, Temporal Fusion Transformer, and others.

Working with TimeSeriesDataset

One of the main classes in the PyTorch forecast package is TimeSeriesDataset.

This class automates everyday tasks, such as:

- Time series scaling and encoding.
- Normalizing the target variable.

- Generating sliding window dataset.
- Converting time series from pandas data frames to torch tensors, and so on.

Let us create **TimeSeriesDataset** object from the UK weather time series dataset which we used in *Chapter 3, Time Series as Deep Learning Problem* **ch8/dataset.py**:

Import part

```
import os
import numpy as np
import pandas as pd
from pytorch_forecasting import TimeSeriesDataSet
```

Creating TimeSeriesDataSet

The following function creates a **TimeSeriesDataSet** object that contains minimal monthly temperature from the *Sheffield* station.

```
def get_weather_dataset():
```

The length of prediction and sliding window:

```
    encoder_length = 120
    prediction_len = 1
```

Loading data from CSV file:

```
    dir_path = os.path.dirname(os.path.realpath(__file__))
    ts_df = pd.read_csv(f'{dir_path}/data/MET_Office_Weather_Data.csv')
    ts = ts_df.loc[ts_df['station'] == 'sheffield']['tmin'].interpolate().dropna().tolist()
```

Creating pandas dataframe:

```
    df = pd.DataFrame(
        dict(
            value = ts,
            group = [0] * len(ts),
            time_idx = np.arange(len(ts)),
        )
    )
```

Creating the `TimeSeriesDataSet` object from the pandas dataframe:

```
dataset = TimeSeriesDataSet(
    data = df,
    group_ids = ["group"],
    target = "value",
    time_idx = "time_idx",
    max_encoder_length = encoder_length,
    max_prediction_length = prediction_len,
    time_varying_unknown_reals = ["value"]
)
return dataset
```

Working with TimeSeriesDataSet object

Let us examine basic `TimeSeriesDataSet` operations:

```
if __name__ == '__main__':
```

Initializing dataset is as follows:

```
dataset = get_weather_dataset()
```

Dataset size:

```
print(f'Dataset size: {dataset.data["target"][0].size()[0]}')
```

>>> Dataset size: 1650

Dataset parameters:

```
print('Dataset parameters:')
print(dataset.get_parameters())
```

Here, we have the list of dataset parameters and their values:

>>>

time_idx	'time_idx'
target	'value'
group_ids	['group']
weight	None
max_encoder_length	120
min_encoder_length	120
min_prediction_idx	0

min_prediction_length	1
max_prediction_length	1
static_categoricals	[]
static_reals	[]
time_varying_known_categoricals	[]
time_varying_known_reals	[]
time_varying_unknown_categoricals	[]
time_varying_unknown_reals	['value']
variable_groups	{}
dropout_categoricals	[]
constant_fill_strategy	{}
allow_missings	False
lags	{}
add_relative_time_idx	False
add_target_scales	False
add_encoder_length	False
target_normalizer	EncoderNormalizer()
categorical_encoders	{'__group_id__group': NaNLabelEncoder()}
scalers	{}
randomize_length	None
predict_mode	False

One of the main **TimeSeriesDataSet** methods is **to_dataloader()** that creates a dataloader for the forecasting model. **batch_size** parameter defines the size of batches in the dataloader:

```
# Convert the dataset to a dataloader
dataloader = dataset.to_dataloader(batch_size = 8)
```

Dataloader is an iterable object:

```
# Show first 2 batches
batch_count = 0
for x, y in iter(dataloader):
    batch_count += 1
    if batch_count > 2:
        break
    print(f'batch: {batch_count}')
```

```
            print(f"X: {x['encoder_cont'].tolist()}")
            print(f"Y: {y[0].tolist()}")
>>>
batch: 1
X: [[[0.8401713371276855], [-0.9969924092292786], …
Y: [[7.800000190734863], …
batch: 2
X: [[[-1.8186951875686646], [-0.550972044467926], …
Y: [[0.5], …
```

`TimeSeriesDataSet` object is a pretty useful wrapper to common time series dataset operations.

Initializing built-in PyTorch Forecasting model

As it was mentioned before, PyTorch Forecasting package has a lot of built-in forecasting models. All of these models inherit a special base class `pytorch_forecasting.models.BaseModel`. This class provides the following functionalities:

- Training and validation is handled automatically.
- Dataloading and normalization is provided by the `TimeSeriesDataSet`.
- Logging training progress, and so on

Let us examine the creation of the PyTorch Forecasting Deep Autoregressive model `ch8/deepar_model.py`.

Import part

```
import random
import torch
from pytorch_forecasting import DeepAR
from ch8.dataset import get_weather_dataset
```

Making script reproducible

```
random.seed(1)
torch.manual_seed(1)
```

Initializing Deep Autoregressive model

The following code initializes the Deep Autoregressive model:

```
dataset = get_weather_dataset()
model = DeepAR.from_dataset(dataset = dataset)
```

Let us examine a summary of the PyTorch forecasting model:

```
print('DeepAR model summary:')
print(model.summarize("full"))
print('==============')
```

Here we have the DeepAR model summary:

>>>

	Name	Type	Params
0	loss	NormalDistributionLoss	0
1	logging_metrics	ModuleList	0
2	logging_metrics.0	SMAPE	0
3	logging_metrics.1	MAE	0
4	logging_metrics.2	RMSE	0
5	logging_metrics.3	MAPE	0
6	logging_metrics.4	MASE	0
7	embeddings	MultiEmbedding	0
8	embeddings.embeddings	ModuleDict	0
9	rnn	LSTM	1.4 K
10	distribution_projector	Linear	22

```
1.4 K      Trainable params
0          Non-trainable params
1.4 K      Total params
0.006      Total estimated model params size (MB)
```

Also, we can examine model hyper-parameters as follows:

```
print('DeepAR model hyper-parameters:')
print(model.hparams)
print('==============')
```

Below the list of model hyper-parameters is provided:

>>>

categorical_groups	{}
cell_type	LSTM
dropout	0.1
embedding_labels	{}
embedding_paddings	[]
embedding_sizes	{}
hidden_size	10
learning_rate	0.001
log_gradient_flow	False
log_interval	-1
log_val_interval	-1

logging_metrics	ModuleList(
	  (0): SMAPE()
	  (1): MAE()
	  (2): RMSE()
	  (3): MAPE()
	  (4): MASE()
	)

loss	NormalDistributionLoss()
monotone_constaints	{}
n_plotting_samples	None
n_validation_samples	None
optimizer	ranger
optimizer_params	None
output_transformer	EncoderNormalizer()
reduce_on_plateau_min_lr	1e-05
reduce_on_plateau_patience	1000
rnn_layers	2
static_categoricals	[]
static_reals	[]
target	value
target_lags	{}

time_varying_categoricals_decoder	[]
time_varying_categoricals_encoder	[]
time_varying_reals_decoder	[]
time_varying_reals_encoder	['value']
weight_decay	0.0
x_categoricals	[]
x_reals	['value']

The following model execution is provided. Take in mind that the model is not trained yet:

```
print('DeepAR model forward method execution:')
dataloader = dataset.to_dataloader(batch_size = 8)
x, y = next(iter(dataloader))
p = model(x)
print(p)
print('==============')
```

We can see that initializing and using built-in PyTorch Forecasting models are pretty straightforward. We will study the complete application of these models in the next sections.

Creating custom PyTorch Forecasting model

It is true, that the use of built-in models has great practical benefits, but we should be able to create custom models. Creating custom models is pretty easy in the PyTorch Forecasting package. Say we have custom deep learning model **ch8/custom_model.py**. This is the same model we used in *Chapter 3, Time Series as Deep Learning Problem*. Let us examine the creation of the custom PyTorch Forecasting model **ch8/forecasting_model.py**.

Import part

```
import random
from typing import Dict
import torch
```

```
from pytorch_forecasting import TimeSeriesDataSet
from pytorch_forecasting.models import BaseModel
from ch8.dataset import get_weather_dataset
from ch8.custom_model import CustomModel
```

Defining PyTorch Forecasting model

Any implementation of the PyTorch Forecasting Model should inherit **pytorch_forecasting.models.BaseModel**:

class ForecastingModel(BaseModel):

Model initialization saves all passed parameters as model hyper-parameters and creates the custom model as follows:

```
    def __init__(self, n_inp, l_1, l_2, conv1_out,
                 conv1_kernel, conv2_kernel, drop1 = 0, **kwargs):
        # saves arguments in signature to `.hparams` attribute,
        # mandatory call - do not skip this
        self.save_hyperparameters()
        # pass additional arguments to BaseModel.__init__,
        #  mandatory call - do not skip this
        super().__init__(**kwargs)
        self.network = CustomModel(
            n_inp = self.hparams.n_inp,
            l_1 = self.hparams.l_1,
            l_2 = self.hparams.l_2,
            conv1_out = self.hparams.conv1_out,
            conv1_kernel = self.hparams.conv1_kernel,
            conv2_kernel = self.hparams.conv2_kernel,
            drop1 = self.hparams.drop1
        )
```

Implementing the forward method

All custom models integrated into PyTorch Forecasting should implement this forward method pattern:

```
    def forward(self, x: Dict[str, torch.Tensor]) -> Dict[str, torch.Tensor]:
```

```
        # x is a batch generated based on the TimeSeriesDataset
        network_input = x["encoder_cont"].squeeze(-1)
        prediction = self.network(network_input)
        # We need to return a dictionary
        # that at least contains the prediction and the target_scale.
        # The parameter can be directly forwarded from the input.
        return dict(prediction = prediction, target_scale = x["target_scale"])
```

The model design is often based on the dataset it is working with, so it is convenient to initialize the model based on the concrete dataset:

```
    @classmethod
    def from_dataset(cls, dataset: TimeSeriesDataSet, **kwargs):
        new_kwargs = {
            "n_inp": dataset.max_encoder_length
        }
        # use to pass real hyperparameters and override defaults set by dataset
        new_kwargs.update(kwargs)
        # example for dataset validation
        assert dataset.max_prediction_length == dataset.min_prediction_length,\
            "Decoder only supports a fixed length"
        assert dataset.min_encoder_length == dataset.max_encoder_length,\
            "Encoder only supports a fixed length"
        return super().from_dataset(dataset, **new_kwargs)
```

Initializing the custom model

Let us initialize the custom model as follows:

```
if __name__ == '__main__':
    random.seed(1)
    torch.manual_seed(1)
    dataset = get_weather_dataset()
    model = net = ForecastingModel.from_dataset(
```

```
    dataset = dataset,
    l_1 = 400,
    l_2 = 48,
    conv1_out = 6,
    conv1_kernel = 36,
    conv2_kernel = 12,
    drop1 = .1
)
```

Following we provide the custom model summary:

```
print('Custom model summary:')
print(model.summarize("full"))  # print model summary
print('==============')
```
>>>

	Name	Type	Params
0	loss	SMAPE	0
1	logging_metrics	ModuleList	0
2	network	CustomModel	231 K
3	network.pool	MaxPool1d	0
4	network.conv1	Conv1d	222
5	network.conv2	Conv1d	876
6	network.lin1	Linear	211 K
7	network.lin2	Linear	19.2 K
8	network.lin3	Linear	49

```
231 K     Trainable params
0         Non-trainable params
231 K     Total params
0.928     Total estimated model params size (MB)
```

Also, let us show custom model hyper-parameters:

```
print('Custom model hyper-parameters:')
print(model.hparams)
print('==============')
```
>>>

conv1_kernel	36
conv1_out	6
conv2_kernel	12
drop1	0.1
l_1	400
l_2	48
learning_rate	0.001
log_gradient_flow	False
log_interval	-1
log_val_interval	-1
logging_metrics	ModuleList()
loss	SMAPE()
monotone_constaints	{}
n_inp	120
optimizer	ranger
optimizer_params	None
output_transformer	EncoderNormalizer()
reduce_on_plateau_min_lr	1e-05
reduce_on_plateau_patience	1000
weight_decay	0.0

Let us examine the model execution. Take in mind that the model is not trained yet:

```
print('Custom model forward method execution:')
dataloader = dataset.to_dataloader(batch_size = 8)
x, y = next(iter(dataloader))
p = model(x)
print(p)
print('==============')
```

Hence, we see that to use the custom model, we need to put this custom model in a PyTorch Forecasting wrapper. Now we can finally study a complete example of solving the prediction problem using the PyTorch Forecasting package.

A complete example

Now, let us study the solution of real-world forecasting problems using the PyTorch Forecasting package. We will consider the UK monthly minimal temperature prediction problem from *Chapter 3, Time Series as Deep Learning Problem*. For this task, we will use the Deep Autoregressive model and the Custom model we considered before **ch8/example.py**.

Importing all required packages:

```
import os
import random
import numpy as np
import pandas as pd
import matplotlib.pyplot as plt
import torch
from pytorch_forecasting import TimeSeriesDataSet, DeepAR
from pytorch_lightning.callbacks import EarlyStopping, LearningRateMonitor
import pytorch_lightning as pl
from ch8.forecasting_model import ForecastingModel
```

Making this script reproducible:

```
random.seed(1)
torch.manual_seed(1)
```

Dataset parameters:

```
# define dataset
encode_length = 120
prediction_length = 1
training_cutoff = 2015   # year for cutoff
dir_path = os.path.dirname(os.path.realpath(__file__))
ts_df = pd.read_csv(f'{dir_path}/data/MET_Office_Weather_Data.csv')
ts_df = ts_df.loc[(ts_df['station'] == 'sheffield')]
```

Train dataset includes the observations before the year 2015 as follows:

```
train_ts = ts_df.loc[ts_df['year'] < training_cutoff]['tmin']\
    .interpolate().dropna().tolist()
test_ts = ts_df.loc[ts_df['year'] >= training_cutoff - (encode_length / 12)]['tmin']\
    .interpolate().dropna().tolist()
```

Creating pandas dataframes:

```python
train_data = pd.DataFrame(
    dict(
        value = train_ts,
        group = [0] * len(train_ts),
        time_idx = np.arange(len(train_ts)),
    )
)
test_data = pd.DataFrame(
    dict(
        value = test_ts,
        group = [0] * len(test_ts),
        time_idx = np.arange(len(test_ts)),
    )
)
```

Creating **TimeSeriesDataSet** objects:

```python
time_series_dataset_params = {
    'group_ids':                   ["group"],
    'target':                      "value",
    'time_idx':                    "time_idx",
    'max_encoder_length':          encode_length,
    'max_prediction_length':       prediction_length,
    'time_varying_unknown_reals':  ["value"]
}
# create the dataset from the pandas dataframe
testing = TimeSeriesDataSet(data = test_data, **time_series_dataset_params)
training = TimeSeriesDataSet(data = train_data, **time_series_dataset_params)
validation = TimeSeriesDataSet.from_dataset(
    training,
    train_data,
    min_prediction_idx = training.index.time.max() + 1,
```

```
        stop_randomization = True
)
```

Initializing dataloaders:

```
bs = 240
train_dataloader = training.to_dataloader(train = True, batch_size = bs)
val_dataloader = validation.to_dataloader(train = False, batch_size = bs)
test_dataloader = testing.to_dataloader(train = False, batch_size = bs)
```

Here, we define the training process with an early stop condition:

```
# define trainer with early stopping
early_stop_callback = EarlyStopping(
    monitor = "val_loss",
    min_delta = 1e-5,
    patience = 1,
    verbose = False,
    mode = "min"
)
lr_logger = LearningRateMonitor()
trainer = pl.Trainer(
    max_epochs = 1000,
    gpus = 0,
    gradient_clip_val = 0.1,
    limit_train_batches = 30,
    callbacks = [lr_logger, early_stop_callback],
)
```

We will implement two different models, our custom model and built-in DeepAR model:

```
custom_model = ForecastingModel.from_dataset(
    dataset = training,
    l_1 = 400,
    l_2 = 48,
    conv1_out = 6,
```

```
        conv1_kernel = 36,
        conv2_kernel = 12,
        drop1 = .1
)
deepar_model = DeepAR.from_dataset(dataset = training)
models = {
        'Custom':                  custom_model,
        'Deep Autoregressive': deepar_model
}
predictions = {}
for model_name, model in models.items():
```

PyTorch Forecasting package defines the optimal learning rate for the current dataset:

```
    # find optimal learning rate
    res = trainer.tuner.lr_find(
        custom_model,
        train_dataloader = train_dataloader, val_dataloaders = val_dataloader,
        early_stop_threshold = 1000.0,
        max_lr = 0.3,
    )
    print(f"Suggested Learning Rate for {model_name}: {res.suggestion()}")
```

Here, in simple line, we perform model training:

```
    trainer.fit(
        custom_model,
        train_dataloader = train_dataloader, val_dataloaders = val_dataloader
    )
```

Predicting on the test dataset:

```
    predictions[model_name] = custom_model.predict(test_dataloader)
```

Let us visualize the results:

```
x, y = next(iter(test_dataloader))
```

```
plt.title('Predictions on Test dataset')
plt.plot(y[0].tolist(), label = 'Real')
for model_name, prediction in predictions.items():
    plt.plot(prediction.tolist(), label = model_name)
plt.legend()
plt.show()
```

Result

Following is the result obtained:

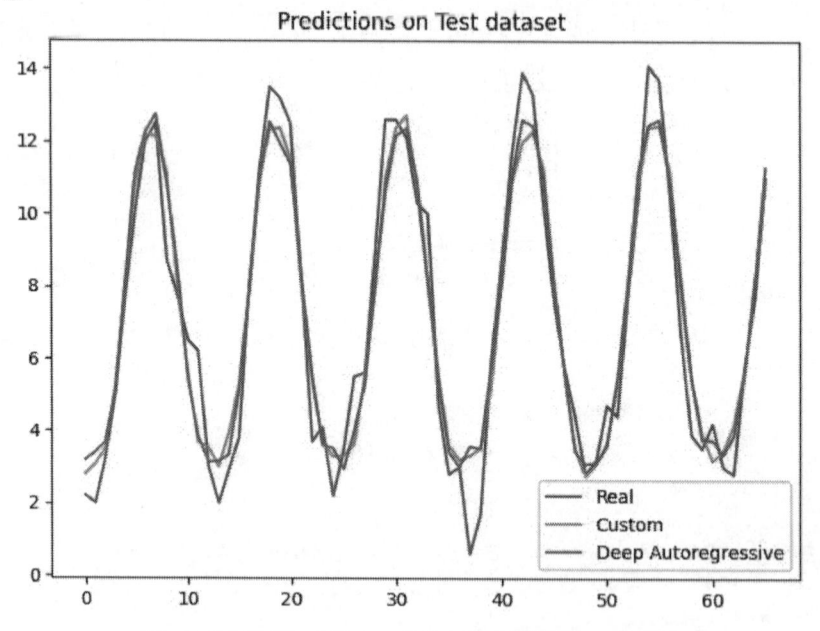

Figure 8.1: PyTorch Forecasting package implementation

As expected, the original DeepAR model and custom forecasting model performed well on the test dataset. In this example, our primary goal was to show the practical application of predictive models using the PyTorch Forecasting package.

Conclusion

In this chapter, we have learned about the basic usage of PyTorch Forecasting packages. These libraries can simplify and facilitate the development and use of predictive models. One chapter is not enough to fully cover all the possibilities of this library. Using these different frameworks, one can significantly reduce the development time, but it does not solve all the problems for you. That is why it is crucial to understand the principles by which a specific approach is implemented.

This chapter concludes the study of applying deep learning techniques to time series prediction. However, this book is not a complete source of all methods and approaches to solving predictive problems. In the next chapter, we will look at the various resources and directions the reader can take to continue exploring time series analysis.

Points to remember

- PyTorch Forecasting package unifies and simplifies the development of the prediction models.
- PyTorch Forecasting package is being under development right now, and it will contain many advanced models for practical usage in the future.

Multiple choice questions

1. **Is it necessary to use the PyTorch Forecasting Package to solve real-world problems?**

    A. Yes

    B. No, but it can save time and development efforts.

2. **Is it possible to use an arbitrary PyTorch model in the PyTorch Forecasting package?**

    A. Yes

    B. No, PyTorch Forecasting package works only with a predefined set of models.

Answers

1. B
2. A

CHAPTER 9
What is Next?

I wanted to congratulate you, as the most challenging part is over! We studied some really advanced deep learning applications to time series forecasting and learned how to use them in practice. Of course, the applications of deep learning to time series forecasting continue to evolve dynamically, and in this chapter, we will see the path to move forward after completing this book.

Structure

In this chapter, we will discuss the following topics:

- Classical time series analysis
- Deep learning
- Studying the best solutions
- Do not be afraid of science
- Expanding your toolbox

Objective

This chapter shows the path for further study in the area of time series forecasting. The resources mentioned in this chapter will keep you notified about the latest advances.

Classical time series analysis

We already know that deep learning models are not black magic boxes that can solve any problem. Each deep learning model is a computational graph that implements various mathematical operations. The architecture of a particular model significantly depends on the problem being solved. There is no need to create a solid border between deep learning methods and classic time series analysis. Both of these approaches can enrich each other and make really effective models.

In *Chapter 6, PyTorch Model Tuning with Neural Network Intelligence*, we saw how hybrid models that use deep learning and classical statistical methods could significantly improve the prediction performance. Often classical statistical methods allow you to make a significant breakthrough in solving problems. Therefore, it is advised to familiarize yourself with the basics of classical time series analysis to be able to combine different approaches in solving problems.

Deep learning

Deep learning methods are rapidly evolving every day. And many different approaches can increase the speed and quality of model training. Also, there are many tools that simplify the deployment and maintenance of deep learning models on remote servers. Therefore, if we use deep learning methods for forecasting problems, we need to continue growing as deep learning experts in general.

Studying the best solutions

One of the best ways to learn is to explore successful solutions to other problems. Learning one practical solution can significantly improve your understanding of various theoretical methods and provide ideas for other solutions.

It is recommended to the readers to examine various solutions to forecasting problems on the Kaggle site: **https://www.kaggle.com/search?q=time+series+in%3Acompetitions**. Many of these solutions contain non-trivial logic, but their study can significantly enrich the reader's experience and give an excellent kickstart to further progress.

Do not be afraid of science

Time series forecasting is a field of science. It combines various areas of mathematics, statistics, and computer science. Usually, the most advanced and revolutionary ideas appear in scientific papers. Yes, reading scientific articles sometimes is not interesting, but not all scientific publications contain complex mathematical concepts and cannot only be understood by professors of mathematics. Many papers include examples of solving practical problems, and most importantly, they have a ready-made implementation of a specific model in Python. Here is an example of a pretty scientific article that analyzes python time series analysis (as shown in *Figure 9.1*):

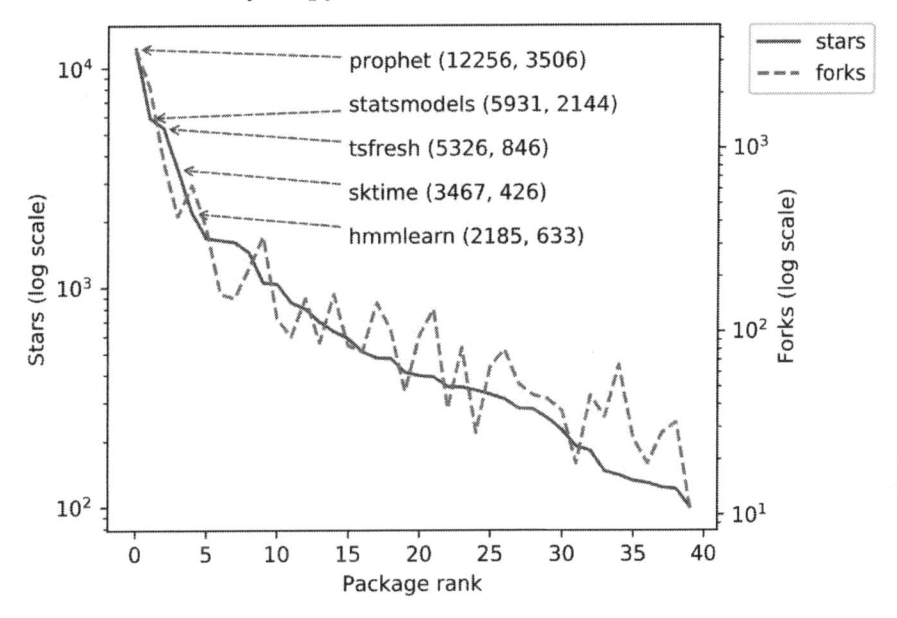

Figure 9.1: A systematic review of Python packages for time series analysis

> **Note: A systematic review of Python packages for time series analysis - https://arxiv.org/pdf/2104.07406.pdf. It is easy to read and can give a lot of useful information.**

Therefore, you can harmlessly start reading scientific papers on a time series topic on scientific resources:

- https://arxiv.org/
- https://www.researchgate.net/
- https://www.sciencedirect.com/
- Other related sites

Expanding your toolbox

At the moment, there are many different python packages that allow you to perform various operations on time series. Learning new tools allows you to become familiar with the concepts that they implement, so it is sometimes helpful to study new packages and, if necessary, inject their functionality into your models.

The following list is the most useful one:

- **PyTorch Forecasting**: https://pytorch-forecasting.readthedocs.io/en/latest/. We already studied this package in *Chapter 8*. This is one of the best PyTorch packages for time series forecasting.

- **Darts**: https://unit8co.github.io/darts/index.html. Python package for easy time series manipulation and forecasting. It contains a variety of models, from classics such as ARIMA to deep neural networks. Moreover, the models can be used in the same way, using fit() and predict() functions, similar to the scikit-learn API style.

- **Prophet**: https://facebook.github.io/prophet/. Prophet is open source software released by Facebook's Core Data Science team for time series forecasting.

- **Sktime**: https://github.com/alan-turing-institute/sktime. Sktime uses shallow machine learning methods for time series forecasting and classification.

- **PyFlux**: https://pyflux.readthedocs.io/en/latest/index.html. PyFlux is a library that implements classical forecasting models like ARIMA, GARCH, GAS, etc.

- **Tsfresh**: https://github.com/blue-yonder/tsfresh. Tsfresh package contains many feature extraction methods and a robust feature selection algorithm.

- **TimeSynth**: https://github.com/TimeSynth/TimeSynth. TimeSynth is an open-source library for generating artificial time series for model testing.

Conclusion

This final chapter listed the most valuable resources and directions for further learning. Deep learning techniques are evolving rapidly and so it is important to stay up to date with all the latest innovations and approaches. This book lays a good foundation in time series forecasting, and hence, it can be a good start for the reader.

Index

A

absolute loss 57
activation function 47
adadelta 58
adagrad 58
Adaptive Moment Estimation (Adam) 58
algorithmic trading
  about 237-243, 247, 248
  evaluating 256, 257
  global parameter 249, 254
  hyper-parameter 254
  hyper-parameter tuning search space structure 252, 253
  model hyper-parameters 249
  prediction model 244, 245
  sliding window dataset 254
  sliding window dataset, preparing 249

alternative model 93, 94
anomaly detection 15
architecture design 92
automatic feature extraction 81-84
autoregressive integrated moving average model (ARIMA) 17

B

built-in PyTorch Forecasting model
  initializing 264
  script reproducible, creating 264

C

casual convolution 156-158
casual convolution layer
  defining 196
  fully connected layer 198
  hybrid model 198
  hybrid model architecture search 200-202

hybrid model search space 199, 200
hybrid model trail 198
obligatory RNN layer 198
classical approaches
　about 16
　autoregressive integrated moving average model (ARIMA) 17
　autoregressive model (AR) 17
　cons 19
　Holt-Winters exponential smoothing (HWES) 19
　pros 19
　seasonal autoregressive integrated moving average (SARIMA) 18
classical time series analysis 280
classification model
　versus regression model 74
computational graph
　creating 30, 31
Convolutional Neural Networks (CNNs) 20, 156
convolution layer
　about 37-40
　types 37
convolution layer, parameters
　about 41
　kernel 41
　padding 42
　stride 43
　weight 41
COVID-19 confirmed cases forecast
　about 223-229
　datasets, converting to tensor 231
　global parameters 229, 234
　input, creating 234
　model hyper-parameters 230
　model, initializing 231

model preparation function 229
prediction, plotting 236, 237
results, obtaining 231-234
results, training 231-234
sliding window datasets, preparing 230
crop layer 163
cross-validation 92

D

datasets 80, 81
decoder layer 148
Deep Autoregressive model
　initializing 265-267
Deep Learning layers
　about 36
　activation function 47
　dropout layer 46
　hyperbolic tangent function (Tanh) 49
　linear layer 36
　pooling layer 44, 45
　ReLU 47
　Sigmoid 48
Deep Learning method 280
Deep Learning model
　about 20
　capabilities 20
　problem statement 74
Deep Learning model trial
　about 181
　dataset 182, 183
　global parameters 182
　model initialization 182, 183
　optimizer 182, 183
dilation 159
dropout 55
dropout layer 46

dynamic processes
  versus static processes 91

E
effectiveness function 91
encoder-decoder model
  about 142-145
  class 149
  datasets, generating 154
  decoder layer 148
  encoder layer 148
  evaluating 151, 152
  global parameters 153
  implementing 147
  initializing 154
  mixed teacher forcing training 147
  recursive training 146
  results, visualizing 154, 155
  script reproducible 153
  teacher forcing training 146
  test dataset, predicting 154
  training 145, 149-151
encoder layer 148

F
forecasting 14
forecasting model development
  stages 94

G
gated recurrent unit (GRU)
  about 112, 123-127
  test dataset, performance 130
  training process 131
Graphical Processing Unit (GPU) 26

H
Holt-Winters exponential smoothing (HWES) 19
hybrid model
  about 192, 193, 195
  casual convolution layer, defining 196
  implementing 196
  search space 196
hyperbolic tangent function (Tanh) 49
hyper-parameter 174
hyper-parameter tuning
  about 174, 175
  NNI API 180
  NNI search 184
  NNI usage 178
  search space 175
  trial 175, 176
  tuner 176
  working 177

K
kernel 41

L
linear layer
  about 36
  parameters 36
long short-term memory (LSTM)
  about 112, 131-134
  evaluating 137
  script reproducible 135
  test dataset, performance 138
  training process 138, 139
Long Short-Term Memory networks (LSTMs) 21, 131

loss function
   about 57, 91
   absolute loss 57
   mean squared error (MSE) 57
   Smooth L1 loss 57

M

Matplotlib 21
mean squared error (MSE) 57
mixed teacher forcing training 147
modelling 15
model optimization 94
Multilayer Perceptron Neural Networks (MLPs) 20
multiple single-step model 80
multi-step forecasting
   about 79
   versus single-step forecasting 78
multi-step model development, approaches
   multiple single-step model 80
   recurrent single-step model 80
   single multi-step model 79
multivariate input - multivariate output
   about 77
   many-to-many 78
   many-to-one 78
multivariate input - univariate output 77
multivariate time series
   versus univariate time series 76

N

Neural Architecture Search (NAS) 186-192

neural network
   testing 92
   training 92
   validating 92
neural network architecture
   about 49-52
   Deep Learning 56
   dropout, using 55
   fully connected network 53, 54
   layer, adding 54, 55
   layer types 53
   performance, improving 52, 53
   ReLU activation, preferring 53
Neural Network Intelligence (NNI)
   about 174
   framework 174
   key features 174
NNI API
   about 180
   search spaces 180
   trail integration 181
NNI built-in tuners
   reference link 177
NNI search
   about 184
   number of trials 184
   search configuration 184-186
   search space 184
NNI usage
   about 178
   search configuration 179, 180
   search space, defining 178
Numerical Python (NumPy) 21

O

optimizer
  about 58
  adadelta 58
  adagrad 58
  Adaptive Moment Estimation (Adam) 58
  Stochastic Gradient Descent (SGD) 58

P

padding 42
pooling layer 44, 45
practical solution
  learning 280
predictive model
  about 206-211
  classical training 215
  Cross Entropy Loss function 215
  datasets, converting to tensors 214
  global parameters 212
  hyper-parameters 212
  initializing 214
  location and features 213
  model preparation function 212
  optimizer 215
  training 216-219
  train-validation split 214
  window dataset, sliding 213
Python for time series analysis
  about 21
  Matplotlib 21
  NumPy 21
  Pandas 21
  PyTorch 22
  Scikit-learn 22
  Statmodels 22

PyTorch
  about 22
  features 22
  setting up 26
PyTorch as derivative calculator
  about 27
  computational graph 31
  computational graph, creating 30
  function creation 27
  function value, computing 28, 29
PyTorch basics
  about 31
  mathematical functions 35
  random tensor 32
  reproducibility 33
  tensor 31
  tensor attributes 34, 35
  tensor creation 31, 32
  tensor method 34, 35
  tensor types 33
PyTorch Forecasting model
  creating 267
  custom model, initializing 269-271
  defining 268
  forward method, implementing 268, 269
PyTorch Forecasting package
  about 260
  features 260

R

real-world forecasting problems
  with PyTorch Forecasting package 271-276
Rectified linear function (ReLU) 47

recurrent neural networks (RNNs)
  about 21, 112-118
  datasets for training, preparing 119
  disadvantages 122
  evaluating 120
  model, initializing 119
  parameters 116, 119
  test dataset, performance 121
  training process 119
  training process, examining 121, 122
recurrent single-step model 80
recursive training 146
regression model
  versus classification model 74

S

Scikit-learn 22
search space 175
seasonal autoregressive integrated moving average (SARIMA) 18
Sigmoid 48
single multi-step model 79
single-step forecasting
  about 79
  versus multi-step forecasting 78
sliding window 89, 90
Smooth L1 loss 57
static processes
  versus dynamic processes 91
Statmodels 22
Stochastic Gradient Descent (SGD) 58
stride 43

T

TCN prediction model
  about 165
  example 166
  test dataset, performance 170, 171
teacher forcing training 146
temporal casual layer 164
temporal convolutional network
  casual convolution 157, 158
temporal convolutional network (TCN)
  about 156
  casual convolution 156
  crop layer 163
  design 160-163
  dilation 159, 160
  implementing 163, 165
  temporal casual layer 164
tensor 31
time series 2
time series analysis
  about 2, 3
  tasks 4
time series analysis problems
  about 14
  anomaly detection 15
  forecasting 14
  modelling 15
time series characteristics
  about 4, 5
  random walk 5-7
  seasonality 11
  stationarity 13
  trend 7-9
time series classification
  problem 75, 76

TimeSeriesDataset
  creating 261
  object, working with 262, 263
  working with 260
time series forecasting
  about 2, 3, 280, 281
  example 59-69
  test dataset 61
  training 61
  validation 61
time series inputs and outputs, types
  multivariate input – multivariate output 77
  multivariate input - univariate output 77
  univariate input - univariate output 77
time series model hyper-parameter tuning
  example 181
time series pre-processing and post-processing
  about 84
  differencing 88, 89
  normalization 85, 86
  trend removal 86
time series regression
  problem 74, 75
toolbox 281, 282
training 56
trial 175, 176
tuner
  about 176
  Gaussian Process Tuner (GP) 177
  grid search 177
  naive evolution 176
  random search 176
  tree-structured parzen estimator (TPE) 177

U

UK minimal temperature prediction problem
  about 95
  alternative model 100, 101
  architecture 97-100
  dataset 95-97
  testing 101-107
univariate input - univariate output 77
univariate time series
  versus multivariate time series 76

Printed in Great Britain
by Amazon